THE NORTH AMERICAN FREE TRADE AGREEMENT

Regional Community and the New World Order

George W. Grayson

Series Editor
Kenneth W. Thompson

Volume III
In the Miller Center Series on
A New World Order

UNIVERSITY
PRESS OF
AMERICA

Lanham • New York • London

The Miller Center

University of Virginia

To
Gisèle Ruth Artura Grayson
and
Thomas Keller Grayson

« »

the finest daughter and son
a loving father could have

Contents

6. The Side Deals (cont.)

7. Evolution of Mexican Lobbying in the United States 151

8. Congress: The Last Best Hope for Victory 167

9. The Showdown Vote 195

CONTENTS

Tables

Foreword

Professor George W. Grayson of the College of William and Mary has combined theory and practice throughout his professional career. He is a theorist in his concern with problems and patterns of democracy, politics, and influence. He is an empiricist in his search for the facts, illustrated by his 30 research trips to Mexico since 1976. His theoretical interests include attention to alliances, negotiations, and national interest. His commitment to public service and his successful quest for electoral office—he has served 20 years in the General Assembly of Virginia—are proof of his qualities as a practitioner. Through it all, he has been a distinguished leader and faculty member of the Department of Government at William and Mary.

The other distinguishing characteristic of Professor Grayson's teaching and research, and no less his public career, has been his continuing concern with values. The first chapter of the present volume reflects this concern, as does his overall view of NAFTA. The underlying assumptions of his interpretation of the defining events in U.S. foreign affairs are rooted in a conception of political ethics. His concept of engagement in world affairs is a standard by which he measures such policies as the Truman Doctrine and the Bricker Amendment.

This approach continues in his discussion of NAFTA and Mexico's new beginning, its new ideology, and the redefinition of its national interests. Grayson's relating of values to politics, interests, and international responsibility is different from that of political theorists who deal only in abstractions and paradigms. He sees not only the world as it is but also as it may become in the 21st century. Basically, his guiding star in analyzing Mexican-U.S. relations is a quest by policymakers for convergences of interests.

FOREWORD

For all these reasons, Grayson's book, along with the McGhee and the Claude books, are invaluable additions to thinking about community and world order. The Miller Center is profoundly indebted to Ambassador George McGhee for providing the intellectual and material means that made this series possible. As on numerous occasions in the past, George McGhee has provided inspiration for the studies and programs of the Miller Center and the resources for carrying them forward.

Kenneth W. Thompson
Director, Miller Center of Public Affairs

Acknowledgments

I want to thank some 50 Canadian, Mexican, and U.S. current and past officials for granting me off-the-record interviews. Although it is fashionable to "bash" bureaucrats, I came to respect even more—in the course of my research—the intelligence, competence, and professionalism of the public servants who make and implement trade policy in North America. They are also articulate teachers, who patiently tried to acquaint me with the intricacies and subtleties involved when 19 working groups spend more than a year hammering out the most ambitious free-trade agreement ever negotiated.

In addition, while not always agreeing with my conclusions, a half-dozen members of environmental organizations painstakingly reviewed the material on NGO lobbying to provide me with insights into the process. I especially benefited from comments offered by Lynn Fisher of the Natural Resources Defense Council and Robert F. Houseman of the Center for International Environmental Law. John Audley of the Sierra Club also opened my eyes to the concerns of environmental groups.

I wish also to express my appreciation to the following individuals for comments on various drafts of this manuscript: Stephen Lande, president of Manchester Associates; B. Timothy Bennett, vice president of SJS Advanced Strategies; John J. Bailey of Georgetown University; Roderic Ai Camp of Tulane University; Carmen Brissette Grayson of Hampton University; and my William & Mary colleagues, Alan J. Ward, C. Lawrence Evans, David A. Dessler, Michael T. Clark, and Ambassador Robert E. Fritts.

To the Foreign Policy Association, I am indebted for their allowing me to draw liberally from a monograph entitled *The North*

ACKNOWLEDGMENTS

American Free Trade Agreement, which I wrote and they published in 1993.

Barbara Wright and Jane Fogarty cheerfully and expertly typed the manuscript; Joe Bates, a William & Mary undergraduate, helped craft the tables; and David Norris, a former William & Mary graduate student, did yeoman's work assisting with research and editing my roughly hewn prose. In addition, Nancy Rodrigues and Michael Abley displayed their wizardry in making certain that several computers effectively accommodated themselves to the text.

Above all, thanks are due to Kenneth W. Thompson, director of the Miller Center of Public Affairs at the University of Virginia, for patiently encouraging my research. Ms. Patricia Dunn of the Center deserves credit for performing the herculean task of preparing the manuscript for publication.

With such abundant help, the defects in this book are obviously my own.

★★★

North American

Free Trade

Agreement

Introduction

At precisely 10:20 p.m. on 17 November 1993, Speaker Thomas S. Foley (D-Wa.) slammed down his maple gavel to quiet the House of Representatives. His purpose was to announce the vote on the proposed North American Free Trade Agreement (NAFTA). "On this vote, the ayes are 234 and the noes 200. The bill is passed," intoned the tall, slightly stoop-shouldered presiding officer, who—just minutes before—had concluded the last speech on behalf of the controversial trade measure with the words: "I go now to the chair to put this question to the House, and I do so with a prayer that it will be the right decision for our people and the right decision for this institution."[1]

After a protracted, acrimonious campaign featuring criss-crossed party and ideological lines, a continental free-trade area would be created on 1 January 1994. The zone would stretch, as pro-NAFTA publicists liked to reiterate, from the Yukon to Yucatán, embracing more than 360 million people whose annual economic activities exceeded $6.5 trillion. As the most ambitious trade accord ever negotiated by the United States, NAFTA would tumble economic barriers between Canada, the United States, and Mexico over a 15-year period. Not only did the pact cover manufactured goods, but it also embraced agriculture, intellectual property, investment, and such services as banking, insurance, and transport. Tripartite parallel agreements authorized the imposition of trade sanctions to provide additional protection to workers and the environment.

During the 11 hours before the vote, 240 members marched to the podium to express their views on the initiative. They articulated dozens of reasons for their support or opposition. Rep. Dan Rostenkowski (D-Ill.), the jowly chairman of the tax- and tariff-

3

writing Ways and Means Committee, concentrated on NAFTA's significance for the United States's role in the world. "We are debating whether America is a confident country, eager to face the future, ready to take on all competitors, or a nation in decline, clinging to memories of our past," he said.[2] In the same vein, Rep. Robert T. Matsui (D-Calif.) declared: "NAFTA is the right thing to do, the productive thing to do, the American thing to do. It creates a vision for the future of our country and of our work force that is based on expansion, growth and change."[3] Such remarks elicited smiles and nods from the platoon of high-ranking Clinton administration officials who crowded into the ornate chamber. They hoped that their boss would not be the first president to lose a trade agreement in Congress since World War II, especially since he was about to fly to Seattle to discuss economic issues with leaders of 14 Asian and Pacific nations.

Opponents also addressed NAFTA's international implications. They warned that lowering protective barriers would propel factories and U.S. jobs to Mexico. "Whose side are we on?" asked Democratic Whip David E. Bonior (D-Mich.). "Are we on the side of the Fortune 500? Or are we on the side of the unfortunate 500,000 who will lose jobs because of this agreement?"[4] On the Capitol steps, devotees of billionaire H. Ross Perot braved a light rain to hoist the placarded message: "Don't Send My Job to Mexico." Meanwhile, five hours into the debate, protesters in the gallery showered the members with bogus $50 bills, shouting "Stop NAFTA Now," as Capitol police hustled them from the building.[5] Emblazoned on the phony bills were the words *Environmental Protection Sold for NAFTA Votes* and *Greenpeace*, the militant ecological group that scorned the pact for relinquishing America's ability to protect its natural resources.

Why did the proposed free-trade agreement arouse such passion and controversy? Would its passage dispatch hundreds of thousands, perhaps millions, of Americans to unemployment lines and welfare offices? Why did a chief executive who concentrated on domestic issues during his surprisingly successful quest for the White House put his reputation and that of his new administration on an issue suffused with foreign policy implications? Was NAFTA a "defining event" with respect to Washington's influence in the world? If so, how?

Chapter 1 of this book describes America's isolationist tradition and identifies the impulse, strongest in the U.S. Congress, for the country to play a diminished role in foreign affairs after the conclusion of the 20th century's hot and cold wars. Chapter 2 analyzes Mexico's remarkable transition from a nation that identified its well-being with protectionism and import substitution to one that strives to link its economy with international markets—a profound change that gave rise to President Carlos Salinas de Gortari's leadership in forging the North American Free Trade Agreement (NAFTA) with the United States and Canada. Chapter 3 concentrates on a pragmatic, uniquely American mechanism— namely, the "fast-track" procedure whereby the executive branch negotiates trade agreements in consultation with lawmakers, who ultimately turn thumbs up or down on such initiatives. Chapter 4, which benefits from the experiences of many of the key participants, focuses on the process and product of 14 months of arduous work by the more than 400 men and women who negotiated NAFTA. Chapter 5 examines the pact as an issue in the 1992 presidential race and the position(s) that Messrs. Bush, Clinton, and Perot staked out on the accord. Chapter 6 presents an analysis of the side deals on import surges, the environment, and labor that Clinton made a *sine qua non* of his backing NAFTA during the 1992 campaign. Chapter 7 zeroes in on the Mexican government's multimillion-dollar attempt to mobilize support, via lobbying and public relations firms, for the continental scheme. Chapter 8 depicts attempts by NAFTA's foes to scuttle the agreement on Capitol Hill. Chapter 9 illumines the campaigns for and against the agreement, leading up to the crucial, fingernail-biting vote in the House of Representatives in November 1993. Chapter 10 speculates on NAFTA's significance for the U.S. role in international affairs, with particular emphasis on the importance of the pact to the Western Hemisphere.

CHAPTER ONE

Defining Events in
U.S. Foreign Affairs

Hostility toward Alliances

The anti-NAFTA sentiments voiced in the early 1990s epitomize the misgivings about international alliances that run like a thread through the tapestry of America's political tradition, often dominating the design and texture of the cloth. Such misgivings extend back to the very beginnings of the Republic. In his *Common Sense* pamphlet, Thomas Paine insisted that "the true interest of America [was] to steer clear of European contentions," thus enabling the young nation to stimulate and safeguard trade with all countries even during wartime.[6] For his part, John Adams implored the Continental Congress to sign only treaties of commerce and "to lay down, as a first principle and a maxim never to be forgotten, to maintain an entire neutrality in all future European wars. . . ." Were the newly independent United States to do otherwise, Adams admonished, "we should be little better than puppets, danced on the wires of the cabinets of Europe."[7]

Early U.S. presidents agreed with Paine and Adams. George Washington, author of the first American neutrality act, was incensed by French Minister Edmond "Citizen" Genet's intrigues against both the Jay Treaty and his administration. Such machinations prompted his warning against the "insidious wiles of

7

foreign influences" in his Farewell Address, delivered on 17 September 1796. "Europe," he emphasized,

> has a set of primary interests, which to us have none, or a very remote relations. Hence she must be engaged in frequent controversies, the causes of which are essentially foreign to our concerns . . . Our detached and distant situation invites and enables us to pursue a different course. . . .[8]

Less than five years later, Thomas Jefferson was no more sanguine about permanent foreign engagements. American merchants took advantage of their country's neutrality during the Napoleonic wars to sell foodstuffs to markets previously closed to them. This profitable trading angered their British counterparts and led London to invoke the Rule of 1756—namely, that commerce restricted during peacetime could not be thrown open during wars. To enforce this arbitrary and capricious doctrine, Royal Navy ships fired across the bow of American merchantmen, boarded vessels bound for and leaving U.S. ports, and impressed American sailors. Such acts poisoned U.S.-British relations and contributed to the War of 1812. No wonder Jefferson, upon swearing the presidential oath in 1801, recommended "peace, commerce and honest friendship with all nations, entangling alliances with none."[9] Such entanglements would, after all, impede the nascent republic's economic development. In this spirit, emissaries of the young nation practiced simple manners and wore unpretentious clothing even when serving in ostentatious European courts. Jefferson, noted for his graciousness as a host, disdained pomp and protocol. He annoyed the foreign diplomatic corps, for example, by refusing to seat them by rank at White House dinners.[10]

After the 1812 conflict, America turned away from Europe to concentrate on its Western frontier: first the Ohio Valley, then the Mississippi Valley, and, ultimately, the Far West and the Plains. Undeveloped lands gained through the Louisiana Purchase, the Mexican-American War, and the acquisition of Alaska further diverted attention from the Old World. Regional rivalries that culminated in the Civil War reinforced America's aloofness from international commitments.

Though careful to avoid such commitments, most 19th-century U.S. leaders rejected isolationism—a word that only migrated from French to the English language in the 1920s.[11] In general, they championed trade, signed commercial accords, welcomed immigrants, and favored cultural exchanges. They cheered on revolts in Spanish America and, through the Monroe Doctrine, endeavored to protect the fledgling states that sprang up from the Rio Grande to Tierra del Fuego (the credibility of this porous *cordon sanitaire*, however, rested on the Royal Navy's discouragement of outside meddling in the region, not American strength). They struggled with England for dominance over the Oregon Territory in the 1840s, observed closely the Greek (1830) and European revolutions (1848), and dispatched Commodore Matthew C. Perry's "black ships" to open up hermetically sealed Japan in 1853. Meanwhile, purchase and conquest continued to expand America's boundaries throughout the century.[12]

Unilateral involvement with other countries was permitted, even encouraged. At the same time, the nation recoiled at alliances or protracted international engagements. Diplomatic historian Thomas A. Bailey disparaged the only accord that implied joint action with another nation, the Clayton-Bulwer Treaty (1850) with Britain that curbed Washington's freedom to construct a transisthmian canal, as "the most persistently unpopular pact ever concluded by the United States."[13] Democrat James Buchanan sneered that, for his statecraft, Secretary of State John M. Clayton deserved a "British peerage."

William H. Seward, a later secretary of state, reaffirmed America's international outlook by rebuffing an 1863 invitation to collaborate with France, Great Britain, and Austria to dissuade Czar Alexander II from grabbing a chunk of Poland. He said:

> Our policy of nonintervention, straight, absolute, and peculiar as it may seem to other nations has . . . become a traditional one, which could not be abandoned without the most urgent occasion, amounting to manifest necessity.[14]

9

A sense of moral superiority infused U.S. disdain for involvement in continental affairs. Americans were democrats; Europeans despots. Americans elected their leaders; Europeans crowned theirs. Americans extolled liberty; Europeans repressed it. Americans pursued peace; Europeans, as practitioners of "power politics," relished wars. "The conclusion was clear: Undemocratic states were inherently warlike and evil; democratic nations, in which the people controlled and regularly changed their leaders were peaceful and moral."[15] Hence, prolonged involvement with Europe threatened to taint, perhaps contaminate, the purity of American democracy and dim the beam of what Emerson called a "beacon lighting for all the world the paths of human destiny."[16]

The lack of a feudal past in the United States militated against the formation of self-conscious classes and the concomitant emergence of ideologically based politics. As a result, pragmatic, "middle class" Americans felt ill at ease with, and lacked an understanding of, European governing systems in which class-inspired doctrines actuated political struggles. The Department of State manifested its aversion to such ideologically driven, often violent political strife by naming lower-ranking envoys (ministers), not ambassadors, to European powers until 1893. The modest growth of the department reflected the limited importance of foreign relations in the post–Civil War period. When inflation is factored in, its budget scarcely increased from 1860 ($1.3 million) to 1890 ($1.8 million), even as the country's population doubled. During this period, the U.S. diplomatic corps expanded from 45 to only 63, while the number of diplomatic missions grew from 33 (1860) to 41 (1890).[17]

Throughout the 1800s the United States—like emerging states of the mid-20th century—was defining itself as an independent nation. Central to forging its own identity was the imperative to distance itself from the economic, political, social, and ideological systems of Europe. Reinforcing this quest for uniqueness was the success America enjoyed. Its capitalist economic system proved productive and innovative; its standard of living moved inexorably higher; and its boundaries expanded through peaceful acquisitions with, to be sure, the exception of the Mexican-American war and conflict with native Americans. The flow of immigrants to U.S.

shores confirmed the country's image of itself as a democratic land of opportunity where fresh starts could be launched and hard work, regardless of one's station in life, rewarded. The United States entered the 1900s as a bustling and independent world power. The events of the 20th century, however, would repeatedly test its reluctance to play a leading role.

The Postwar Impulse to Withdraw

The impulse to retreat from world affairs has been especially strong at the conclusion of wars, hot and cold, in the 20th century. First, years of human and economic sacrifice weary the American people of shouldering international burdens. During hostilities, they see their young people maimed and killed, they pay higher taxes, and they endure rationing and other restrictions on personal freedom. Amid economic dislocations and social disorganization, the public yearns to recapture the "good old days." Such times were uncomplicated by the horror of death on encrimsonated battlefields with unpronounceable names. The apparent ungratefulness of allies for U.S. contributions to the conflict serves only to exacerbate national fatigue and suspicion of foreigners. Such distrust was sharpened by the 1917 Russian revolution and led to a mounting fear of Bolshevism. A rash of "Communist-led" strikes contributed to a crackdown on trade unionists and the deportation of aliens after World War I.

Second, the domestic problems that were neglected or masked during wartime demand attention after hostilities have ceased. Often such problems have risen rapidly up the scale of national priorities, having worsened because of the diversion of tax dollars from schools, hospitals, and roads to tanks, aircraft, and guns. Race riots launched by poor African-Americans afflicted New York and other cities following the 1918 Armistice with Germany. The anti-Vietnam War and the civil rights movement impelled a concerted drive for women's rights, beginning in the 1970s.

Third, the conflict itself raises the consciousness of new groups who were, formerly, at the margin of the political system. Having hoisted the Stars and Stripes in combat, they demand their share of the American dream. Truman's post–World War II integration of the armed forces encouraged black veterans, many of whom were recruited from Southern farms but demobilized in Eastern cities, to pursue political and economic rights by working through the system rather than assaulting it. Litigation in the 1950s and 1960s was complemented by militant, often bloody, demonstrations as white liberals joined the crusade for social justice. The employment of women during World War II foreshadowed both a permanent place for females in the work force and the subsequent political and legal struggle for gender-based equality.

Fourth, the domestically focused Congress looks askance at the internationalist president who led the country into battle. Their wariness is all the greater because the conflict enabled the chief executive to extend the metes and bounds of his authority at the expense of the legislative branch. A shift of emphasis to internal affairs gives senators and representatives an opportunity to expand their policy-making role vis-à-vis a White House that dominates foreign affairs during the fighting.

Fifth, even if the United States emerged victorious from the fray, counter-elites arose to exploit the national fatigue. They criticize the conduct of hostilities, the terms of the peace, the wartime profiteering, or the general hard times in such a way as to diminish the public's appetite for additional foreign entanglements. Following World War I, for example, celebrated American authors spawned an influential school of "disillusionist" literature, which helped mold public perceptions. On Capitol Hill, inveterate isolationists inveighed against British propagandists, arms merchants, and other self-serving interests that had stampeded the country into war.[18] In 1950 Wisconsin's burly Senator Joseph R. McCarthy railed against "twenty years of treason" practiced by Democratic administrations. Roosevelt and Truman were, he averred, responsible for the Soviet hammerlock on Eastern Europe and the loss of China to the Reds. A stalemate in Korea drummed up support for his conspiracy theory. If the United States was the world's strongest nation, the Asian impasse could not be explained by North Korean superiority; rather, internal subversives—those supposedly 205 "known communists" in the State Department and their malefic accomplices—had sapped our strength, collaborated with the enemy, and prevented victory. McCarthy ranted, raved, and ravished careers until the Senate censured him in late 1954. Rush Limbaugh, a chubby, 42-year-old broadcaster, has stepped forward to exploit the widespread angst and uncertainty that afflict millions of Americans in the aftermath of the Cold War. He offers black-and-white analyses during complex, confusing times. Two hardbound Limbaugh polemics, *The Way Things Ought to Be* (1992) and *See, I Told You So* (1993) have been among the biggest-selling nonfiction books of all time. In addition, 610 AM stations, which reach more than 16 million people, air his radio program; some 210 stations carry his late-night TV show; and a monthly newsletter disseminates Limbaugh's aggressively simplistic "wisdom" to an estimated 300,000 subscribers, whom the entertainer refers to as "dittoheads."[19]

Defining Events in U.S. Foreign Policy

One or more "defining events" that occur soon after the conclusion of a conflict indicates what role the United States will play in the postwar period. As discussed, the advent of peace generates intense pressures for the country to diminish its international entanglements, bestowing a higher priority on domestic issues neglected during the wartime years. Members of Congress are especially tempted to endorse a cautious, constrained, and less ambitious foreign policy. In contrast, presidents are inclined to favor advance over retreat in the form of continued, active international engagement. Institutional factors help to explain this preference: in the 20th century, wars and international involvement have strengthened the executive's authority at the expense of the legislative branch; the public, relatively uninformed about world affairs, often accords the chief executive greater leeway in foreign than in domestic policy; and the president's reacting to fast-breaking developments abroad draws both TV cameras to the White House lawn and public attention to his leadership qualities. Defining events reveal whether Washington seeks to project its values as a world leader after a conflict or turn inward, reassessing its participation in world affairs. Such events have followed each of the major conflicts of the 20th century, beginning with World War I.

The Versailles Treaty

Exemplifying a "defining event" was the Senate's post-World War I defeat of the Treaty of Versailles. Four outstanding provisions graced the document's 440 articles and 75,000 words: revised boundaries for dozens of countries and the dismemberment of the Austrian-Hungarian empire, reparation payments by the vanquished Central Powers, the disarmament of Germany, and the establishment of a League of Nations. President Woodrow Wilson, the League's chief architect, considered the organization a crucial mechanism for resolving international disputes through cooperation rather than violence. Article X of the League Covenant embraced the concept of collective security—that is, by vote of its Council, League members would jointly employ economic sanctions or military force to punish an outlaw state. Initially, the public applauded the efforts of *Wilson le juste*, as the French people hailed him, to make the world "safe for democracy." Thirty-two state legislatures passed resolutions endorsing the League, 33 governors threw their support behind the concept, and the *Literary Digest* found broad approval among newspaper editors (718 supportive; 478 supportive with reservations; only 181 against).[20] Wrote one newsman, "To reject this proposition is to repudiate the blood-sacrifice of our boys"; argued another, "We believe it would be the most stupendous error in all history for our nation not to be a part to the League. The world demands it."[21]

Key politicians gravitated toward one of three groups with respect to the initiative. Wilson and many Democratic leaders urged that the treaty be ratified with no major changes or compromises. Their antagonists were such "irreconcilable" isolationists as Senators William E. Borah (R-Idaho), Hiram W. Johnson (R-Calif.), and James A. Reed (R-Mo.). Reed, for example, ridiculed the League as "a sort of international smelling committee." Between the president and the isolationists lay the largest group, led by Senate Foreign Relations Committee

Chairman Henry Cabot Lodge (R-Ma.). These "reservationists" were willing to ratify the treat provided amendments sharply reduced America's international obligations, especially the delegation of war and peace decisions from the U.S. Senate to the League Council.

Lodge and other Republican defenders of American sovereignty added 14 "reservations" to the treaty. The intractable Wilson, enfeebled by a stroke, reacted to the proposed changes by urging defeat of the legislation. "In my opinion," the president wrote Senate Democrats, "[the Lodge resolution] does not provide for ratification but, rather, for the nullification of the treaty. I sincerely hope that friends and supporters of the treaty will vote against the Lodge resolution of ratification."[22] On 19 November 1919, following eight months of deliberation, only 39 senators backed the treaty to which Lodge had attached amendments. A Democratic attempt to obtain approval without reservations lost 38 "yeas" to 53 "nays." The imperious president had nothing but contempt for "pygmy-minded" legislators who, he believed, elevated partisanship above the national interest. The isolationists jeered Wilson's inflexibility by revising his 1916 campaign slogan to read, "He Kept Us Out of Peace."[23] Senator Borah acclaimed the outcome as "the second winning of the Independence of America" and "the greatest victory since Appomattox."[24]

Although 24 countries formed the League of Nations without U.S. participation, such key members as England and France lacked the will to thwart the rise of dictators in Italy, Germany, and Spain. In the 1920 presidential contest, the American electorate overwhelmingly sent to the White House Warren Gamiel Harding, a bespectacled, boorish Ohioan, who promised "normalcy not nostrums." For political reasons, the GOP nominee had hedged his League position during the campaign. After his inauguration, however, he made no bones about his stance. "My administration," he proclaimed, "doesn't propose to enter now by the side door, back door, or cellar door."[25] Despite Harding's hostility, the Senate gave impulse to the Five-Power Naval Limitation Treaty of Washington (1922) that imposed a ten-year holiday on the construction of capital ships. The United States also promoted the Dawes and

Young plans to restructure and reduce Germany's debt obligations, while advocating the Kellogg-Briand Pact to abolish war.

Although monitoring League activities through a mission in Geneva, the United States resisted continuous involvement in European affairs. Mesmerized by the "Roaring 20s" and struck by the Great Depression of the 1930s, America shifted its attention to domestic concerns, not to play a pivotal international role until Japanese bombers left the country no choice. The New York *World* foresaw the folly of this course when it wrote: "We have lost courage, confidence and resource; we have made the Declaration of Independence parochial instead of universal, and we have withdrawn selfishly and afraid from complications that can never be settled without our help."[26]

The U.N. and the Truman Doctrine

As World War II was drawing to a close, new defining events revealed that the United States should not retreat to its pre-war isolationism. In February 1945 Franklin Roosevelt, Joseph Stalin, and Winston Churchill reported the convening of a meeting to draft the United Nations Charter. This announcement followed a week-long conclave of the "Big Three" at the Crimean resort of Yalta. Secret accords reached at the Yalta conference encompassed the status of Poland, zones of occupation in Germany, and territorial concessions to Moscow for entering the war against Japan. Even before Germany and Japan surrendered, 50 nations dispatched delegates to San Francisco to create the United Nations. They completed their work in just two months, with the signing ceremony held on 25 June 1945.

Overwhelming grass-roots support propelled the document through the Senate. In mid-1945, for example, four out of five Americans favored U.S. membership.[27] Nevertheless, at the public hearings, a few witnesses excoriated the U.N. Charter as a "Communist plot" and a "godless and unconstitutional document" drafted by wicked foreigners. One critic even denounced the initiative as a "British-Israel World Federation movement" to establish "a world state with the Duke of Windsor as King!"[28] Less flamboyant detractors such as isolationist senators Henrik Shipstead (R-Minn.) and William Langer (R-N.D.) insisted that the U.N. represented a superstate and that U.S. membership would violate the Constitution.[29]

Unlike Lodge in 1919, Senator Tom Connally (D-Tex.), who chaired the Senate Foreign Relations Committee, strongly endorsed the treaty. Recalling the death of the League of Nations Covenant, he shouted: "Can you not still see the blood on the floor?" On 28 July 1945, the Senate approved the initiative by a vote of 89 to two. That the United States enjoyed a veto in the U.N. Security Council helped overcome most objections. Still, Senator Hiram Johnson, an irreconcilable who had fought Wilson hammer and tong 26 years before, sent word from his deathbed that if in the chamber he would have voted "no" to the United Nations.[30]

Shipstead and Langer's grousing aside, a bipartisan alliance buttressed Congress's commitment to internationalism. Central to this alliance was Senator Arthur H. Vandenberg, Jr., an extremely influential Republican from Michigan whose strong isolationist views gave way to internationalism upon the bombing of Pearl Harbor.[31]

With Vandenberg's enthusiastic backing, President Harry S Truman filled the vacuum left when the United Kingdom unexpectedly advised its allies in 1947 that it could no longer provide full-scale economic assistance to Greece and Turkey. The withdrawal of British aid increased the possibility that Communist guerrillas, aided and abetted by Yugoslavia's Marxist regime, would seize power in Greece. Turkey's situation seemed equally precarious. To forestall left-wing takeovers, Truman made a surprise appearance before Congress on 12 March 1947. He told a hushed audience:

> One of the primary objectives of the foreign policy of the United States is the creation of conditions in which we and other nations will be able to work out a way of life free from coercion . . . We shall not realize our objectives, however, unless we are willing to help free peoples to maintain their free institutions and their national integrity against aggressive movements that seek to impose upon them totalitarian regimes. This is no more than a frank recognition that totalitarian regimes

imposed on free peoples, by direct or indirect aggression, undermine the foundations of international peace and hence the security of the United States.[32]

Within two months, Congress had appropriated $400 million for Greece and Turkey. The vote in the House was 287 to 107; in the Senate, 67 to 23. In comparison to subsequent aid donations, the sum may have been modest, but the political statement resounded beyond Capitol Hill. "For the first time in its history, the United States had chosen to intervene during a period of general peace in the affairs of peoples outside North and South America."[33] Not only did the assistance bolster regimes in Athens and Ankara, but it also set the stage for the Marshall Plan, approved in 1948, which helped revive Western Europe's war-ravaged economies.

Bricker Amendment

Despite bipartisan support on major foreign policy initiatives, Republicans had little love lost for Truman, whom they viewed as a Midwest perpetrator of Roosevelt's imperiousness. They berated him as a "gone goose" at the party's 1948 convention, whose delegates arrived in Philadelphia buoyed by the feeling that their nominee would be the next chief executive. Former Congress-woman Clare Booth Luce brought the conventioneers to their feet when she inveighed against the Democrats as a party divided into "a Jim Crow wing, led by lynch-loving Bourbons . . . a Moscow wing, masterminded by Stalin's Mortimer Snerd, Henry Wallace . . . and a Pendergast wing run by the wampum and boodle boys . . . who gave us Harry Truman in one of their more pixilated moments."[34] They resented the bare-knuckled, confrontational style that found Truman summoning the GOP-dominated 80th Congress back into session before the 1948 election to expose its "no-account, do nothing" record. Truman's subsequent come-from-behind victory over Governor Thomas E. Dewey in 1948 stunned Hoover's legatees, out of the White House for 15 years, who believed the keys to the presidential mansion lay within their grasp.

Republicans did not oppose Truman's resolute, highly popular dispatch of forces to prevent Pyongyang's troops from overrunning the entire Korean Peninsula in mid-1950. They did, however, excoriate his leadership when public opinion—which fluctuated with the fortunes of war—soured on the Asian venture. Although 81 percent of Americans initially approved of Truman's decisive action to combat aggression, fully two-thirds of respondents to an early 1951 Gallup Poll favored pulling out of Korea—with only 25 percent continuing to approve the action and 9 percent undecided.[35]

Truman had sent more than a million troops abroad under U.N. auspices, not by a declaration of war but through executive agreements. During the conflict, he had deployed four American divisions to Germany in accord with obligations arising out of membership in the North Atlantic Treaty Organization. Analysts described such forces as a "trip wire" to commit Washington to war against the Soviet Union should it take advantage of hostilities in Asia to invade Germany. In April 1952 the president, acting as commander in chief, placed the nation's steel mills under government control to avert a strike that could disrupt the flow of armaments to U.S. forces in Korea. This action, later declared unconstitutional by the Supreme Court, ignited a firestorm on Capitol Hill.

To rub salt in the lawmakers' wounds, Truman blithely asserted that his constitutional powers—"repeatedly recognized by Congress and the courts"—allowed him to move troops anywhere in the world. Subsequent presidents made even more sweeping claims, and executive agreements became the chief mechanism for presidential war making during the Cold War.[36]

Senators, who perceived themselves as the constitutionally designated stewards of foreign alliances, decried the arrogance with which Roosevelt and Truman had single-handedly (and, sometimes, secretly) decided matters of war and peace, forged pacts with foreign nations, dispatched fighting units around the world, and undertook bold acts on the home front. Even more objectionable to many lawmakers was the possibility that the U.N. Charter, the Universal Declaration of Human Rights (adopted in 1948), and other international agreements might be employed to control education, civil rights, interstate commerce, and other domestic

19

policies. Senator A. Willis Robertson (D-Va.), for example, worried that the federal courts might rule that the U.N. Charter invalidated the states' segregation laws.[37] Frank E. Holman, president of the American Bar Association in 1948–49, argued that "ardent internationalists" would use "a variety of devious maneuvers and clever resorts to semantics, to transform the United Nations into a 'World Government'" that infringed on the sovereignty and independence of the United States.[38]

The vehicle for reining in imperious presidentialism was the so-called "Bricker Amendment," named after its chief sponsor, Senator John W. Bricker (R-Ohio). Bricker, an isolationist whom detractors berated as an "honest Harding," was Dewey's right-wing running mate in 1948. He decried Roosevelt's New Deal and Truman's Fair Deal, equating Washington's accumulation of power with Soviet communism. His eponymous legislation, which went through a number of iterations between 1951 and 1954, required congressional approval of both treaties and executive agreements. One provision even opened the door to state interference with international accords.

President Dwight D. Eisenhower feared that Bricker's handiwork would reinstitute the weakness of the Articles of Confederation. "Every treaty of the future and possibly of the past would be subjected to ceaseless challenge by any of the states under Article X," he wrote in his memoirs. "Lawsuits, controversy, and confusion would replace the simple and efficacious processes visualized by the Founding Fathers, and . . . chaos in international affairs would result."[39] Senator William J. Fulbright (D-Ark.) claimed the amendment constituted a "retreat from the world." Ex-President Truman averred that the legislation would "ruin any attempt of the President to carry out foreign policy" and that "Eisenhower knows that they are trying to cut his throat." In a lighter vein, Eisenhower himself quoted a wag's comment that the Ohio senator was attempting to demolish the Constitution "brick by brick by Bricker."[40]

Still, Senator Bricker forged ahead with his crusade to protect the American form of government from the dangers of "treaty law." Clearly, the fate of his amendment would be a defining event for America's Cold War identity. Joining Bricker were 56 Senate co-sponsors and dozens of national organizations, including the American Legion, the Veterans of Foreign Wars, the Catholic War Veterans, the Chamber of Commerce of the United States, the National Grange, the American Council of Christian Churches, the American Medical Association, and the American Bar Association. Greatly outnumbered were opponents, whose meager ranks included the Americans for Democratic Action, the American Jewish Congress, the American Federation of Labor, B'nai B'rith, the American Association for the United Nations, United World Federalists, the American Civil Liberties Union, and the American Association of University Women.[41]

Despite the Eisenhower administration's vehement opposition to Bricker's initiative, Senate Majority Leader William F. Knowland (R-Calif.) stated that he could not "ignore a dangerous tendency toward executive encroachment on legislative powers."[42] Enough Democrats rallied behind the president to defeat Bricker's Amendment by a 50-to-42 vote on 25 February 1954. The following day, a substitute offered by Senator Walter F. George (D-Ga.) that contained the core of Bricker's language failed to muster the necessary two-thirds vote by 60 to 31. The last vote—a "no" cast by Senator Harley M. Kilgore (D-W. Va.)—decided the outcome.[43] As a result, Congress failed to curtail the executive's freedom of action in foreign relations.

War Powers Act

The Vietnam War (1962–75) proved to be the most divisive foreign conflict in U.S. history. Television brought pictures of fire-fights, carnage, massacres, and mayhem into America's living rooms each evening, demystifying the warfare to a new generation raised on G.I. Joe dolls and patriotic war bond commercials. Anti-war activists burned draft cards and flags as "Middle America" watched with disgust. White House and Pentagon policymakers miscalculated and misled the public as to troop levels and strategy. Ugly confrontations on campuses and in courtrooms, over the airwaves and on city streets, stretched thin the nation's sense of civic unity.

As the body count rose, Congress endeavored to limit the president's "imperial" policy-making. Lyndon Johnson had last consulted legislators over war powers when he submitted the Gulf of Tonkin Resolution, which breezed through the House and Senate in 1964. Still, there was no formal declaration of war. Congress remained a group of 535 spectators between 1969 and 1972, as Nixon pursued Vietnamization, air and ground offenses against Cambodia and Laos, normalization of relations with China, détente, linkage, the mining of Haiphong harbor, and the Christmas bombing of North Vietnam.[44]

Legislators employed the budget process to curb presidential assertiveness. Beginning in 1970, Congress included provisions in all military appropriations bills that forbad military assistance to Cambodia, except where necessary to accomplish the removal of U.S. troops from Southeast Asia or to obtain the release of war prisoners. In mid-1973, after the withdrawal of American forces from Vietnam, Congress voted to cut off all funds for further U.S. operations in Cambodia. Although vetoing the measure, President Nixon agreed to a compromise that halted funding on 15 August.

Some members of Congress filed a lawsuit that challenged the constitutionality of the air war in Cambodia. The approach came a cropper in July 1973 when the U.S. Court of Appeals for the Second Circuit ruled that the issue amounted to a "political question" and was not within the province of the federal judiciary. The Supreme Court refused to intervene.

Manifest congressional impotence vis-à-vis the White House prompted Senator Jacob K. Javits (R-N.Y.) to introduce legislation that would limit executive war making. Under this initiative, the president could lawfully commence hostilities under only four specified conditions: (1) repelling an attack on the United States; (2) protecting American armed forces overseas; (3) protecting the lives of Americans abroad; and (4) fulfilling U.S. military obligations encompassed in a specific law. Once initiated by the president, he would have to report his actions to Congress immediately. Presidential war making could not be continued for more than 60 days without formal authorization by Congress.

The Senate passed the so-called War Powers Act in 1972 and 1973, and it finally became law in October 1973 over a Nixon veto.

The measure reflected Congress's desire for presidents to curtail unilateral involvement in foreign matters in favor of making policy in concert with the legislative branch—a recipe for greater attention to internal rather than international affairs. Did the legislation accomplish this goal? So broad is the act's language that the commander in chief can still initiate almost any kind of military action deemed in the national interest.[45] By starting from the premise that the chief executive must be free to move rapidly in a crisis, the legislators "gave the game away."[46] It is naive to believe that Congress, even when confronted with a large-scale presidential war, would muster the political courage to terminate hostilities—or that the White House would give more than cursory attention to legislative opposition. "By wrapping himself in the flag and appealing to the patriotism—and the jingoism—of the public, the president could keep his war going."[47] A series of assets— legitimacy in foreign affairs, access to intelligence, entrée to the media, the fast-breaking nature of international events, centralized decision making (contrasted to congressional fragmentation)— ensures the White House's dominant role in world affairs. In fact, neither Congress nor the president has invoked the provisions of the War Powers Act.

Yet behind the legislation's puny legal facade lay a powerful political restraint on presidential adventurism: the nation's abhorrence over Vietnam. The conflict had devoured tens of thousands of lives and billions of dollars in national treasure. Even worse, it had opened a fault-line in American society: many university students disdained the political objectives and social values of their parents' generation; "hawks" and "doves" lost respect for national institutions that seemed unable to win or lose with dignity; Vietnam veterans condemned a government that sent them to war as sons and daughters but received them home as orphans; and scores of African-American leaders criticized a society that appeared indifferent to the disproportionate sacrifices that blacks had made in the rice paddies of Southeast Asia. Even the "Great Communicator," Ronald Reagan, limited himself to a whirlwind assault on the tiny nation of Grenada and a proxy war on Nicaragua, lest he arouse the ire of the two-thirds of Americans who regularly expressed misgivings about a Vietnam-style involvement in Central America.[48]

Desert Shield/Desert Storm and NAFTA

The year 1989 will loom as one of the most important dates in the 20th century. At the beginning of the year, communism held sway over a crescent that stretched from the Elbe to the Sea of Japan. By year's end, U.S.S.R. President Mikhail Gorbachev had slashed weapons spending by 20 percent, announced the withdrawal of 200,000 troops from Asia, recognized the Solidarity movement's victory in Polish parliamentary elections, and proclaimed that the future of Poland and Hungary was "their affair." Equally important, on 9 November he witnessed the opening of the Berlin Wall and the ensuing exodus of hundreds of thousands of East Germans to the West.

The Cold War had ended, not with the communization of the world but with breadlines that exposed the Soviet system's inability to meet its people's fundamental needs. As in the aftermath of hot wars, pressures built to diminish the United States's global role. This role had proven costly. America lost 100,000 people (45,000 in Korea; 55,000 in Vietnam) containing communist expansion. In 1945 its national debt was $259 billion; 45 years later it surpassed $3 trillion. Defense expenditures had contributed to dramatic economic growth in the post-World War II period. By the 1990s, however, U.S. leaders faced a plethora of domestic challenges: inadequate schools, widespread homelessness, an overburdened health care system, mounting crime, ubiquitous drug use, a deteriorating transport network, and a high unemployment rate.[49]

The peace dividend would furnish at least some of the wherewithal to confront internal needs. Expenditures on defense and foreign aid declined as domestic concerns assumed an ever greater importance. Would Washington be satisfied to observe, rather than shape or manage, the changes that were sweeping the post-Cold War world? Would post-Cold War defining events signal a turn inward for the planet's sole remaining superpower?

The U.S. chief executive's answer to these questions was "no." In response to Iraqi President Saddam Hussein's August 1990 invasion of the oil-rich desert sheikdom of Kuwait, for example, President George Bush assiduously marshalled support in the U.N. Security Council for a land, sea, and air blockade of Iraq. After an extensive debate, the U.S. Congress reluctantly endorsed a resolution authorizing the use of "all necessary means" to expel Iraq from Kuwait. Such a resolution, the chief executive wrote, "would help dispel any belief that may exist in the minds of Iraq's leaders that the United States lacks the necessary unity to act decisively."[50] During three days of impassioned speech-making, most Democrats advocated continued economic sanctions; Republicans gave a green light to commencing hostilities. The Senate vote, held on 12 January 1991, was 52 to 47; minutes later, the House of Representatives backed the resolution 250 to 183.

On 16 January, the Pentagon launched air attacks on Iraq, converting Desert Shield into Desert Storm. Ultimately, the president deployed 400,000 troops in the Mideast, the largest American contingent sent abroad since Vietnam. By early March, Iraq's generals accepted allied terms for a formal end to the Persian Gulf War. An ecstatic George Bush, his approval rating near 90 percent, said: "By God, we've kicked the Vietnam syndrome once and for all."[51]

Was he correct? Were the American people supportive of U.S. involvement in global affairs? Although prepared to back a brief (42 days), successful war fought over a vital interest, the voters were most concerned about problems closer to home. The paladin of Desert Shield/Desert Storm, the man who appeared politically invincible in the spring of 1991, lost his reelection 18 months later. No single factor ever explains satisfactorily the defeat of a popular incumbent, but clearly the electorate resonated to challenger Bill Clinton's pledge to change the nation's priorities from international to domestic pursuits. Also noteworthy was the public's growing disenchantment with Operation Restore Hope, President Bush's December 1992 dispatch of troops to Somalia, and widespread opposition to the involvement of U.S. armed forces in Bosnia and Haiti.

The salience of domestic issues threatened to thwart Clinton's first important foreign policy challenge: approval of the North American Free Trade Agreement, which had been negotiated by the Bush administration. As reflected in the 17 November congressional debate, a broad spectrum embracing Patrick J. "Pat" Buchanan, H. Ross Perot, Ralph Nader, the American Federation of Labor-Congress of Industrial Organizations (AFL-CIO), large environmental organizations, and key Democratic congressional leaders decried the proposed free-trade pact as a "threat to U.S. sovereignty" and an "assault on American workers."

The president, on the other hand, called action on NAFTA crucial to America's future. "This is the end of the Cold War. This is the dawn of the 21st century," Clinton said in an address at the John F. Kennedy Library. "In these moments we have to reach deep into ourselves to our deepest values to our strongest spirit and reach out, not shrink back." The chief executive added:

> Our generation must now decide, just as John Kennedy and his generation had to decide at the end of World War II whether we will harness the galloping changes of our time in the best tradition of John Kennedy and the post-war generation to the well-being of the American people, or withdraw from the world and recoil from our own problems as we did after World War I.[52]

For him, NAFTA constituted a "decisive moment" for the United States. As with the defeat of the Versailles Treaty, the ratification of the U.N. Charter, and the other post-conflict "decisive moments" before it, NAFTA's passage, signaling engagement over retreat, would indeed constitute another defining event for America. Amplifying NAFTA's importance was the likelihood that trade would rival, if not surpass, weapons as the focus of international competition in the post-Cold War era. In short, the ability to successfully export high quality goods and services would be crucial to our economic well-being at home and to the projection of our influence abroad.

Even though the U.S. economy was relatively open, at least compared to those of Japan and Western Europe, further liberalization would give rise to "winners" and "losers." At the grass-roots level, the former tended to remain inert; they had no idea that a new job or lower costs for items consumed would flow from diminished protectionism. On the other hand, the latter were more likely to belong to labor organizations prepared to fight hammer and tong against freer trade. In view of the controversy that formally integrating the U.S. and Mexican economic systems would spark in Washington, it was not surprising that the initiative for this venture lay with Mexico's daring chief executive.

CHAPTER TWO

NAFTA:
Mexico's New Beginning

Introduction

If a Mexican Rip Van Winkle sprang from bed in the mid-1990s after slumbering 20 years, he would blink his eyes in amazement. He would see that his country's youthful, former president, Carlos Salinas de Gortari, had opened Mexico's once hugely protected economy to imports, while welcoming foreign investors formerly reviled as imperialist agents who threatened the sovereignty of this cornucopia-shaped country of 90 million inhabitants. The newly awakened observer would notice, much to his surprise, a leaner, more efficient government, one that was urging entrepreneurs to take over activities that the state had aggressively monopolized when he began to sleep.

Most astonishing of all, he would notice Mexican officials, in concert with their U.S. and Canadian counterparts, implementing the North American Free Trade Agreement. Previously, such a pact was unthinkable because it evoked images of Uncle Sam meddling in Mexican affairs. Now it is viewed as a "win-win-win" opportunity for the three countries of North America. Salinas and his successor, Ernesto Zedillo Ponce de León, believe that the pact will spur trade, impel investment, create jobs, and curb illegal immigration from Mexico to the United States.

The interplay of ideology, interests, and institutions help explain the sharp change that Mexico underwent while our friend dreamed in the arms of Morpheus.[53] Ideology involves a mosaic of "symbolically-charged beliefs and expressions that present, interpret and evaluate the world in a way designed to shape, mobilize, direct, organize and justify certain modes or courses of action and to anathematize others."[54] The concept will be employed less pretentiously here as the Mexican government's pattern of behavior in economic affairs. Interests are synonymous with "national interests," which have been defined as "the total values and purposes of a state applied to a particular set of circumstances, and seen in relation to the means available for their realization."[55] And institutions refer to "persistent and connected sets of rules (formal and informal) that prescribe behavioral roles, constrain activity, and shape expectations."[56]

ISI and Mexico's Economic Miracle

The ideology that drove Mexico's economic development in the mid-20th century was import substitution industrialization (ISI)—a concept widely accepted throughout the hemisphere in the 1930s. This idea involved erecting protectionist barriers to foster domestic industries that could produce goods previously purchased from abroad. Such hemispheric nations as Argentina, Brazil, and Chile employed this strategy to cope with the catastrophic effects of the Great Depression. The sharp contraction of the U.S. and European economies slashed external demand for the one or two items that most nations of the region relied upon to earn foreign exchange. Importers slammed their doors to the sugar, wool, copper, silver, tin, oil, and beef that they had traditionally purchased. A drop in both the unit price and quantity of Latin American exports meant that their total value between 1930 and 1934 was 48 percent below that of the 1925-29 period.[57] Latin American leaders viewed import substitution as a means of reducing dependence on their traditional suppliers of food products, clothing, and such consumer durables as automobiles and household appliances, of generating employment for a restive and expanding work force, and of broadening their array of potential exports.

Mexico concentrated on internal priorities during the 1930s to implement elements of the 1917 "revolutionary" constitution. In particular, President Lázaro Cárdenas del Río (1934-40) sought to uplift, organize, and recruit for the ruling revolutionary party peasants, workers, and other neglected segments of the population. To achieve these objectives, he vigorously expanded land reform, nationalized the railroads and petroleum industry, and recognized an expanding number of labor unions and peasant associations.

Domestic priorities gave way to international concerns as World War II severely curtailed the nation's access to imports. As a result, successive chief executives, beginning with Manuel Avila Camacho (1940-46), constructed a tariff wall to shield virtually every new industry established in their country from foreign competition. Avila Camacho's successor, Miguel Alemán Valdés (1946-52), depended even more heavily on tariffs to stimulate private sector investment. He kept duties low on raw materials purchased abroad, while imposing rates that often exceeded 100 percent on imported manufactured items. By the late 1950s, Mexico had replaced tariffs with import licenses as the principal tool of protectionism. These permits both stimulated industrialization and conserved valuable foreign exchange for the importation of essential goods.[58] The exchange devaluations of 1949 and 1954 provided an additional safeguard to nascent industries by markedly undervaluing the peso and, thereby, discouraging imports.[59]

Incentives to entrepreneurs complemented the protectionist barricade composed of tariffs, import permits, and a cheap currency. These incentives included tax concessions, low interest loans, inexpensive energy, a malleable union movement, and the construction of an elaborate system of highways, rail lines, airports, harbors, and communication facilities. Foreign investors joined the domestic business community in taking advantage of these benefits. U.S. investment, followed by loans, flowed across the border, expanding fivefold between 1950 ($566 million) and 1970 ($2,822 million). Among the industrial giants that flocked to Mexico were General Motors, Dow Chemicals, Pepsi-Cola, Coca-Cola, Colgate, Goodyear, John Deere, Ford, Proctor and Gamble, and Sears,

Roebuck.[60]   This government-directed policy catalyzed an "economic miracle" manifest in a growth rate that averaged more than 6 percent for nearly four decades before opportunities for producing goods internally waned.

Mexican National Interests

The inward focus of import substitution industrialization dovetailed with Mexico's low-key foreign policy. Washington's military and diplomatic intrusiveness during the Mexican-American War (in which Mexico lost more than half its national territory) and the 1910 revolution (during which the U.S. Marines occupied Veracruz and General John J. "Black Jack" Pershing pursued Pancho Villa across the New Mexico border) sensitized Mexican leaders to the Hobbesian nature of a world where adversaries prowled, where civilized discourse often failed, where might triumphed over right, and where the best hope for a weak, vulnerable nation was lofty principles of international law. Salient among these tenets were national sovereignty, the juridical equality of nations, national self-determination, and nonintervention in the internal affairs of other states.

Franklin D. Roosevelt's "Good Neighbor Policy" helped to ease the tensions arising from Cárdenas's expropriation of the U.S.-dominated oil industry in 1938. An improved relationship was evident in Mexico's close cooperation with its northern neighbor during World War II. Specifically, Mexico declared war on the Axis powers in 1942, sent 400,000 *bracero* workers to labor-drained fields in the United States, and dispatched three air force squadrons to the Philippines, where they saw limited action near the end of hostilities in 1945.

In the postwar period, Mexico deemed its national interests advanced by active efforts to spur economic development at home complemented by relative inactivity abroad. During this period, Mexican diplomats concentrated on maintaining good—or, at least correct—relations with Washington. After all, the United States supplied nearly two-thirds of Mexico's imports and provided the chief market for its exports.

Such attention to domestic economic progress did not diminish Mexico's devotion to codes of international conduct. This enthusiasm was evident in the aftermath of the 1962 Cuban missile crisis, when President Adolfo López Mateos strongly backed the creation of a nuclear-free zone in Latin America. On 14 February 1967, at a ceremony in Tlatelolco, the section of Mexico City near the Foreign Ministry, representatives of 21 Latin American countries signed the Treaty for the Prohibition of Nuclear Weapons in Latin America. In a joint declaration, the signatories praised the so-called Treaty of Tlatelolco "as a first step toward global disarmament and ultimately towards complete and universal disarmament." The treaty entered into force on 22 April 1968, following its endorsement by the U.N. General Assembly four months earlier.[61]

Mexican leaders also perceived that a more ambitious pursuit of principled foreign policy goals could advance both their international and domestic agendas. Such a strategy was evident in President López Mateos's refusal, in the face of pressures emanating from Washington and the Organization of American States, to sever diplomatic and commercial relations with the Castro regime in Cuba. His policy conformed with Mexico's commitment to nonintervention in the affairs of other countries. In addition, this populist dimension of foreign policy deprived domestic leftists of a sensitive issue and diverted attention from an industrialization scheme that benefited the privileged few at the expense of the impoverished masses.[62]

Institutional Support

It was precisely ISI's beneficiaries who provided the institutional support for this program. Clearly, corporations that flourished thanks to protectionism backed the system that had fattened their profits. Many of these firms belonged to national business organizations. These groups included the Confederation of Chambers of Commerce of Mexico (CONCANACO), the Confederation of Industrial Chambers (CONCAMIN), and the National Chamber of Manufacturing Industry (CANACINTRA).

The myriad permits, tariffs, rules, and regulations required to implement protectionism spawned a vast state apparatus that had a stake in preserving and expanding government controls. The ranks of bureaucrats grew proportionate to government intervention in the economy. Thanks to nationalizations, accomplished largely in the 1970s, the number of public firms mushroomed and the state soon generated more than half of national economic activity. By the early 1980s, the federal government employed more than three million people.

The official Institutional Revolutionary Party (PRI) and its leaders also took advantage of import substitution to further their interests. An expanding and intrusive federal regime provided employment for the party faithful and their allies. In addition, party chiefs stood ready to slash the red tape that confronted a businessman or consumer seeking an official document required for an economic transaction. The quid pro quo for such a favor might be assisting the PRI in an upcoming election or conferring a financial consideration on the helpful party activist.

Problems with ISI

For several reasons, import substitution proved a mixed blessing for Latin American economies. First, hopes of curbing reliance on industrialized nations faded as developing states found themselves dependent on machine tools and other sophisticated capital goods imported by the infant industries that they had nurtured. Dependency was not eliminated; only its form changed. Second, these imported manufactures commanded increasingly higher charges compared to world market prices for many of Latin America's major exports. Expressed simply: adverse terms of trade meant that ever more bags of coffee, wheat, or sugar were needed to purchase a tractor, generator, or machine tool. Third, having copied First World production techniques, many infant industries were capital-intensive and, therefore, created relatively few jobs. Fourth, continued protection for the infant industries, even after they had matured, shielded them from competition. Such hot-house conditions enabled these firms to produce goods that were dear in price and cheap in quality. The result was a consumer-to-producer income transfer that benefited the incipient industrialists and their network of managers and professionals at the expense of workers, peasants, farmers, and the lower middle class. Finally, opportunities for corruption multiplied apace with import substitution. Unscrupulous (and, often, ill-paid) bureaucrats and party activists regarded the intricate transactions suffusing protectionism as a ticket for exacting bribes, known as *mordidas*, political favors, or both.

By the late 1960s, many of Mexico's spry, eager infant industries of the previous generation had grown pot-bellied, lethargic, whiny, and inefficient. Sheltered from competition, hundreds of these firms turned out expensive items of inferior quality that were uncompetitive in foreign markets. The first "captains of industry" had shown entrepreneurial talents that earned the respect of the authorities. Such respect faded over time as the private sector became more dependent on protectionist measures. "Hence, the second- and third-generation *empresarios* were more subordinate to, and dependent on, the government, and more risk-adverse."[63]

Just as the protectionist Smoot-Hawley Tariff chilled international commerce and alerted U.S. lawmakers to the pitfalls of protectionism in the early 1930s, Mexico's experience with infant industries demonstrated the shortcomings of import substitution in the late 1960s. As an economics student at the National Autonomous University of Mexico (UNAM), Carlos Salinas witnessed a confrontation between the regime of President Gustavo Díaz Ordaz and segments of the middle class that symbolized the exhaustion of ISI-inspired growth.

During the protracted economic miracle, the political system had furnished opportunities for members of this growing and increasingly heterogeneous class. They did look askance at the authoritarianism, corruption, and curbs on free expression that marred the regime; yet the system generated both jobs for themselves and the prospect of social mobility for their children.

Flagging growth, however, exacerbated the essentially political tension that burst forth in the 1968 student movement, which Salinas observed without joining. "The majority of middle-class members, intellectuals, students, and business people were altogether relegated to a nonparticipant role, one that simply did not fit with either their social or economic status or their aspirations. They shared this relegated status with labor and peasants, who had also lost in the economic arena."[64]

Student dissatisfaction with political conditions and economic inequality sparked at least 47 separate demonstrations between 23 July and 10 August. In mid-August, the student strike committee shifted from a series of minor protests to a mass rally that drew 150,000 demonstrators to the Zócalo plaza on 13 August. There they linked President Díaz Ordaz to police and army violence, as indicated in placards that proclaimed: "Criminal," "Hated Beast," and "Assassin."[65] Sharpening government concerns about the mounting protests were the impending Olympic Games to be played in Mexico City. This international competition, it was hoped, would portray Mexico to the world as a developing, innovative, and unified country. The climax to the government-student conflict took place on 2 October 1968, when army and police units fired on several thousand unarmed students, housewives, and office workers protesting the lack of freedom in their country.

Díaz Ordaz, broken by the Tlatelolco massacre, increasingly delegated responsibilities to Luis Echeverría Alvarez, his government secretary who supervised the bloodbath. In 1970 Echeverría became president. Not only did the new chief executive continue ISI despite its obvious limitations, he expanded governmental intervention in the economy to stimulate growth and boost employment. Government spending, which totaled 13.1 percent of GNP in 1970, rose to 39.6 percent in 1976. Meanwhile, the number of state companies grew like Topsy—to exceed 700 under Echeverría before soaring to 1,155 in the early 1980s. The president bypassed a generation of politicians who aspired to rewards for their loyalty to the "revolutionary" family. Instead, to fill posts in new and expanded federal agencies, he recruited younger loyalists, many with technocratic rather than political credentials. Salinas, for example, and many of the U.S.-trained senior officials in his government began their public service at this time. Any qualms that they might have had about the politically correct statist policies of the 1970s were carefully concealed.

In the absence of higher taxes, prices rose steadily during the *sexenio* (six-year term), even as the business community—which intensified its political organizing—suffered from an erosion of profits.[66] Their hostility to his populism prompted Echeverría to decry "greedy industrialists" and other "bad Mexicans." Such diatribes offended the business community, which every other Mexican president had courted since World War II.

Echeverría's mercurial behavior, erratic pronouncements, and inept handling of economic problems alienated both the right and left: the former because of resentment toward the government's blustering, excessive intrusion into the economy, combined with official disdain for the private sector; the latter because the performance of the self-styled "people's president" failed to match his rhetoric of reform. Conflicts were subsidized, not resolved. To avoid harsh political and economic choices, the government increased spending—in an indiscriminate and profligate fashion that ballooned the foreign debt from $3 billion in 1970 to $19.6 billion in 1976. In an attempt to divert attention from his economic missteps at home, Echeverría launched various initiatives to diminish the Third World's reliance on industrialized countries and Mexico's dependence on the United States. In fact, this dependence increased because of his need to agree to an austerity plan fashioned by the International Monetary Fund (IMF) to stabilize Mexico's shaky economy.

The wrongheadedness of excessive state intervention became further evident during the administration of Echeverría's successor, José López Portillo, who campaigned on the innocuous, mollifying slogan, "We are all the solution." Immediately upon donning the red, white, and green presidential sash, the weight-lifting, karate-practicing ex-finance secretary took advantage of his country's newly discovered petroleum deposits to spur economic growth and enhance Mexico's role as a leader of both the region and the Third World. Expanding exports of "black gold" increased the gross domestic product by approximately 8 percent each year between 1978 and 1982. This growth generated vast profits for the private sector and helped create one million new jobs annually.

Mexico's success became the envy of a world floundering in recession. Such glamour, however, diverted attention from the beginnings of "petrolization." This neologism connoted a superheated economy fueled by oil revenues, an overvalued currency, mounting dependence on external credits to import escalating amounts of food, capital, and luxury goods, a moribund agricultural sector, and—above all—outsized budget deficits spawned by prodigious spending by a rapidly expanding bureaucracy. López Portillo insisted that his country was "not so much underdeveloped as underadministered." Compounding Mexico's problems was the shortage of skilled workers amid widespread unemployment, as well as bottlenecks in port services, storage, and transport. The government had built highways to handle one-fifth the traffic of the 1980s,[67] while the railroads had changed little since the days that Pancho Villa and his troops rode them during the revolution. Rather than raising taxes, Mexican leaders chose to cover budget shortfalls by printing stacks of crisp new peso notes to pay for social programs, lavish subsidies, large-scale infrastructure projects, and other capital investment.

Excessive spending drove prices ever higher. The rate of inflation dropped from 20.7 percent in 1977 to 16.2 percent in 1978 only to climb back to 28 percent in 1980. A dearer peso with respect to the dollar discouraged tourism, inhibited the export of relatively labor-intensive manufactures, and intensified dependence on oil and its derivatives to generate dollars. Petroleum, which accounted for 21.9 percent of the nation's export earnings in 1977, produced three-fourths of these revenues six years later.

Like a heroin addict who sells his blood in the morning to get a "fix" from an eager, well-heeled supplier at night, Mexico reacted to petrolization pressures by exchanging oil for loans. All told, the country's private and public obligations exceeded $100 billion. In the spring of 1981, however, foreign bankers stopped flooding into Mexico City when an international oil glut appeared, and the seller's market for oil shifted to one favoring buyers. Determined not to "rat on OPEC," with which Mexico had coordinated policy, the country adhered to overvalued oil prices—even as clients abandoned Pemex either for random sales on the so-called spot market or exporters offering discounts. Disquieting changes occurred within an eight-week period beginning 3 June 1981: Mexico cut its prices $4 a barrel; Jorge Díaz Serrano, a López Portillo confident, Pemex's director-general, and architect of the sharp price reduction, abruptly resigned under fire. Patrimony Secretary José Andrés Oteyza, an inveterate nationalist-populist from the Echeverría school, assumed control of oil policy; and Pemex shipped 109.15 million barrels to the U.S. Strategic Petroleum Reserve. When the smoke cleared, López Portillo faced the reality that Mexico earned just $14.6 billion from oil, gas, and petrochemical sales for the year, barely two-thirds of the amount projected.

Only a $10 billion rescue scheme, fashioned by the Reagan administration in response to a desperate August 1982 appeal from Mexico City, prevented the country from defaulting on its foreign debt. López Portillo's agreeing to an IMF stabilization plan was crucial to the success of the bailout. The chief executive became increasingly withdrawn, sleeping late, failing to shave, padding around the Los Pinos presidential palace during the day in his dressing gown. To those familiar with his condition, he appeared as a "hermit," a man who wished to shield himself from the perceived perfidy of Díaz Serrano over oil prices and the abject failure of his presidency. "The President is sounding defensive and apologetic and—that's the worst thing that can happen in Mexico," said a prominent politician, emphasizing the importance of each Mexican chief executive as a symbol of power and stability.[68] López Portillo seemed to be handing over the reins of economic decision making to Miguel de la Madrid Hurtado, the PRI's presidential candidate in the 1982 election. The incumbent named close associates of de la Madrid to head the Central Bank and Finance Ministry.

Still, López Portillo was determined to have his last hurrah. While negotiations with the IMF were hanging fire, he sought to brandish his revolutionary credentials by expropriating the private banking system—an impromptu act that caught all but the Mexican leader's closest advisers by surprise. The man who had once warned his countrymen to end "panic-stricken and frantic activity," justified the 1 September 1982 nationalization on the grounds that bankers had "betrayed" Mexico by facilitating speculation against the peso, which had lost 75 percent of its value during 1982. "I can affirm," he said, "that in recent years a group of Mexicans . . . led, counseled, and supported by private banks, have taken more money

39

out of the country than all the empires that have exploited us since the beginning of our history."[69]   Indeed, it was gross financial mismanagement, not a plot by banking gnomes, that had sparked the capital flight.   Nevertheless, the nationalization inflicted a long-felt trauma on the country's private sector, which had recorded huge profits during the four-year oil boom.   After all, the banks controlled scores of major corporations through stock, debt obligations, and board memberships.

This "profoundly revolutionary measure" by an outgoing leader elicited memories of Echeverría's populism.   It was designed to arrest the chief executive's plummeting popularity, identify a scapegoat for his earlier failure to remedy the country's social ills, secure for himself a place alongside Lázaro Cárdenas in the country's pantheon of heroes, and mollify the left.   At the PRI's behest, some 300,000 workers, peasants, and civil servants flocked to Mexico City's central plaza to praise the intrepid action of "the patriotic president."   In the opinion of one writer, "López Portillo was looking increasingly like a bullfighter awarded both ears and the tail" because of his undaunted move.[70]   Demagoguery reached its zenith when the president began collecting "voluntary" contributions from laborers, campesinos, and government employees to compensate the owners of Mexico's banks—a program in which the military refused to participate.[71]

Arguably, López Portillo was the worst president in modern Mexican history, especially because he participated in egregious corruption and squandered resources that could have been used to achieve sustained development and improve the plight of the 50 percent of Mexicans who live as rag-pickers at the base of a squat social pyramid.   One of his last major political acts, however, did pave the way for a more enlightened economic strategy.   He named as his successor the moderate, reserved de la Madrid, who avoided the extreme acts of his two immediate predecessors.   After almost three years of experimenting with central planning, López Portillo's successor championed a new, market-oriented development plan.

De la Madrid's was not an easy presidency.   During his early years in office, the IMF and foreign bankers hailed Mexico as a model for other Third World debtors to emulate.   The chief executive reduced the inflation rate from 100 percent in 1982 to 60 percent in 1984, and his country was the first to negotiate postponements in repaying the principal of its $96-billion external debt. Yet in mid-1984 the government began to spend freely—with an eye to improving the PRI's performance in the July 1985 congressional and state elections. The result was a failure either to reduce inflation below 60 percent or to achieve the goal of 5 percent annual growth between 1985 and 1988. When oil prices plunged again in early 1986, the president cut approximately $1 billion from a federal budget that overflowed with red ink. Still, the IMF exerted enormous pressure on Mexico to pursue the kinds of measures—reduced subsidies, higher taxes, and tighter monetary policy—that had contributed to a sharp recession three years before. Such actions appeared a prerequisite for a $1.6 billion credit from the international body, whose imprimatur was needed for additional loans from private bankers. IMF officials cheered de la Madrid's easing the rules for foreign investors, granting exceptions to the majority-domestic-ownership requirement for new businesses, shutting down a white elephant steel plant, and beginning to privatize other state industries. They wanted, nonetheless, higher fees and lower subsidies on fertilizer, staple foods, and electricity. Public transport fares and telephone rates were also quite low.[72]

The economic cabinet met continually throughout the late winter and spring of 1986 in an attempt to craft a strategy that would pry more monies out of the international financiers without requiring draconian measures that could spark widespread social discontent just a year before the next presidential campaign would begin. By June Jesús Silva Herzog Flores, 51, Mexico's Yale-trained, flamboyant globe-trotting finance secretary, was advocating a temporary suspension of interest payments to conserve the country's $2 to $3 billion in foreign reserves. Reportedly, he recommended reducing the budget deficit to 8-9 percent of GDP, several points less than the IMF proposed. His preference was for decreased spending, an unpopular move that Salinas as secretary of budget and planning (SPP) would have to implement, rather than tax increases, for which Silva Herzog's own ministry would be responsible. To offset the political impact of the projected cuts, Silva Herzog is said to have proposed a 90-day suspension of $1.6

billion of the $3.6 billion in interest on Mexico's $98 billion debt to foreign creditors, which fell due in the second half of the year.[73]

A middle-level Mexican official, who knew that a halt in debt payments would make his country a pariah in the eyes of world bankers, warned the U.S. Embassy of the possibility of drastic action. He urged that President Reagan personally phone de la Madrid or that Federal Reserve Chairman Paul A. Volcker, a key player in the 1982 bailout, visit Mexico to spell out the dire consequences of unilateral action. Personnel from the State Department, Treasury Department, and CIA dispatched urgent messages to Washington. On 9 June, Volcker flew in to confer with Silva Herzog and Miguel Mancera Aguayo, the moderate, extremely professional head of the Central Bank who had resigned when López Portillo nationalized the banking system only to be later reappointed by de la Madrid.

After Volcker's departure, Silva Herzog—his public populism notwithstanding—reportedly urged larger budget cuts than were acceptable to his colleagues. The meeting proved tempestuous and the finance secretary alienated the decorous de la Madrid by "losing his cool," in the words of an observer. "He was completely alone in recent cabinet meetings," said one well-placed source.[74] SPP Secretary Salinas opposed reductions in food and transportation subsidies and cuts in other popular programs on the grounds that they would exacerbate discontent in a country already flailed by a 90 percent inflation rate. In contrast to Silva Herzog's isolation, Salinas had used his SPP post, which entailed allocating resources to government agencies, to cultivate allies within the cabinet. His network extended even to Mexico City Mayor Ramón Aguirre Velázquez, a de la Madrid confidant, and the president's top aide Emilio Gamboa Patrón.[75] Although not actively cooperating with Salinas, other presidential hopefuls—Government Secretary Manuel Bartlett Díaz and Energy Secretary Alfredo del Mazo—were not adverse to seeing the finance secretary fall on his face. Salinas and his cohorts convinced the chief executive that Silva Herzog had become an apologist for, and defender of, the IMF, and was insufficiently attuned to the domestic repercussions of its proposals. For his part, the arrogant Silva Herzog, whom an international magazine had named "finance minister of the year" in the early

1980s, neglected to build alliances. Three factors account for this failure: Silva Herzog's hubris, his exceptional intellect complemented by an extraordinarily engaging personality that some labeled charismatic, and his long-time, close personal and professional ties to de la Madrid, who would select the nation's next president. The upshot of this donnybrook was the secretary's "irrevocable resignation," and his replacement by Gustavo Petricioli Iturbide, 57, a close friend of the president with whom Salinas enjoyed productive relations. Silva Herzog's departure had several consequences: It set the stage for a reasonable compromise with the IMF and international bankers, many of whom feared that the ambitious Salinas would be more difficult to deal with than the ousted finance secretary; it removed the leading contender to succeed de la Madrid from the race that would begin in 1987; and it enabled Salinas, previously an aggressive champion of state planning, to fashion Mexico's liberal economic policy, which proved a stepping stone to the presidency for the recent convert to the magic of the marketplace.

New Ideology

Even as Salinas pursued a nationalistic approach to debt negotiations, he and de la Madrid realized that business-as-usual statism would condemn Mexico to economic purgatory. Thus, they championed a new growth strategy keyed to market forces rather than ubiquitous state involvement in an inward-looking, heavily protected economy. They began to rip apart this protectionist cocoon in order to boost labor productivity, stimulate investment, and activate the domestic business community that, because of the interventionism promoted by Echeverría and López Portillo, viewed the government as a menacing adversary. They also sought to obtain foreign loans, attract state-of-the-art technology, spur non-petroleum exports, and combat inflation. As a first step toward integrating their nation into the international economic system, de la Madrid signed a Bilateral Subsidies Understanding with the United States in 1985. This accord stipulated that his country would phase out export subsidies in exchange for an injury test in countervailing-duty litigation. For example, U.S. steel producers would have to demonstrate actual harm suffered from Mexican steel imports that benefited from unfair trade practices before penalties could be imposed on these goods. Before the Understanding was signed, U.S. firms could instigate Commerce Department investigations of allegedly subsidized Mexican exports even without submitting proof that their businesses had been injured.

To build on this important foundation, the two nations entered into a Bilateral Trade and Investment Framework Understanding in November 1987. This accord enabled either country to request consultations with the other on any matter concerning bilateral trade and investment. The document also called for annual cabinet-level consultations between the two governments to review outstanding issues. This pact paved the way for agreements on textiles, steel, and alcoholic beverages. Two years later, the United States and Mexico took advantage of the work begun earlier and concluded a second trade and investment understanding.

Meanwhile, Salinas and de la Madrid championed their country's membership in the General Agreement on Tariffs and Trade (GATT) in 1986. GATT is a Geneva-based, multination organization devoted to promoting trade by lowering barriers and conferring reciprocal benefits on members.

De la Madrid gave impetus to the idea of market forces by nominating Salinas as his successor. The selection of the "atomic ant"—so called because of his energy, self-discipline, and attention to details—brought cheers in bank towers and board rooms. Less enthusiastic were peasants, bureaucrats, and denizens of the shantytowns that suffuse and surround Mexico City and other urban centers. They resonated to Cuauhtémoc Cárdenas Solorzano, son of the beloved, late President Cárdenas, who urged retention of an interventionist economic model to cope with acute stagflation and high unemployment. The actual election proved difficult for Salinas. Only after a protracted vote count was the cerebral ex-SPP secretary awarded a slight majority in a three-way contest. The defeated Cárdenas organized the Party of the Democratic Revolution (PRD) to consolidate his electoral base and advance his statist views.

Once ensconced in the presidential palace in December 1988, Salinas continued to reduce impediments to imports in order to force domestic corporations to compete with their foreign counterparts. "Our first challenge was privatizing the private sector," stated Finance Secretary Pedro Aspe Armella.[76] In the process, Mexico dropped its average tariff rates from 27 percent to 13.1 percent and jettisoned licensing requirements for 86 percent of the nation's goods purchased abroad.

In the six years after joining GATT, Mexico achieved as much trade liberalization as the United States attained in the 40 years after reaching its protectionist zenith with the Smoot-Hawley Tariff. Mexico's opening catalyzed an increase in exports to $46.2 billion for 1992, while imports exceeded $62.1 billion. The ever-larger trade deficit sprang from imports of machinery and other goods by a private sector gearing up for greater competition, particularly from U.S. and Canadian producers.

National Interests Redefined

A redefinition of national interests informed Salinas's commitment to a local version of perestroika, designed to vault Mexico from the Third to the First World. Under Echeverría and López Portillo, national interests involved shielding domestic producers from the global economy. Safeguards not only took the form of high tariffs and ever present import permits; they were also enshrined in investment restrictions, Third World solidarity schemes, cooperation with the Organization of Petroleum Exporting Countries, and a refusal to join GATT.

As both cabinet secretary and chief executive, Salinas argued, in essence, that all politics is global. He emphasized that the world was changing, as evidenced by the internationalization of markets, financial interdependence among states, and mounting commercial competition. For Mexico to close its economy to these forces would mean not progress, but stagnation—and the nation's consignment to the status of an economic backwater. The result would be an increasing inability to sell its goods abroad, create jobs, attract investment, and increase income. Salinas warned that:

Those nations that do not adapt themselves creatively will not be able to maintain their integrity. Those who do not do so in time will allow the opportunities offered by the new situation to pass by and will be forced to suffer the disadvantages one by one: stagnation; technological insufficiency; social tension; and finally, national weakness, which means an effective loss of sovereignty.[77]

Institutional backing for Salinas's market-focused reforms came largely from high-ranking officials with whom he had served in the de la Madrid administration, as well as from individuals whom he recruited to senior posts in the Central Bank and in the ministries of Finance and Public Credit (SHCP), Commerce and Industrial Development (SECOFI), and Budget and Planning (SPP).[78] Most of these technocrats share several traits: they grew up in comfortable, middle-class, political families, earned undergraduate degrees in economics in Mexico, received advanced training in economics, public administration, or related fields at prestigious U.S. universities, speak English fluently, belong to the PRI, and have pursued careers in the Central Bank, Finance Secretariat, or related agencies. Many of these men have long been concerned with social questions. Salinas, for example, wrote his Ph.D. thesis on rural development; Manuel Camacho Solís, who served as mayor of Mexico City from 1988 to 1993, conducted research on labor unions; Aspe focused his academic work on income distribution; and Zedillo prepared his Yale dissertation on how undisciplined fiscal policy accentuated Mexico's public debt crisis.[79]

Several highly respected intellectuals wrote and lectured continually about the need for market reforms. These include political economist Luis Rubio F., director of the Centro de Investigación para el Desarrollo, A.C.; Rogelio Ramirez de la O, head of the ECANAL business consulting firm; Luis Pazos, president of the Mexico City-based Center for Free Enterprise Research; and Enrique Krauze, author and deputy editor of the monthly magazine *Vuelta*.

Washington also encouraged Mexico's newfound enthusiasm for market-focused policies. Salinas's Mexico had the distinction of becoming the first beneficiary of the 1989 Brady Plan for diminishing Latin America's commercial debts. Under this initiative, named for U.S. Treasury Secretary Nicholas F. Brady, the banks offered Mexico three options or a blend thereof: a 35 percent reduction on the principal of loans, a corresponding cut in interest rates to 6.25 percent, or refinancing amounting to 60 percent of annual interest charges. This was the first time since the debt crisis had erupted in the early 1980s that the United States had proposed lower interest rates for greatly overborrowed countries. Mexico's reasonableness on the debt question enhanced the Americans' receptivity toward negotiating a free-trade agreement with its Spanish-speaking neighbor.

CHAPTER THREE

NAFTA faces a Fast-Track Showdown[80]

Introduction

Salinas was in office for more than a year before he embraced the idea of a free-trade agreement with the United States. A decade before, continental economic integration, especially in the energy field because of the 1970s oil crisis, had emerged as one of the few innovative proposals of the 1980 U.S. presidential campaign. Republicans Ronald Reagan and John Connally and Democrat Edmund G. "Jerry" Brown, Jr., pronounced themselves in favor of the concept.[81] Reagan even talked at length with López Portillo about the desirability of a comprehensive arrangement, covering trade, capital, and labor. The Mexican leader, who had resisted Washington's encouragement to enter GATT, listened politely before refusing to endorse a proposal that he deemed unrealistic. "He told us that our children, and probably our grandchildren, would never see the day [that economic integration would occur]," recalls Reagan's campaign manager.[82]

At that time, Mexican politicians perceived the issue as a political "third rail." Nationalists even castigated the idea of constructing a pipeline, designed to export excess gas from Mexico's Southeast to the Texas border, as a potential land-based Panama Canal, vulnerable to seizure by the U.S. Marines in the event of a crisis. As Heberto Castillo, erstwhile leader of the Mexican

Workers' Party, now a part of the PRD, expressed it: " . . . to construct the *gasoducto* to Texas will leave our sons and grandsons in ruins. A future generation of Mexicans will damn, perhaps still in Spanish, the government official who plundered their country."[83] Publicly favoring such a scheme would have ended the career of most politicians in defensively nationalistic Mexico, where the "colossus of the north" is frequently blamed for all kinds of real and imagined evils.

An example of this near-paranoia surfaced in mid-1980, when Mexican officials and newspapers had a field day accusing Washington of stealing rain by diverting hurricanes from Mexico's shores. The villain was the U.S. National Oceanic and Atmospheric Administration, whose hurricane-hunter aircraft had allegedly intercepted a storm named "Ignacio" off Mexico's Pacific coast in October 1979, thereby contributing to the country's worst drought in 20 years. Mexican observers, including the director of the country's National Meteorological Service, apparently believed that Yankee ingenuity was so great that Uncle Sam could bend Mother Nature to his indomitable will.[84]

Salinas's Misgivings about an FTA

In a display of concern about Mexico's powerful neighbor, Salinas said just before his inauguration, "I am not in favor of such a proposal [for integration]. There is such a different economic level between the United States and Mexico that I don't believe such a common market would provide an advantage to either country."[85] As late as October 1989, during a visit to Washington the Mexican chief executive spoke with U.S. officials about a sector-by-sector opening, not about sweeping economic integration. Salinas won a disputed election to gain the presidency; a majority of respondents told pollsters for the *Los Angeles Times* that they thought populist, leftist Cárdenas had captured more votes.[86] In contrast to his PRI predecessors who garnered 70 to 80 percent of the ballots casts, Salinas's official tally was only 50.7 percent. In view of the new chief executive's weakness upon taking office, he could hardly have advocated a new relationship with Washington that would have flown in the face of Mexico's neuralgic nationalism.

Salinas, once confidently ensconced in power after a series of bold moves had lofted his popularity, changed his mind about a free-trade agreement. Contributing to this volte-face was his failure to broaden Mexico's commercial and financial ties with Western Europe and Japan. In early 1990, the Mexican chief executive spent ten days in Western Europe, where he met with the leaders of Britain, West Germany, Belgium, Switzerland, and Portugal. Although then-Prime Minister Margaret Thatcher encouraged his efforts, the other hosts graciously conveyed a disheartening message: "We admire your market-oriented strategy to open and modernize Mexico's hidebound economy, but East Europe will be the target of our capital investment, finance, and commercial activities." For their part, the Japanese also praised Salinas's accomplishments but emphasized that their greatest economic interests lay in the Asian littoral.

These polite rebuffs reinforced Salinas's belief, as trading blocs emerged in Western Europe, in the Pacific Rim, and between Canada and the United States, that Mexico must find another dynamic partner to avoid becoming a stagnant backwater, while arming itself against protectionist threats. The United States was an obvious choice. Location, tradition, and a spiderweb of economic ties pointed Salinas northward. Also impressive was the success of the 1989 U.S.-Canada Free Trade Agreement (CFTA) in stimulating bilateral trade and attracting investor attention to Canada. The bonds between Mexico and the United States were already noteworthy, as evidenced by the 1989 flow of exports ($25 billion), investment ($5.5 billion), and traveler expenditures ($5.7 billion) from the United States to its southern neighbor. For their part, Mexican consumers purchased U.S. goods and services valued at $27.2 billion, making Mexico the third-largest export market for the United States in 1989. Almost 2,000 *maquiladoras* (border assembly plants), employing a half-million Mexicans, fortified the bilateral linkage, as did the growing interrelations between the New York and Mexico City stock exchanges.

Other signs of mounting United States–Mexican interdependence included increased migration, tourism, telephone calls,

51

telegraph messages, and media contacts. Data on such transactions appear in chapter 10.

In addition, *Petróleos Mexicanos* (Pemex), the state oil monopoly, had furnished 44 percent of the almost 600 million barrels of oil stored in the U.S. Strategic Petroleum Reserve. As well, Pemex and private Mexican firms purchased upward of $100 million worth of oil equipment and services from U.S. suppliers in 1989.

Consensus-building at Home

Following his return from Europe in early 1990, Salinas was determined to push for a free-trade agreement with the United States. To begin with, he had to make certain that President Bush, who had voiced support for a continent-wide pact during the 1988 campaign, was still receptive to the idea. To find out, Salinas phoned Bush in late February and, subsequently, dispatched two of his most trusted advisers—Chief of Staff José María Córdoba Montoya and Commerce Secretary Jaime Serra Puche—to talk with their U.S. counterparts. Private consultations with Secretary of State James A. Baker III, National Security Adviser Brent Scowcroft, U.S. Trade Representative Carla A. Hills, Commerce Secretary Robert A. Mosbacher, and Council of Economic Affairs Chairman Michael J. Boskin, encouraged the Mexican envoys about the possibility of negotiating an accord, although Washington did not give the green light until late March or early April.[87]

Mexico's highly centralized political system, buttressed by ubiquitous official influence in the media, guaranteed broad acceptance of the presidential initiative. Taking their cue from Los Pinos presidential palace, most PRI leaders applauded a free-trade pact; many editorial writers wrote glowingly of the venture; major business associations backed an accord; and even the Confederation of Mexican Workers (CTM), the 5.5 million-member trade union federation that forms part of the PRI's corporatist structure, grudgingly advocated a bilateral economic agreement as a means to create jobs and boost wages.[88] On 21 May the Mexican Senate recommended that the government negotiate a free-trade pact.

The president gave SECOFI responsibility for NAFTA. To lay the groundwork for negotiations, SECOFI established an "ideas group" (*grupo pensante*). This body was coordinated by Herminio Blanco Mendoza (SECOFI), 40, who received his doctorate in economics from Yale and served as undersecretary for foreign trade before being named Mexico's chief NAFTA negotiator in September 1990. Its other members were Jaime Zabludovsky Kuper (SECOFI), 34, who held master's and doctorate degrees in economics from Yale and was responsible for technical matters, including contacts with Canada and other countries with FTA experience; Jesús Flores Ayala (SECOFI), 40, recipient of a master's degree in economics from the University of Warwick, who was in charge of logistics, specifically identifying the resources available for the negotiations and proposing how to organize them; and Guillermo Aguilar Alvarez C. (International Court of Arbitration of the CCI, Paris), 32, who had studied law at UNAM and the University of Montpelier and concentrated on the legal aspects of a free-trade accord.

Salinas's clear mandate to SECOFI to prepare for talks with United States militated against public opposition from other ministries, which had misgivings about the venture. Pemex and the Federal Electricity Commission, for example, were among the agencies that expressed, in the words of an insider, "extreme caution" about NAFTA. Serra Puche and Blanco showed themselves to be consummate diplomats in handling free-trade skeptics who worried about incursions onto their bureaucratic turf. "You have the expertise needed to make the president's initiative work; ours is simply a coordinating role," was the message disseminated from the SECOFI building. The Finance Ministry had long championed free trade and worked hand-in-glove with Commerce officials to prepare for negotiations. Serra Puche and Blanco enjoyed the full and effective cooperation of not only Aspe, but of undersecretaries José Angel Gurría Treviño, Guillermo Ortiz Martínez, Carlos Ruiz Sacristán, and Francisco Gil Díaz. At the president's directive, Agriculture Secretary Carlos Hank González and Undersecretary Luis Téllez Kuenzler also threw their wholehearted support to the NAFTA venture.

On 5 September 1990, SECOFI established an Office for NAFTA Negotiations to lead and coordinate discussions with the United States. Approximately 100 specialists in different economic fields, which—in terms of the high quality of personnel, relatively small size, and singularity of purpose—was patterned after the Office of the United States Trade Representative (USTR). Also created was an Intersectoral Commission of NAFTA that embraced the federal agencies with the greatest stake in an agreement—namely, SECOFI, Treasury, Foreign Relations, Social Development, Labor, the Central Bank, and the Presidency. Finally, Serra Puche formed a Treaty Advisory Council to keep major constituencies (labor, agriculture, business, and academia) informed about the free-trade process.

Salinas loudly trumpeted the issue at home. He did so in part because he wanted to mobilize support for the initiative, and in part because he believed that positive publicity about the pact would help the PRI politically in the July 1991 midterm congressional elections.[89] His party's strong showing in these contests provided to the Salinas administration the legitimacy it had failed to achieve in the controversial 1988 election. The fact that PRI's president, Luis Donaldo Colosio Murrieta, directed the landslide victory lofted his political stock. This triumph was an important factor in Salinas's selecting him as the official party's 1994 presidential standard-bearer. Tragically, an assassin's bullet removed him from the contest on 23 March 1994.

U.S. Reaction

Once they agreed on the wisdom of exploring a free-trade pact, the chief executives directed officials from their nations to begin discussing such a accord. Serra Puche and Córdoba participated actively in these sessions, as did Carla Hills and Ambassador Julius L. Katz, the number-two official in USTR, the nation's pivotal agency in trade matters. During this period, Robert B. Zoellick, the State Department's counselor and a Baker confidant, developed a close working relationship with the French-born Córdoba, deemed the most influential adviser to Salinas. Following months of these unofficial, exploratory contacts, the Mexican leader formally told Bush in early fall that he wanted to commence talks on a free-trade area.

Earlier, the U.S. bureaucracy had been divided over the urgency of forging such a pact. From the outset, the National Security Council, along with the departments of Commerce, State, and Treasury, welcomed the idea of an accord and urged full-speed-ahead on the proposal. Initially, the USTR and the Department of Agriculture both expressed caution about the initiative. The USTR, in particular, knew from its protracted efforts on the U.S.-Canadian Free Trade Agreement in the late 1980s how much groundwork had to be laid with Congress and the private sector before negotiations could prosper. Ambassador Hills was also concerned that embarking on NAFTA would delay completion of GATT's "Uruguay Round." Mexico, after all, purchased less than 5 percent of U.S. goods and services shipped abroad, while GATT members accounted for nearly 100 percent. The USTR was also skeptical of whether Mexico knew what major negotiations would entail or how far it would have to go to reach a successful accord. Did Mexico want to negotiate only trade issues—or was it prepared to extend the discussions to investment, intellectual property, services, agriculture, and other subjects of importance to Washington? By spring, however, USTR was convinced that NAFTA would complement, not conflict with, efforts to conclude the GATT talks.

The Uruguay Round involved contentious, multilateral bargaining, commenced in the Uruguayan resort city of Punta del Este in 1986. These parleys transcended the traditional GATT agenda of manufactured goods to address obstacles to trade in financial services and agricultural items, as well as the protection of patents, trademarks, copyrights, computer software, and other intellectual property. An agreement between the United States and Europe was crucial to the success of GATT negotiations. A conflict over price supports and export subsidies between the European Community and a U.S.-led coalition of agricultural exporters, however, paralyzed the global talks, thereby giving added impetus to NAFTA.

To diversify America's trade options, U.S. Trade Representative Hills recommended to President Bush the initiation of formal negotiations with Mexico on a comprehensive free-trade agreement, following preliminary consultations with private sector representatives and Congress. Serra Puche made a similar proposal to Salinas.

In a letter dated 21 August 1990, Salinas formally proposed to Bush the initiation of negotiations on a bilateral FTA. On 25 September, the U.S. president, in accord with domestic law, notified Ways and Means Committee Chairman Rostenkowski and Lloyd Bentsen (D-Tex.), chairman of the Senate Finance Committee, of trade negotiations with Mexico. The communication also apprised the committees of the expressed desire by the Canadian government to participate in the negotiations—with the goal of achieving a trilateral trade pact. In early February 1991, Bush informed the chairman of the Ways and Means Committee that he, Salinas, and Canadian Prime Minister M. Brian Mulroney had agreed, on the basis of three-way consultations, to seek NAFTA. On 1 March, Bush requested an extension of fast-track procedures, for two years ending 1 June 1993, to facilitate completion of both the Uruguay Round and the proposed continental trade pact.

Later in the month, Speaker Foley reconstituted a Trade Agreement Coordinating Group, originally established in the 102nd Congress. It was chaired by Rostenkowski and included the Majority Leader, the Minority Leader, co-chairs of the Democratic Trade Task Force, and chairmen and ranking minority members of the nine standing committees with jurisdiction over subjects involved in trade negotiations.[90] This group was the primary coordinating mechanism in the House for monitoring the progress of the NAFTA negotiations and, later, for consulting informally with the Clinton administration on developing the draft implementing legislation.[91]

Canada Comes Abroad

Participation in the NAFTA parleys was not an easy decision for Canada. Prime Minister Mulroney had been caught off guard when, just before he made a March 1990 visit to Mexico, Secretary of State Baker informed him of possible U.S.-Mexican trade negotiations. At first blush, Mulroney, in office since 1984, was leery of seeking to inject Canada into any such discussions.

56

Detractors of his Progressive Conservative party had, after all, blamed the CFTA for a deepening year-long recession; Mulroney's public approval rating had fallen to 12 percent, making him the most unpopular prime minister in the 50-year history of Canadian polling.[92] So unpopular was he that in Toronto, students threw wet macaroni at him, while in Edmonton, posters warned, "Brian Mulroney is coming to Alberta. Stop him."[93] Extraordinarily contentious efforts to craft a constitutional arrangement between the federal government and Canada's 10 provinces also militated against Ottawa's entering yet another round of controversial free-trade negotiations. Underground publications—a legal version of the *samizdat* that had sprung up in pre-Gorbachev Russia—pilloried the trade deal with the United States and inflamed public opinion. Such anti-CFTA polemics as Marjorie M. Cohen's *Women and Free Trade* and Marjorie Bowker's *On Guard for Thee* reached tens of thousands of readers. Bowker, a 72-year-old retired family court judge from Alberta, warned that the accord even threatened Canada's extremely popular social programs, including old-age pensions, medical insurance, and unemployment benefits. American companies, she reasoned, might attack such programs as "unfair subsidies" to their Canadian competitors.[94]

Soon, party divisions erupted over NAFTA. The populist New Democrats, whose president was vice president of the Canadian Labour Congress, and a wing of the Liberals opposed Canada's entry into the negotiations just as they had strenuously objected to the CFTA.[95] Nor was the leadership of the Progressive Conservatives solidly behind Canadian involvement. Mulroney and Finance Minister Michael H. Wilson favored their country's participation. Their enthusiasm for participation was matched by that of the Canadian ambassador to the United States, Derek H. Burney. Although a career civil servant, Burney was a Washington insider with political skills that invited comparisons with House Speaker Thomas P. "Tip" O'Neill, Jr. In contrast, Deputy Prime Minister Donald F. Mazankowski, International Trade Minister John C. Crosbie, External Affairs Minister Joe Clark, and the prime minister's chief of staff, Hugh Segal, initially expressed misgivings about a trade pact. They believed that their country had more important priorities and that negotiations would probably coincide with the next general elections. Because Canadian governments seldom survive more than two terms, these promised to be difficult contests. Mexico, moreover, was only Canada's 17th largest trading partner, and although Mexico City was geographically closer to Toronto than to Vancouver, psychologically it was much further away. At one point in early 1990, Crosbie was quoted as saying that there was "zero pounds of pressure per square inch" in Canada pushing for a deal with Mexico. One senior External Affairs official, on perceptions of NAFTA within the top layers of the federal bureaucracy, said: "There are arguments on both sides, but some people in the trade establishment in Ottawa look on this with alarm. Their position is that we are still trying to digest the effects of the Canada-U.S. Free Trade Agreement, and this is the worst possible time to tackle something new."[96]

In March 1990 Mulroney appointed a small task force, headed by Donald Campbell, a career diplomat, to evaluate the impact of NAFTA on Canada. By spring it was evident that U.S.-Mexican negotiations would commence if the Bush administration obtained negotiating authority. Subsequently, the Canadian cabinet sought even deeper and broader studies, including the impact of a continental pact on the automobile sector. By August Mulroney and his ministers considered several options for Canada's status at the talks: (1) nonparticipant; (2) observer; (3) semiparticipant—that is, taking part in negotiations in just a few sectors;[97] and (4) full participant.

Ultimately, full participation emerged as the only rational choice. So vital was the U.S. market to Canada that the Mulroney government could not risk Mexico's achieving benefits there that Ottawa did not enjoy. As one Canadian diplomat explained: "We didn't want to compromise the preferences that we bought and paid for through tough concessions made in the CFTA." Moreover, Canada did not wish the United States to enmesh itself in a series of hub-and-spoke commercial arrangements.[98] In such a configuration, Washington, as the commercial hub, would enjoy preferential access for its exports to spoke nations (e.g., Mexico and other Latin American states), which—in turn—might not have similar entrée into the markets of other spoke countries. On a positive note, Canada's trade with Mexico had begun to grow, albeit slowly, and it wanted the same entry to the expanding Mexican market that U.S. traders would enjoy. Ottawa also realized from its CFTA experience that negotiating a free-trade agreement tends to thrust participants into the international limelight. Might not such attention lure investors to the countries involved? At least, by joining NAFTA, Ottawa would be in a better position to ensure that investment dollars were not diverted from Canada to Mexico and the United States. If the latter became a hub country, it would be especially attractive to European and Asian entrepreneurs whom the Canadians were anxious to entice to their economically troubled nation. Additionally, the Mulroney government viewed the NAFTA discussions as an opportunity for resolving trade problems that had emerged with the United States in recent years. There was even the chance to obtain clearer and more predictable rules of origin, an extension of duty drawback provisions, and an improved mechanism for consultation and dispute settlement.

In April 1991, Mulroney appointed a "Core Group" of 12 to 15 participants at the assistant deputy minister level to determine how Canada should approach the negotiations. Represented in this body were External Affairs, International Trade, Finance, Investment Canada, Agriculture Canada, and Industry, Science, and Technology Canada (ISTC). The issue of which minister would spearhead Ottawa's negotiations was resolved when Mulroney, in an April 1991 shake-up of his 40-member cabinet, conferred upon Wilson, formerly finance minister, the newly created "superministry" of International Trade and Competitiveness, crafted from elements of several existing cabinet departments. Initially a NAFTA skeptic, John Crosbie, a "Jesus by thunder Newfoundlander," was moved to the fisheries ministry.

At first both Washington and Mexico City were concerned lest Canadian involvement slow or hobble negotiations that had the biggest payoff for their two countries. The departments of State, Treasury, and Commerce were especially apprehensive. A senior USTR official speculated, off the record, that Mexico appeared hopeful that Washington might veto Ottawa's involvement. According to a Canadian diplomat who asked to remain anonymous, Senator Bentsen expressed his opposition to three-way talks by saying, "When you talk with your wife in the bedroom, you don't want an observer."

U.S. Chief Negotiator Julius Katz, however, stood firm for Canada's inclusion. A 40-year champion of free trade, Katz disliked the concept of a network of bilateral agreements. Instead, he preferred a core agreement that would grow to include other countries. Some of his colleagues in other U.S. agencies argued that Mexico and Canada might, in the course of bargaining, "gang up" on the United States. "So what," he replied. "We can simply follow Nancy Reagan's approach [to their position] and 'just say no.'"[99] As a practical matter, there was no one in official Washington who was going to tell Mulroney—one of the United States's closest, perhaps the closest, ally—that the NAFTA door was shut to him. In addition, Canada's presence would ensure negotiations that focused on three-way trade and not simply the provision of U.S. aid to Mexico.

In a conciliatory gesture, Ottawa pledged to withdraw from the talks if it constituted an impediment to their conclusion. "If we couldn't stand the heat, we would graciously leave the kitchen—and not slam the door behind us," stated a Canadian diplomat.[100] The United States and Canada also agreed that during NAFTA negotiations, no changes would be made in their free-trade agreement without the consent of both parties. As things turned out, Canada's participation actually assuaged some Mexican fears that their country, with 1/20th the gross domestic product of the United States, would be overwhelmed if it entered the proposed trade configuration alone with an economic behemoth. The presence of a third party at the table also afforded the Mexicans some respite from direct U.S. pressure. "Conflicts between the Americans and Canadians provided a change of pace and some breathing space for us," confided one Mexican negotiator.

What is Fast Track?

What is fast track? How does it affect trade legislation? The musings of some humorists aside, it is neither a speedy racecourse, a zany dance step, nor a high-speed sports event. Rather, fast track reflects the American genius for hammering out compromises. The U.S. Constitution empowers the president to conduct foreign affairs, including trade agreements; Congress is vested with authority over foreign commerce. Yet legislators found out in 1930 that trying to write tariff legislation could boomerang. In that year, as noted above, the House and Senate passed the infamous Smoot-Hawley Tariff to protect Depression-injured industries. What architects of this legislation failed to anticipate was the swift retaliation that Smoot-Hawley provoked from trading partners. The result was a downward spiral in both world commerce and the U.S. economy. Congress corrected its error in the Reciprocal Trade Agreements Act of 1934. From that legislation through the Trade Expansion Act of 1962, the lawmakers delegated authority for trade negotiations. They authorized the president to cut U.S. tariffs (within specified numerical limits) in exchange for reductions by our trading partners. The final deal would be implemented by presidential proclamation, without Capitol Hill's involvement.[101] Despite occasional outcries from adversely affected industries, the arrangement worked well for negotiators. Their credibility at the bargaining table grew because the deals they cut would become law. In the late 1960s, however, antidumping codes, customs appraisals, and other nontariff barriers (NTBs) began to figure more prominently in trade talks. There was no advanced authorization system for NTBs, and Congress refused to implement two important nontariff commitments agreed to by the Johnson administration in 1967. Indeed, the Senate was so alarmed over investing the White House with authority that could transcend trade issues, it even turned down President Nixon's 1973 proposal for a congressional veto over NTB agreements.[102]

How, then, could the executive branch enjoy the necessary leeway and credibility to negotiate intricate trade arrangements, including NTBs, without hostile legislators disfiguring its masterpiece through a barrage of amendments that could delay and cripple controversial bills? The answer turned out to be fast track. This mechanism authorizes presidential representatives to forge a trade deal with one or more foreign governments. Congress must then accept or reject the accord as a package; no changes are allowed.

This concept, embedded in the Trade Act of 1974, established an executive-legislative partnership in trade affairs. The Omnibus Trade and Competitiveness Act of 1988 further provided that fast-track authority could be extended for two years if the president so requested, on the condition, of course, that neither a key committee (Ways and Means in the House; Finance in the Senate) nor either legislative chamber passed a disallowing resolution within 90 days of the White House request. Absent congressional disapproval, expedited procedural protection would apply to any trade agreement submitted 90 calendar days before the expiration of fast-track authority. In the case of NAFTA, the deadline for submitting the pact was 1 June 1994.

Fast track allows expedited trade negotiations to take place under the following formal and informal procedures:

- The president provides at least 60 days' notice to the House Ways and Means and Senate Finance Committees of his intention to commence trade negotiations with a foreign country;

- The president informs the House of Representatives and the Senate of his intention to enter into an agreement at least 90 calendar days before he signs the accord;

- After signing the agreement, the president submits it to the House and the Senate, along with an implementing bill crafted in concert with congressional leaders, a statement of administrative action proposed to implement the agreement, and detailed supporting information explaining how the agreement achieves the United States's negotiating objectives;

- Provided the executive branch has met all procedural hurdles, the House (45 days in committees; 15 days on the floor) and the Senate (15 days in committees; 15 days on the floor) may take up to 90 legislative days to consider the legislation. Speech-making in each chamber is limited to 20 hours. Debate time in the House is split equally between proponents and opponents; in the Senate, the time is divided between the majority and minority leaders;

- Finally, the House of Representatives votes first on the unamendable legislative package, which cannot be filibustered in the Senate.

In 1991 proponents advanced several arguments in favor of fast track. First, the mechanism ensured that the initiative for trade negotiations lay with the executive branch, while conferring upon Congress ultimate control over an agreement's fate. To deprive the president of this authority would remove an important incentive for him to involve legislators in the negotiating process. Second, a vote for fast track endorsed process, not substance. Members could reject an agreement considered harmful to the nation or to their constituents. Third, extending fast track was crucial to continued U.S. efforts to reduce trade barriers in a world where protectionism was alive and well. Fourth, the process had served the United States well in concluding free-trade agreements with Israel (1985) and Canada (1989). Finally, foreign countries would deem it futile to negotiate with Washington if any agreement were subject to being overturned or adorned with "Christmas-tree amendments" in Congress to protect certain U.S. industries.

With respect to the last point, Representative Sam M. Gibbons (D-Fla.), a free-trader and chairman of the Subcommittee on International Trade of the Ways and Means Committee, pointed out that Congress conceived of fast track after defeating two agreements negotiated under the GATT's Kennedy Round (1964–1967). The reaction of our trading partners was, he said: "Listen, unless you reform your congressional procedures, we aren't dealing with you anymore. You are not a reliable bargainer."[103]

Opponents of NAFTA, on the other hand, got their licks in against fast track. First, they insisted that, while appropriate for negotiations among 100-plus GATT members, accelerated approval authority was not intended for talks with just a country or two. Second, they claimed that the Mexicans were so eager for NAFTA that fast track was unnecessary; in the words of Senator Howard M. Metzenbaum (D-Ohio), "The Mexicans initiated these trade talks.

The Mexicans want this agreement. And the Mexicans will continue to negotiate with or without the fast-track."[104]   Third, critics contended that the Reagan administration had failed to consult Congress sufficiently on the U.S.-Canada Free Trade Agreement, and that Bush's representatives would likewise engage only in pro forma contacts with the legislative branch. "In my experience, the [Bush-Congress] consultations have not been meaningful," said Senator Thomas A. Daschle (D-S.D.). "Muggers meet directly with their victims, too, but we don't call it consultations."[105]   Although some detractors admitted that Bush's team might truly consult with the Ways and Means and Finance committees, they argued that rank-and-file legislators who belonged to neither panel would be frozen out of the loop. Deprived of the chance to submit floor amendments, such members would have little or no influence on the trade talks.   Fourth, a few members viewed fast track as an unconstitutional abridgement of the checks-and-balances system, while others, who conceded its legality, berated the process as an "abdication," "abrogation," or "surrender" of legislative prerogatives. They inveighed against giving the White House a "carte blanche," "blank check," or "keys to the store."[106]   Fifth, Representatives Charles B. Rangel (D-N.Y.) and Frank J. Guarini (D-N.J.) complained that the proposed trade negotiations would ignore the influx of drugs from Mexico.[107]

A final argument against the special negotiating authority touched on the merits of the pact itself. An amalgam of labor, environmental, consumer, and religious organizations submitted that fast track would facilitate a fundamentally flawed agreement. NAFTA, they argued, would eliminate American jobs as factories migrated across the border to take advantage of "sweat-shop" conditions amid lax environmental rules and human rights abuses. Mike Clark, president of Friends of the Earth, charged that "the fast track is a slippery track, a wrong track and it should be stopped dead in its tracks." In a similar vein, the Reverend Pharis Harvey, executive director of the International Labor Rights Education and Research Fund, compared a free-trade accord with Mexico to a "shotgun wedding" that could lead to a "lose-lose" situation for both countries.   Added Harvey: "The administration is giving us a blueprint for a train wreck."

Fast track's critics took advantage of a prolonged recession and high unemployment in the United States, NAFTA foe Harris Wofford's upset victory in a Pennsylvania Senate race, and the White House's preoccupation with Operation Desert Shield/Desert Storm to press their case with Congress. At the same time that U.N. forces were routing Saddam Hussein, the anti-fast-track coalition was attempting to vanquish NAFTA through lobbying on Capitol Hill. As late as February, Mexican Congress-watchers deemed that, while the Senate would approve fast track, the administration was 80 votes short of winning approval in the House of Representatives.[108]

Bush Enters the Fray

Nearly two months after Iraq's defeat in March 1991, President Bush began his counterattack on behalf of fast track. In this battle, he enjoyed enthusiastic backing from the Coalition for Trade Expansion, which constituted a veritable "Who's Who" of major American corporations (many of which belonged to The Business Roundtable and later affiliated with the United States Alliance for NAFTA, Inc. coalition). The chief executive and his business allies argued that since 1986, U.S. exports to the increasingly open Mexican market had doubled to $28.4 billion, creating 315,000 export-related jobs in the United States, and that NAFTA would generate 113,000 new trade-focused jobs in Texas alone. "If Americans are honestly concerned about their environment, the standard of living in Mexico and about democratization," averred MIT Professor Rudiger Dornbusch, "they cannot escape the recognition that a thriving, open market economy will raise living standards, foster individual freedom, decentralize political power and allow people to organize around local issues."[109]

Prospects brightened for fast-track approval after Bush, fearful of a setback, announced bilateral discussions keyed to the concerns of labor and environmental groups. These talks produced a memorandum of understanding on worker health and safety signed by U.S. Labor Secretary Lynn Martin and her Mexican counterpart. This document provided for the exchange of information on worker health and safety, working conditions, labor standards enforcement, resolution of labor-management disputes, collective bargaining agreements, social security, credit institutions, labor statistics, labor quality, and productivity. NAFTA would make it possible, Secretary Martin said, "to move earnestly with our neighbors to the south to address child labor and safety and health concerns and improve the lives of our working men and women."[110]

In addition, Bush assured Congress of his commitment to:

- Strict health and safety standards for agricultural imports, to prevent Mexican products that do not meet U.S. health or safety requirements from entering the United States;

- Transition periods of more than ten years for the reduction of U.S. tariffs in certain sectors and industries;

- Worker adjustment programs for workers who may lose their jobs as a result of an agreement with Mexico; and

- Exclusion of labor mobility and immigration laws from the negotiations.

At the direction of Bush—the self-styled "Environmental President"—and Salinas, authorities in both countries also devised an Integrated Environmental Plan for the Border. Following 17 public hearings, the United States ($384 million in 1992-1993) and Mexico ($460 million in 1992-1994) pledged substantial resources to implement the first phase of this program. Their highest priority was wastewater treatment projects for twin-cities along the border (San Diego/Tijuana, Imperial Valley/Mexicali, Nogales/Nogales, and Laredo/Nuevo Laredo). Monies were also promised for law enforcement, environmental health, emergency planning and response, and the monitoring and mitigation of transboundary air pollution. This initiative was designed to blunt the charge that Mexico would remain a "pollution haven" for unscrupulous foreign firms if NAFTA were approved. In March 1991 Salinas aggressively raised his ecological profile by closing the aged, sulfur-belching Azcapotzalco oil refinery in Mexico City, which had employed 5,000 workers.

Between 1989 and 1991, the environmental and natural resources budget for Mexico's Secretariat of Ecology and Urban Development (SEDUE)—succeeded in 1992 by the Secretariat of Social Development (SEDESOL)—shot up from $6 million to $36 million, and the agency closed 28 border businesses for environmental infractions in 1991. SEDESOL's team of 200 inspectors ensured, among other things, that the amount of hazardous waste from *maquiladoras* that was properly disposed of doubled from 14.5 percent in 1990 to 31 percent a year later.

The 1 May 1991 Action Plan revealed Washington and Mexico City's attentiveness to ecological issues and helped to split the labor-environmental axis arrayed against fast track. With the promise that environmental organizations would be represented on panels advising U.S. Trade Representative Hills, the National Wildlife Federation (NWF), the National Audubon Society (NAS), the Natural Resources Defense Council (NRDC), and the Environmental Defense Fund (EDF) expressed cautious support for negotiations. In a *New York Times* column, NWF President Jay D. Hair illuminated the progress made by ecologists:

> When a handful of environmental groups first stepped into the free-trade discussion, they were greeted with condescending incredulousness by financial experts who viewed the talks as belonging to a closed club devoted exclusively to commercial considerations. That presumption—that environmentalism and economics don't mix—has been punctured.[111]

Hill's good-faith support for environmental protection obviated the need for Hair to withdraw support from the free-trade initiative as he threatened to do if the Bush administration reneged on its commitment.

Enhancing the prospect for fast-track authorization was the resolute backing that NAFTA enjoyed from key U.S. policymakers, many of whom were Texans. In addition to President Bush, fellow Texans Secretary of State Baker, Commerce Secretary Mosbacher, Senate Finance Committee Chairman Bentsen, Senator Phil Gramm (D.-Tex.), and Representative Bill Archer (R-Tex.), ranking minority member of the House Ways and Means Committee, knew firsthand of Mexico's crucial importance to the United States. House Speaker Foley, House Majority Leader Richard A. Gephardt (D-Mo.), and Ways and Means Chairman Rostenkowski also cast their lot with fast track. Gephardt, on whom organized labor had counted to defeat fast track, made clear that his support for accelerated negotiating authority did not commit him to vote for a NAFTA that failed to address labor and environmental concerns. Of his intended vigilance, the majority leader warned: "I am serving notice today that Congress will [keep the pressure on]. Chairman Rostenkowski, Senator Bentsen, and I will sound like the song by the [P]olice that goes, 'Every breath you take, every step you take, every move you make, we'll be watching you.' Trust but verify: that will be our policy."[112]

The Fast-Track Vote[113]

Ultimately, the president succeeded in elevating fast-track approval to a referendum on protectionism. "Having already opposed [the extremely popular] Bush on the use of force in Iraq," wrote David S. Cloud of the *Congressional Quarterly Report*, "many Democrats fear[ed] a vote that would be portrayed as economic isolationism."[114] A Republican strategist said: "If there was one case in which the Persian Gulf paid off for him [Bush], this was it."[115] In mid-May 1991, Congress killed resolutions to disallow fast-track authority. On 23 May, the House of Representatives voted 231 to 192 against a disallowing motion sponsored by Representative Byron L. Dorgan (D-N.D.); the next day the Senate, by a 59-to-36 vote, turned its thumbs down on a similar measure proposed by Senator Ernest F. Hollings (D-S.C.). In fact, Hollings could muster only 14 co-sponsors for his resolution, compared to 37 for a like measure in 1990. In explaining this drop in co-sponsors, the South Carolinian said: "The Carla Hills bazaar opens, and she goes around to my colleagues and says, 'I will take care of you if you get off that resolution.'"[116]

With 85 percent of Republicans in both houses supporting fast-track extension, the overwhelming majority of opponents were

Democrats (170 of the 192 "noes" in the House; 31 of 36 "noes" in the Senate). These votes followed rejection of anti–fast-track initiatives by the House Ways and Means Committee (27 to 9) and the Senate Finance Committee (15 to 3)—bodies that have principal jurisdiction over trade legislation.

In the House, several groups were conspicuous for their opposition. Twenty-two of 25 Congressional Black Caucus members (88 percent) opposed the initiative, 18 of 27 female members (64.7 percent) voted no—with Barbara Vucanovich (R–Nev.) voicing opposition but not voting—and 69 of 125 congressmen serving their eighth term or more casting negative votes (54.8 percent). Most opponents represented states with smokestack industries and strong unions (the Northeast and the "rust belt"), major textile sectors (Georgia and the Carolinas), and those states along the northern U.S. border, where many people perceived the CFTA to be harmful to their agricultural, seafood, textile, or footwear industries.

Among the House supporters were 29 of 45 freshmen (64.4 percent), six members of the nine-person Hispanic Caucus (66.7 percent), and two of three Asian-Americans (66.7 percent), as well as representatives from coastal states (56.1 percent), and states bordering Mexico (72.7 percent). Interestingly, the California delegation narrowly favored the legislation, even though it is the state with the largest Hispanic-American population. Labor and environmental groups apparently helped persuade 17 of the state's 45 representatives to vote "no"—with two members (Dornan and Levine) not voting. On average, pro–fast track members were younger (51.8 years) than opponents (53.7 years). Fast track enjoyed more support in the House than reflected in the 231 favorable votes. According to observers, once the critical mass of 218 votes was achieved to ensure extension, support tapered off—in part, because several California representatives, who had asked the leadership for leeway to oppose fast track if their votes were not required for passage, voted no.

Many of the same geographic and interest-group factors seemed to influence the Senate vote, except that members in all tenure classifications backed fast track, including a majority of freshmen (58.6 percent).[117] The northeast and east south central regions were the only two sections of the country whose senators voted opposite of House members: the northeast senators favored fast track and the east south central senators opposed it. Both Asian-American senators (Daniel Inouye and Daniel Akaka, Democrats from Hawaii) voted "no," while the two female senators split, with Nancy L. Kassebaum (R-Kan.) voting "yes," and Barbara Mikulski (D-Md.) voting "no." Like their House counterparts, the average pro–fast-track senators were younger (55 years) than opponents (60.7 years).

NAFTA benefited from the fact that a two-year extension of fast track was crucial to completing the Uruguay Round. Many legislators who expressed qualms about the North American scheme were reluctant to capsize global negotiations that had been churning along for five years. "If we were able to have a separate vote up or down on U.S.-Mexico [fast track], we'd win," claimed Senator Donald W. Riegle, Jr., (D-Mich.).[118] He objected to free trade with Mexico because, in his view, it would spur automobile producers to move assembly plants south. Even GATT, however, was not universally popular. A case in point was the northern plains states. There, legislators opposed the Uruguay Round because Washington was proposing a sharp reduction in (or phase-out of) agricultural subsidies in exchange for the opening of the European Community to U.S. foodstuffs. Two area lawmakers, Senator Max Baucus (D-Mont.) and North Dakota's Representative Dorgan, emerged from the fast-track debate as influential spokesmen on NAFTA.

Further evidence that the fast-track outcome was no harbinger of the ultimate NAFTA vote came in House Resolution 146, sponsored by Gephardt to propitiate the AFL-CIO (union members picketed him during a visit to his St. Louis district following the fast-track vote). This nonbinding legislation, which was overwhelmingly approved, expressed the "sense of the House" that the Congress could suspend the accelerated negotiating authority if the administration failed to keep its 1 May commitment to environmental safeguards, employee safety, and worker adjustment assistance. HR 146 not only put Bush on notice that Congress would hold his feet to the fire, it also provided cover for legislators concerned about offending trade unionists. "There are members on both sides of the aisle who want to vote for something satisfying, as much as they can, labor's demands," commented Rostenkowski.[119] Initially, Bush feared that the resolution would offend Mexico and resented being, in the words of the Ways and Means chairman, "nickeled and dimed."[120]   In the view of the *Congressional Quarterly Weekly Report*, the president wound up supporting the measure in hopes that it would attract more votes to fast-track extension and bolster the U.S. position in the troubled GATT talks in Geneva.   Ambassador Hills publicly doubted that lawmakers would actually pull the rug from under fast track anyway.   "To change the rules midway would undoubtedly cause our trading partners such offense that they might walk from the negotiations," she warned.   "But that's not the way government should work . . . I would hope that members of Congress would not change the rules."[121]

Conclusion

Its architects designed fast track to facilitate the orderly negotiation of trade agreements: throughout the talks, the executive branch would consult key lawmakers—with the Senate and the House of Representatives ultimately casting up-or-down votes on the completed package.   This mechanism proved crucial to NAFTA's eventual success.   Had not the Bush administration obtained fast-track authorization, the final pact would have suffered asphyxiation through filibuster and amendment.   As it turned out, fast track also proved crucial to Bill Clinton's defeat of the forces of retreatism that threatened to weaken America's role in global affairs.

CHAPTER FOUR

The Negotiations

Introduction: The USTR

Once the fast-track prerogative was secure, the trade ministers formally launched the NAFTA talks on 12 June in Toronto, at what became the first of seven Trilateral Ministerial Oversight meetings, involving Hills, Serra Puche, and Wilson. For Washington, responsibility for the conduct of negotiations was vested in the United States trade representative. The Trade Expansion Act of 1962 created the Special Representative for Trade Negotiations, predecessor to the USTR, an agency within the Executive Office of the President that was obligated to report to Congress. Thus, the legislation removed prime responsibility for trade matters from the State Department, which allegedly stressed broad foreign policy goals at the expense of trade, was too attuned to the interests of foreign governments, and had become a "fudge factory" that was slow to reach decisions. Neither could such responsibility be entrusted to the Commerce Department, whose powerful business constituency, some argued, prevented it from bringing an objective national perspective to trade policy.

Compared to the somnambulant, hidebound Commerce Department, with some 31,000 employees spread around the world, the USTR is a dynamic, take-charge agency with approximately 165 officials. "No one ever retires from USTR," averred an alumnus of the trade agency who asked not to be cited. "They are men and women with 'Type A' personalities who work their behinds off for ten years or so and then move elsewhere in the federal government or get rich lobbying." Other insiders call them "Texas Rangers for whom 12-hour work days constitute the norm." USTR's small size and talented personnel means that their negotiators have both "long leashes" when bargaining and, when necessary, "direct access" to the United States trade representative, a Cabinet member.[122] Critics call USTR a "negotiating swat team" that swoops in to negotiate agreements—often with considerable technical support from the Commerce Department—that other agencies then have to implement.

Although none is monolithic, key U.S. bureaucracies tend to be either relatively free-trade oriented (Treasury, State, and Council of Economic Advisers) or protectionist (Commerce, Labor, and Agriculture). At its inception, USTR was squarely in the free-trade camp and still gravitates to that end of the spectrum. Over the years, however, two factors have contributed to a growing pragmatism within the agency. To begin with, it has established good consultative relations with Congress, especially with the Senate Finance Committee and the House Ways and Means Committee. In recent years, USTR has shown sensitivity to Capitol Hill's concern about the expanding size of trade as a portion of GNP, in general, and growing U.S. trade deficits, in particular. An example of the agency's propitiation of lawmakers came during hearings on the 1988 trade expansion act. The USTR supported strong authority for reprisals against nations that continually register large trade surpluses with the United States. Such legislation, known as Super 301, has never been used, but USTR likes having this club behind the door when negotiating.

At the same time, under a legislative mandate, USTR has developed an alphabet soup of business consultative groups known as Industry Functional Advisory Committees (IFACs) and Industry Sectoral Advisory Committees (ISACs). Ambassador Hills used the IFACs and ISACs as forums for soliciting advice from the chief executive officers of major corporations. She was especially attentive to large, export-active firms such as producers of chemicals, pharmaceuticals, and lumber. Meanwhile, USTR sought to neutralize such natural enemies of liberalization as the steel, textile, glass, and the maritime industries.

Even as it nurtures effective ties with Congress and the corporate community, USTR—an executive branch agency—has cultivated productive relations with the White House. Hills was a visible and forceful member of the Bush Cabinet. Her chief of staff during her last year at USTR, Steve Farrar, had formerly worked in the White House. Another USTR official, Warren Maruyama, had served as President Bush's special assistant for international economic policy. Hills' successor, Mickey Kantor—a Los Angeles lawyer, longtime party activist, and close friend of the Clintons—chaired the Democratic nominee's successful presidential campaign.

The Negotiators

The trade ministers were bright, tough, strong-willed, and well-connected to their chief executives. A former prosecutor in California, an assistant U.S. attorney general from 1974 to 1975, and secretary of housing and urban developing in the Ford administration, Hills, 57, neither suffered fools gladly nor enjoyed "schmoozing." Educated at Stanford and Yale, extremely intelligent, named by *Time* magazine as one of ten Women of the Year in 1976, at ease in Washington's corridors of power, and possessed of a prosecutor's élan, she liked to cut to the heart of issues without wasting time on peripheral matters. "If she has a weakness," a Canadian official observed, "it's her tendency to press for additional concessions beyond the best interests of the parties concerned." The less intense Wilson, 53, was a prominent Toronto securities broker before joining the Mulroney cabinet in 1984. Before taking charge of the NAFTA talks for his country, he held the crucial portfolio of finance minister. In that position, he acquired the reputation of being a policy "nerd" because of his Bill Clinton–like fascination with the details of major issues. The extroverted Serra Puche, 39, was a *wunderkind* in Mexico's financial bureaucracy. After earning a Yale Ph.D. in economics, he held key posts in the Office of the Presidency and the Finance Secretariat before Salinas named him secretary of commerce and industry in December 1988. The three leaders relished delving into the nuts and bolts of issues and were anxious to monitor the negotiations closely. Hills and Wilson, who had been criticized for not doing more to move the meandering Uruguay Round to completion within five years, seemed determined to demonstrate strong political leadership in the NAFTA sessions—even if it meant micromanaging complicated issues. Nonetheless, a good working rapport developed among the three, who not only met frequently but stayed in continual phone contact—a major difference with the CFTA negotiations. "The upshot was smoother negotiations, rather than everything peaking at the endgame," according to a mid-level Canadian official.

The chief negotiators—Julius Katz, John Weekes, and Herminio Blanco—presented a study in contrasts. The flinty, 65-year-old Katz, a highly regarded veteran of the State Department, USTR, and public policy and trade consulting firms, continually strove to move negotiations ahead and enjoyed substantial leeway for making decisions. Weekes, an unpretentious civil servant in his late 40s, had distinguished himself as Canada's ambassador to GATT. His measured, understated negotiating style demonstrated none of the passion with which he pursues cross-country and downhill skiing. Katz and Weekes knew each other from early Uruguay Round negotiations. This meant that the 41-year-old Blanco was the new boy on the block, but his colleagues quickly learned that he was nobody's fool. Miguel Leaman, the Mexican embassy's experienced economic counselor, said that Blanco had the intelligence to play five chess matches simultaneously.[123]

Herman Von Bertrab, a former Jesuit and university instructor, remembers encountering Blanco in an advanced international economics course at the Technological Institute of Monterrey, often called Mexico's MIT and one of the nation's top universities. The movie-star handsome 20-year-old sat sphinx-like at his desk, neither bothering to open a book nor take a note. "This guy is just wasting his father's money and my time," thought the instructor. Well into an intricate problem involving the Mundell-Fleming Model of fixed and flexible exchange rates, Von Bertrab realized that he had made a mistake. As he pondered how to extricate himself from what is every teacher's nightmare, Blanco slowly raised his hand. "Professor, if we go back three steps and change the value of the variable from x to y, wouldn't we arrive at the proper answer?" the young man correctly suggested. Von Bertrab recalls that his first thought was, "Give me a machine gun so I can wipe out this kid."[124] In fact, the professor and student became fast friends, and Von Bertrab wound up directing SECOFI's NAFTA office in Washington.

In addition to at least six chief negotiators' meetings, Katz, Weekes, and Blanco talked frequently by telephone. The respect that shaped relations among the three men contrasted markedly with the tension between the taciturn, secretive, and unpredictable Peter Murphy and the much older, smart, choleric, and tantrum-prone S. Simon Reisman—the respective U.S. and Canadian chief negotiators—during the CFTA talks. Said an aide to a U.S. senator who followed the bargaining closely: "These negotiations are a set of talks between a man who can't talk [Murphy] and a man who can't listen [Reisman]."[125] Murphy, a gangling Rhode Islander, sometimes did not even confide in his closest working colleagues; Reisman, known as "the rhinoceros" by colleagues for his toughness, once demonstrated his hair-trigger temper by extinguishing his cigar on an American negotiator's shiny desk, rather than using an ashtray. So dysfunctional did the Murphy-Reisman relationship become that Secretary of State Baker and Finance Minister Wilson, along with Canadian Ambassador Derek Burney, had to step in to complete the deal when the 68-year-old Reisman stalked away from the bargaining table in September 1987, stating that—in his view—the "negotiations are over."

As a supporting cast behind Hills and Katz, the main bureaucratic players in Washington shared the same interests. They viewed NAFTA as a means to lock in the market-focused reforms enacted by the de la Madrid and Salinas regimes; they wished to expand opportunities below the Rio Grande for U.S. financial institutions and other investors; they sought greater access for U.S. exports to Mexico; they wanted to eliminate burdensome licensing requirements confronting grains and other farm exports; and they championed access for American truckers and bus lines into Mexico's interior. Viewing relations from a geopolitical vantage point, they insisted that NAFTA meant investment, growth, job-creation, and—above all—stability in a neighbor with which the United States shares a 2,000-mile-long border and a sometimes stormy political relationship.

As mentioned above, President Salinas also regarded NAFTA as giving momentum to the sustained development needed to advance his country to developed status. Not only would increased continental trade attract North American investment, it would also draw capital from Europe, Asia, and elsewhere in Latin America, where entrepreneurs coveted opportunities presented by a secure, expanding trade zone encompassing the United States. In addition, dismantling protectionism would force Mexico's business community to increase efficiency or risk bankruptcy. And just as the Americans saw NAFTA as institutionalizing Mexico's market opening, Salinas regarded the accord as a means of protecting his country against any U.S. reversion to protectionism. Salinas thus found it encouraging that the struggle over fast track had strengthened the bonds between Hills and Serra Puche. Ottawa, which was still assimilating the CFTA that had sparked such a heated internal controversy, acted defensively until the NAFTA bargaining began, when it increasingly engaged itself in the negotiations.

The USTR designated the "lead agency" for each of 19 working groups. Even though USTR assumed a lion's share of the leads (seven), it assigned a dozen leads to agencies with functional responsibility for the subject under review. Thus, the Department of Agriculture headed the Agriculture Working Group, the Department of Transportation led the Land Transportation Working Group, the Treasury Department took charge of the Financial Working Group, and so forth. Five considerations explained USTR's meting out of responsibility: (1) its desire to take advantage of agency expertise; (2) its extremely small staff, already heavily committed to the Uruguay Round; (3) its previous success with lead-sharing in the CFTA; (4) the commitment to collegiality by Chief Negotiator Katz; and (5) its belief that involving seven large departments in negotiating NAFTA would ensure their support for the final version of the pact. By awarding the Commerce Department three leads (Automotive, Insurance, and Trade Remedies), for example, USTR helped assuage the initial concerns of a few of its officials about NAFTA, arising from the

CFTA, about the scope of tariff reductions and the resolution of dumping and subsidies disputes.

Foreign Trade Minister Wilson also apportioned leads among Canadian ministries to capitalize on expertise and foster bureaucratic harmony. He assigned nine leads to External Affairs (Foreign Trade's twin agency), four to Finance, three to ISTC, and one apiece to Transport Canada, Investment Canada, Agriculture, and Energy and Mineral Resources.[126] Such lead-sharing contrasted with the CFTA negotiations. Then Mulroney, who had opposed a free-trade accord with the United States before his election, knew that its foes would depict such a pact as compromising Canada's sovereignty and national identity. To ensure careful management of the talks, he vested full responsibility for their conduct in a Trade Negotiations Office, headed by a confidant, Simon Reisman, who reported directly to the prime minister.

Initially, all Mexican leads were officials in, or men detailed to, the Commerce Secretariat—a practice that vexed other agencies. Once negotiations were well underway, SECOFI assigned the Treasury and Agricultural ministries responsibility for, respectively, Financial Services and Agriculture.

The U.S. government named five or six officials from different agencies to each working group; the Canadians appointed three or four; and the Mexicans, with markedly fewer personnel at the outset, generally appointed several officials but added negotiators as the talks progressed and they realized the complexity of the issues. The U.S. and Canadian lead negotiators were in their 40s, exhibited negotiating experience thanks to having participated in the CFTA or GATT, and were usually officials from agencies vested with functional responsibility for their working group's subject matter. Although continuity and professionalism are hallmarks of the Canadian bureaucracy, it was unusual for Washington to have so many experienced negotiators at the table, most of whom were career civil servants. The success of Republicans in three consecutive presidential elections contributed to continuity of personnel responsible for trade matters. Expanding the pool of U.S. talent was the fact that departments with trade responsibilities had been heavily involved in both the Uruguay Round and the free-trade accord with Canada.

Differences characterized the three teams. At the beginning of negotiations, the United States had five women serving as lead negotiators and the Canadians two. In contrast, all leads for the hurriedly assembled Mexican team were male; most Mexican leads were in their 30s; and they boasted little or no previous negotiating experience. "Bright but inexperienced" was the label that trade insiders initially applied to the Mexicans, many of whom held degrees from Ivy League or other prestigious U.S. universities. The Mexicans' academic prowess prompted some Americans to joke: "These guys graduated from schools that we couldn't get into and that wouldn't even put our children on their waiting lists." The Mexican negotiators compensated—in part, at least—for their anemic backgrounds in trade bargaining by working extremely hard to master the issues confronting them, taking maximum advantage of computers and mathematical models, coordinating more closely among themselves than did their Washington and Ottawa counterparts, and hiring as advisers first-class American and Canadian lawyers, commercial experts, and economists. Most prominent among these counselors was Robert E. Herzstein, who is discussed in chapter 7. He advised the Mexicans on U.S. laws, ranging from fast-track procedures, to statutes affecting the sugar industry, to antidumping and countervailing duty practices. Chris Thomas, a private Canadian attorney who had served on the staff of former Trade Minister Pat Carney during the CFTA parleys, advised the Mexicans on how to respond effectively to U.S. demands and proposals. A contract with Nathán Nitco, a Mexican researcher working in Canada, gave the Mexican team access to mathematical algorithms he had developed that pertained to rules of origin—that is, the percentage of North American content that a product had to contain to benefit from newly negotiated preferences. Before the talks began, the Mexicans used Nitco's model to calculate how various rules of origin would affect some 250 economic sectors—information that proved invaluable in dealing with the Americans and Canadians.[127]

In contrast to the Americans and Canadians, Mexican leads had responsibility for several working groups, with the exception of the Working Group on Energy and Petrochemicals, whose lead, Jesús Flores, had but one assignment. That a half-dozen or so men covered 19 working groups fostered coherence within the Mexican team, which kept in continual communication with its senior officials. Of course, the heavy load also led to frazzled nerves and exhaustion.

Although variations existed among working groups, the Mexican leads had less bargaining discretion than their U.S. and Canadian counterparts. This condition sprang partly from their "greenness." More important, however, was the centralized nature of Mexico's political system. Its hierarchical structure meant that top officials, possibly even the president, made decisions that involved particularly sensitive issues—such as energy relations with the United States. As it turned out, SECOFI representatives were engaged in several sets of talks: with the United States and Canada; with federal agencies concerned about the impact of trade concessions on their bailiwicks; and with Mexican business interests. The government helped to organize the latter through the Coordinator of Foreign Commerce Business Organizations (COECE), which had prepared studies examining the strengths and weaknesses of 114 economic sectors. On the other hand, the U.S. negotiators had to worry about Congress; in matters such as countervailing duties and antidumping rules, the Americans had substantially less room to maneuver than did the Mexicans and Canadians. In general, however, lawmakers did not home in on specifics or technical aspects of the deal. Their concerns rested more with political questions, the most prominent of which was: "How can we ensure that working people are well treated under NAFTA?" USTR was also constrained by the need to preserve private-sector support for the agreement.

For their part, the Canadians were reluctant to move away from the CFTA in many areas. After all, the increasingly unpopular Mulroney feared that a bold new pact would constitute a palpable liability in his nation's upcoming national elections.

Sacred Cows

Each country had certain "taboo" issues that were non-negotiable. For Washington, these were Mexican immigration to the United States and "set asides" and other preferences in government procurement benefiting minorities, veterans, and small businesses. Also off limits was the so-called Jones Act, named for an early-20th-century senator from Washington state whose legislative mission was to shield American maritime interests from competition. The latter stipulates that cargo shipped between U.S. ports, including trade with the nation's territories and possessions (except the Virgin Islands), be carried on vessels built in the United States, documented under the U.S. flag, and manned by American crews. Ottawa literally had a sacred cow in that its negotiators fiercely safeguarded dairy farming, as well as poultry production. Even more sensitive was the protection of publishing, radio and television production, film making, and other cultural industries, lest Canadian society be penetrated—and, according to detractors, contaminated—even more by Hollywood and American media. At the same time, Mexico refused to modify Article 27 of its constitution, which reserves to the state the ownership, exploration, and development of petroleum. Three months into the talks Serra Puche underlined the delicacy of energy matters when he articulated the "five noes" to which Mexico's negotiators zealously adhered. They said "no" to diminishing Mexico's control over the exploration, development, refining, and processing of hydrocarbons and primary petrochemicals; to guaranteeing oil supplies to another country; to relinquishing the state monopoly over the commerce, transport, storage, and distribution of energy; to permitting risk-contracts in exploration and production; and to allowing foreign-owned gasoline stations. Apparently, Salinas hoped for breakthroughs, notably in areas of the oil sector not protected by his nation's Constitution. A senior U.S. official, who refused to have his name used, reported that the chief executive told the head of a major American oil company, "You guys keep pressing Pemex for greater access." Agriculture and financial services were other acutely sensitive issues for the Mexicans.

The Rhythm of Negotiations

The first few months of negotiations concentrated on "clearing away the underbrush," according to a key member of the Auto Working Group. That is, the countries sought to determine the scope of a possible agreement in their areas by swapping detailed information on each nation's sectors, their regulatory mechanisms, their trade practices, and their legal framework and organization. The negotiators also became acquainted with their counterparts, whom they began to probe for concessions. In most working groups, the United States and Canada advanced language employed in, or similar to, that of the CFTA. Equally important to the learning by government officials was the benefits that accrued to business communities throughout North America during the initial phase of talks. They began to perceive the complexities of crafting an ambitious, trilateral agreement. They also found out that their competitors' strongly held positions would be difficult to change. Additionally, some U.S. congressmen began to have their eyes opened about a continental pact.

Katz had hoped that the exploratory or pre-negotiation period could have taken place between October 1990 and June 1991. To his dismay, he found that the Mexicans were not prepared to begin talks this early. Moreover, the Bush administration found that it had to concentrate on procedure rather than substance—that is, gaining approval for fast track. As a result, initial discussions did not commence until after the second ministerial meeting convened in Seattle in August 1991.

U.S. and Canadian negotiators in such working groups as energy, government procurement, and subsidies—areas in which the Mexicans postponed concessions until the eleventh hour—dismissed the first six months as a "waste of time" or a "pointless rhetorical exercise." "If I heard the Mexicans say *interesante* one more time, I thought I would throw up," said a Commerce Department official attached to the Energy Working Group.[128] A Canadian also active in the energy negotiations suggested that one meeting would have been sufficient to lay the groundwork for substantive bargaining. Other negotiators were more sanguine about the exploratory phase.

In the area of dispute resolution and countervailing duties, for instance, the Americans and Canadians took advantage of this period to learn about the *amparo*, a powerful Mexican constitutional device, roughly analogous to habeas corpus, to protect citizens against the state. In addition, after five months of preliminary discussions, the Mexicans modified their interpretation of the Calvo clause following passage of a Foreign Ministry- backed Law on Treaties in early 1992. This clause, which appears in Mexico's Constitution, stipulates that a foreign national or corporation renounces any claim to diplomatic assistance from his own country in the event that litigation arises with the host government. The Mexicans also sought to acquaint their fellow North Americans with the intricacies of their Automotive Decree, which governed the manufacture of, and trade in, vehicles in Mexico. A high SECOFI official believed that this educational effort did not bear fruit until the so-called Doubletree plenary meeting, held in Arlington, Virginia, in early June 1992.

Particularly productive exchanges took place in the working group on financial services. The CFTA chapter in this area was sketchy, to say the least, with a set of rules that were unenforceable. Thus, the Americans and Canadians were anxious to improve upon the language of their bilateral agreement while exploring opportunities in Mexico's closed market. The Mexicans, in turn, who had recently reprivatized their banking industry, sought to acquaint themselves with such practices in the United States and Canada as "reservations," "prudential carve-outs," "regulatory carve-outs," "national treatment," and "nonbanking lenders." These initial conversations helped produce one of NAFTA's most impressive chapters.

Generally speaking, little of importance with respect to the final pact occurred during the fall. On the average, the working groups met once a month for up to three days—with the most notable event being an exchange of preliminary tariff offers on 19 September 1991. Five weeks later, Ambassador Hills joined Serra Puche and Wilson to review the progress of the working groups at the Third Trilateral Ministerial Oversight session in Zacatecas. In terms of reaching agreements, these "ministerials" produced more smoke than substance. Ambassador Hills, it was said, "never saw a briefing book that was too thick." She was also impatient with aides who provided incoherent or internally inconsistent material. She prepared meticulously for these meetings, as did Serra Puche and Wilson, who shared her voracious appetite for mastering the details of an issue. The result was that these highly publicized one-day sessions raised expectations. In fact, the participants were often overinformed; they involved themselves in issues that had yet to ripen; and they diverted attention from the hand-to-hand combat that was just commencing in the working-group trenches over rules of origin, snap-back triggers, phytosanitary standards, and other unglamorous issues. Several working-group leads confided their trepidation over ministerial meetings. They feared that the involvement of the bright, dynamic cabinet members in the subject matter of their working group would jeopardize the fragile achievements that had been made.

The lack of progress in most working groups during the first few months could also be traced to the presence at each bargaining site of dozens, sometimes scores, of Mexican private-sector representatives. They often stayed at the same hotel as their country's working groups, with whose leaders they sometimes met between bargaining sessions. What accounted for the omnipresence of these business "camp followers"? To begin with, the prospect of competition from an economic heavyweight and an economic middleweight endowed the talks with life-or-death significance for Mexican corporations. They were on guard because the de la Madrid administration had infuriated entrepreneurs by consulting them little, if at all, before joining GATT. The academic or bureaucratic backgrounds of virtually all Mexican negotiators persuaded the business community of the imperative to acquaint them with the practical consequences of any concessions granted. SECOFI, moreover, had encouraged Mexican industries to articulate their concerns about NAFTA through COECE, while discouraging the petrochemical industry and other sectors from hiring their own lobbying firms in Washington. Thus, many Mexican companies believed it crucial to have eyes and ears present at the negotiating sites. Although retarding progress in the early months, extensive discussions with Mexico's business community throughout the negotiations ensured this influential interest group's support of—or, at least, acquiescence in—the final agreement. This protracted dialogue also deepened communication channels between the government and the private sector, forced the latter to resolve internal grudges, built bridges between small, medium, and large producers, and alerted entrepreneurs to the imperative to reform their corporations to compete effectively with foreigners.[129]

USTR convened a meeting of U.S. leads every two weeks to review progress, harmonize positions, identify opportunities, prepare for upcoming talks, and warn the delegation to "time bombs that might explode." Also participating in these sessions were representatives of the White House's Domestic Council and the National Security Council, who frequently expressed impatience over the slow pace of the negotiations. The domestic policy analysts generally comprehended the intricacies of a continental free-trade pact. In contrast, the NSC staff members were on the prowl for two or three "wedge issues" that President Bush could resolve with Salinas to propel the bargaining to a speedy conclusion. Their unrealistic outlook may have sprung in part from meetings that high-level Mexican officials had with General Scowcroft. Even Mexican cabinet members, including Serra Puche, had unreasonably optimistic views on how long it would take to complete negotiations. For relentlessly describing the difficulties that lay ahead, the USTR gained the reputation among colleagues from other agencies of "playing wet *serape*." "I told them," said a ranking USTR official, "that we can complete the agreement tomorrow, but you won't like it and Congress won't pass it."[130]

Composite Text

Between the Zacatecas session and year's end, the negotiations of most working groups entered a second stage. At the 9-10 October Meech Lake meeting of chief negotiators, Weekes took the lead in urging the delegations to "table texts"—that is, to crystalize their positions on concept papers and exchange them with their counterparts by the end of November. The American (21 November), Mexican (2 December), and Canadian (4 December) texts were exchanged in late fall. Before and on New Year's Day, lawyers from the three countries met at the Canadian consulate in Dallas to organize the material from the working groups in a consistent manner. They wanted to be certain that key words and concepts employed in the different drafts conveyed the same meaning. The goal was to combine the papers to facilitate a narrowing of the differences between them. The draftsmen crafted a "run-on text" that conveyed the consensus of the negotiators. In several working groups, there was no pretense at integrating negotiating positions. These texts carried little more than the position of each country, listed one after another—the Canadian position in bold typeface, the United States in plain print, and the Mexican in italics. In groups responsible for five controversial subjects (agriculture, energy, textiles, automotive, and trade remedies), either the Americans or the Mexicans failed even to produce tentative chapters. In the final analysis, the run-on text alerted the leads to how much work lay ahead of them, while demonstrating to political leaders in the three nations just how far apart the negotiators were. Of course, it was the unusual politician who could make sense out of the gap-filled, "cut and paste" draft.

Crafting a "composite," integrated text provided the focus for a lengthy session held at Georgetown University's Leavey Center in early January 1992. Much to the amazement of the Americans and Canadians, the Mexicans arrived in Washington with a computerized composite prepared in both Microsoft and Word Perfect format. This informatic *tour de force* required thousands of man-hours.[131] The Georgetown gathering was the first at which all of the working groups were present, infusing the process with synergism.[132] The deputy chief negotiators, who enjoyed an unusually warm rapport, took charge of the week-long meeting. These were Charles E. "Chip" Roh, Jr. (U.S.), Jaime Zabludovsky (Mexico), and Robert Clark (Canada). In negotiations, a high correlation exists between the size of one's retinue and the degree of posturing. Because Roh, Zabludovsky, and Clark frequently met alone or in extremely small groups (or communicated by phone), they spoke frankly. In so doing, they could float proposals and candidly assess their counterparts' trial balloons. They would try to resolve major disputes at the working-group level, although final decisions rested with more senior officials. These men also devoted hundreds of hours to domestic constituencies. As such, they functioned as a human early warning system, apprising chief negotiators and ministers of actual or potential problems on their home fronts. Helpful to the deputies was their ability to avoid the glare of publicity that haunted the trade ministers and chief negotiators.

The Georgetown conference produced no major break-throughs, even though a composite was produced—with key, unresolved issues highlighted by brackets. In several chapters, bracketed areas consumed more space than points of consensus. Yet the positions of the three countries began to converge in standards, telecommunications, and intellectual property. These advances occurred in large measure because of progress in these fields accomplished in the Uruguay Round.

The "bracket reduction" stage, which began at Georgetown University, continued throughout early 1992. U.S. negotiators battled for concessions in all areas, including energy, investment, and government procurement. Two factors actuated their assertive-ness. To begin with, the Americans realized that they had not arrived at a comprehensive trade agreement or even one that was as good as the CFTA or the prospective Uruguay Round accord. To have settled for a "half-assed agreement," in the view of one important participant in the process, "would have cost us badly needed support within the business community at a time of intense labor union opposition." Washington, moreover, believed that if the Mexicans failed to open their market, they could never achieve the sustained growth necessary for eventual prosperity. Although crucial to Mexico, such prosperity would also benefit the United States economically and geopolitically. Three additional considerations underlay American pressure for broader liberaliza-tions: (1) knowledge of NAFTA's greater importance to the relatively underdeveloped Mexico, where the pact commanded twice the support found in the United States (Mexican pollster Miguel Basañez found that 71 percent of Mexicans, desperate for change after a decade of economic crisis, favored unrestricted continental trade);[133] (2) the fact that Mexico's tariffs were, on average (10 percent), at least twice as high as those of the United States (4 percent) and Canada (5 percent); and (3) the possibility that

Congress might reject any accord that failed to contain conspicuous benefits for the United States.

Lending credence to this last point was a continual flow of communications from Capitol Hill urging the negotiators to protect U.S. interests with every breath in their bodies, while battering down Mexico's protectionist door. For example, a mid-March 1992 letter from Senator Pete Domenici (R-N.M.) and six other energy state senators proposed "guiding principles" for U.S. negotiators in energy matters. Although couched in terms that would apply to North America as a whole, these tenets took aim at Serra Puche's "five noes." They included, *inter alia*, permitting private equity participation through risk contracts in oil and gas exploration, allowing market forces to determine hydrocarbon prices, and ensuring direct, nondiscriminatory access to all markets for foreign investment in pipeline construction.[134] Such public boldness notwithstanding, the individual oil patch legislators privately told the negotiators: "Look, we know what you're up against with Article 27 [the Mexican Constitution's ban on private oil activities]; cut the best deal that you can."

Legislators regularly spoke out because they were kept abreast of the progress of the talks and because trade, which increasingly affected local factories' employment levels, had an impact on so many congressional districts. The Reagan administration's tendency to play its cards close to the vest in crafting the CFTA had raised hackles among lawmakers and in the business community. Ambassador Hills was determined to obviate such criticism of NAFTA by submitting updated drafts of the agreement to appropriate offices on Capitol Hill. Meanwhile, she arranged briefings by USTR officials and negotiators with members of Congress and their staffs, especially those on the 18 House and Senate committees with jurisdiction over trade. In February 1992 the USTR head also led a delegation of 11 members of Congress and 27 private sector advisers to Mexico City. There they discussed the proposed pact with President Salinas, his key cabinet secretaries, the Mexican negotiating team, and representatives of Mexico's private sector. Contacts with the business community flowed through formal and informal channels. Individual agencies and negotiators received a steady stream of visits, phone calls, facsimiles, and letters from companies, unions, and individuals concerned about one or more facets of the negotiations.

Despite such herculean efforts in communication, Democrat Gephardt complained about the public's being kept "in the dark" about NAFTA. "This secret process, I believe, could seriously undermine the ability of Congress to affirm an agreement at the end of the day," he informed Hills, in what appeared to be an election-year attack on the GOP administration.[135] Later, Chairman Rostenkowski contradicted this charge when he lauded USTR for its "relentless" efforts to keep Congress informed.

While generally considered a frustrating, unproductive event by the U.S. team, a Mexican official reported a breakthrough for his side at the 9-10 February meeting of trade ministers in Chantilly, Virginia. For the first time, he said, his country comprehended that NAFTA would be based not on horse-trading over the removal of barriers but on a set of principles—a concept that Washington and Ottawa had endorsed from the beginning. In other words, greater access for American corn to Mexico would not result from the United States' agreeing to import more Mexican-made autos. Rather, the three countries would strive to remove, over time, all tariffs. Four key tenets of a principles-based accord were (1) complete elimination of all impediments to trade, (2) equal treatment in each country for all goods and services produced in North America, (3) a commitment not to erect additional commercial obstacles between and among the signatories once the pact was signed, and (4) the extension to North American partners of most-favored-nation treatment accorded a third country. If, for instance, Mexico agreed to open its oil fields to exploration, development, and ownership by Spanish companies, it would have to confer the same opportunities on U.S. and Canadian firms.

Dallas Breakthrough

At the 17-21 February 1992 plenary session in Dallas, Chief Negotiator Katz and his Mexican and Canadian counterparts, Herminio Blanco and John Weekes, made an important advance. This was the first so-called "jamboree" inasmuch as all of the working groups were present and the countries had each others' draft texts before them. Still, the negotiations remained bogged down after two-and-a-half days, even though the Mexicans gave lip-service to accelerating the discussions. Katz wanted to wrap up the negotiations in time for congressional action before the November election. He was frustrated by an inability to extract decisions from the Mexicans. They had been warned at the Chantilly ministerial meeting that they had not offered enough concessions to achieve a deal. Something had to be done or the negotiators would continue to wrestle with an unwieldy composite text—Katz called it a "monster"—that was suffused by unresolved issues. At this point, according to observers, Katz "blew his top." He emphasized, in no uncertain terms, that Mexico's simply making tit-for-tat concessions—that is, the barrier-based approach—to the United States and Canada was unacceptable. He stressed, and Blanco acknowledged, that Mexico, as the most closed of the three economies, would have to reduce its protectionism by more than its partners if economic integration were to be achieved.

Word of this understanding rippled throughout the two floors of the Dallas Trade Mart and energized the activities of the 400 working-group members. Katz and his colleagues met with each of the leads, sometimes with the entire working group, to cajole, drive, push, interrogate, and determine how close the officials were to resolving outstanding issues. In some cases, the chief negotiators provided general guidance to the negotiating teams and sent them back to the bargaining table; at other times, they sat down at the table to help find a solution. This was a "hands on" effort to integrate the activities of the 19 working groups whose members had previously met independently.

Mexican officials, and some American and Canadian participants, downplayed the "Katz temper tantrum" explanation of the progress recorded at Dallas. Rather, they attributed the headway attained to the availability of a composite text, the heightened expectations for concluding an accord, and the fact that the Mexican team had "jelled" in terms of developing the confidence, expertise, and clarity of objectives essential to proceeding more rapidly.

Whatever the explanation, Dallas produced clear progress in autos, rules of origin, customs, services, investment, and financial services. Still, ups and downs followed the jamboree. A leaked copy of the 478-page, heavily bracketed "Dallas Composite" text revealed that the negotiations, as of the Texas conclave, were far from complete.[136] In financial services, for example, the Mexicans were still dragging their feet on bestowing "national treatment"—the same legal treatment accorded domestic enterprises—on U.S. and Canadian firms. Furthermore, Mexico wanted to open only 12 percent of its financial services market to its North American neighbors by the year 2002, while the United States and Canada were seeking full entrée.[137] Agriculture was another focus of controversy and remained so until the final day. Predictably, the United States resisted Mexican demands for both immediate access to the American market for fruits and vegetables and the maximum possible protection for its own corn, sorghum, pork, and dairy products. While attempting to safeguard vulnerable U.S. producers, the American working group pressed the Mexicans to open their market to corn and other grains.[138] Having recently privatized its telephone system, the Mexicans were also striving to shield the telecommunications sector from foreign competition until at least 1999.[139] Meanwhile, the leaked text revealed that the parties had agreed on national treatment of investors and the free movement of transport (with some Mexican restrictions on railroads) throughout the continent.[140]

Although a Washington-based publication, *Inside U.S. Trade* kept close tabs on the negotiations, the Dallas Composite was the only draft text to reach the media. Because the leak apparently occurred in Canada, possibly through an opposition-controlled provincial government, Ottawa began monitoring even more carefully the circulation of working drafts. The leak only mildly annoyed U.S. and Canadian negotiators, who were used to having "classified" government documents show up in the press. In contrast, the Mexicans, accustomed to operating amid greater secrecy, were livid at the public distribution of the Dallas text, via Canada, to NAFTA critics, opposition congressmen, and journalists in Mexico City. As things turned out, the leaked material was too complicated, obscure, and opaque for the press to understand.

The leaks aside, the pace of negotiations quickened in late winter, and Ambassador Hills soon reported that the 1,200 brackets in the Dallas Composite had been reduced to a "few hundred." The working groups met more often, some convening every week; the chief negotiators got together at least once a month; and the ministers kept in touch by telephone. The line of progress was, in Katz's words, "wavy," but the six weeks following the Dallas plenary spurred advances in the chapters on investment, intellectual property, textiles, standards, sanitary practices, customs administration, financial services, banking, and surface transportation. The tendency was to have one good meeting followed by a bad one. Fairly positive sessions (27 April-1 May plenary and 25-26 July ministerial) held in Mexico City were complemented by relatively unproductive meetings in Montreal (6-8 April ministerial) and Toronto (13-15 May plenary). It was at the late July Mexico City ministers' meeting that conspicuous progress took place in the contentious area of dispute resolution.

In proposing the formula that was adopted in this controversial field, the Mexicans showed that their newness to international trade negotiations could produce fresh ideas. Guillermo Aguilar, the legal expert who played an increasingly important role in the negotiations, worked with Fernando Salas, a member of his country's Financial Services Working Group who held a Ph.D. in industrial organization, to devise incentives for settling disputes. They sought a method that would achieve objectivity while ensuring that checks and balances protected all parties. Their solution was designating a five-member dispute resolution panel through "reverse selection." Specifically, the complaining country would select two panelists from a trilaterally approved list of eminent trade, legal, and other experts from the defending country; the defending country would choose two panelists from a similar roster of complaining country specialists; and these four panelists would name the chairman, who would be from a nondisputing country.[141] In Mexico City, Katz, Blanco, and Weeks also tabled a text on autos.

End Game and Post-End Game

By mid-summer the "end game" commenced as Chief Negotiators Blanco, Katz, and Weekes and team members settled in at Washington's renowned Watergate Hotel for marathon sessions beginning on 29 July. Three days later, they were joined by the ministers, who hoped that the deal could be completed rapidly. Wilson, for instance, brought an overnight bag with two shirts, not expecting to remain in Washington nearly two weeks. The rule of thumb is that 90 percent of the work is done on the most controversial subjects in roughly the 10 percent of the entire negotiating period consumed by the end-game stage. Table 1 classifies the subjects in terms of relative difficulty in reaching an agreement. During the end game, working groups with unresolved issues met at length before queuing up to present outstanding questions to the chief negotiators. After listening to the three leads present their differences, Blanco, Katz, and Weekes attempted to devise a solution or, more likely, narrow the controversy. The working groups then returned to the negotiating table until the next impasse sent their leads back to the chief negotiators for assistance. Especially sensitive items—autos, energy, government procurement, investment, and final tariff issues—had to be "bumped up" to the ministers or to chief executives for resolution. Ad hoc one-on-one contacts completed the formal negotiations. On several occasions, for example, Serra Puche sought out Alan M. Dunn, a Commerce Department official and U.S. lead of the Trade Remedies Working Group, to restart stalled negotiations in this area.[142]

TABLE 1

DIFFICULTY OF CONCLUDIING NAFTA CHAPTERS

1 (relatively easy)	Tariffs/nontariff barriers; safeguards; land transportation
2 (neither easy nor difficult)	Textiles*; standards; principles for services; telecommunications; intellectual property; dispute settlement
3 (relatively difficult)	Rules of origin; government procurement; energy and petrochemicals; subsidies and trade remedies; financial services; insurance services; agriculture; investment; automobiles

*Category 2 for Mexico; Category 3 for Canada.

For the millions of tourists who descend on Washington each year, the Watergate complex evokes beguiling images of the 1972 break-in of the Democratic party's sixth-floor headquarters, a scandal that sent 25 Republican operatives to jail and President Richard M. Nixon into forced retirement. After exchanging proposals and counterproposals from dawn to dusk (or later) at the Watergate Hotel, the negotiators had a less romantic sense of the venue. When asked his impressions of the building, Steven Jacobs, a Commerce Department official assigned to the Auto Working Group, said: "My most vivid memories are of a sea of bilious green carpets, lousy lighting, 15 of us squeezed into a room, lots of coffee and Coca-Cola, long waits to see the trade negotiators . . . and yet a spirit of excitement, a sense of making history, particularly among the relatively young U.S. team members."[143]

Another key actor compared the Watergate weeks to "boot-camp," while Deputy Assistant Secretary of Commerce Ann H. Hughes, U.S. lead for the Auto Working Group, recalled "excruciating boredom" as teams waited for their counterparts to react to offers before meeting with the chief negotiators or trade ministers to address intractable issues.[144] Other participants remembered the ubiquitous bowls of green Peruginos mints provided by the Watergate. Chip Roh ate so much junk food during this period that he referred to Peruginos and potato chips as NAFTA's "two basic food groups."[145] Meanwhile, participants in the Trade Remedies Working Group resorted to a liquid diet of gin, scotch, and tequila to help break logjams. The head of Mexico's Working Group on Energy and Petrochemicals said that "it was as if we were in jail: we watched through the windows as people enjoyed summer; then summer turned to fall—and we were still in jail."[146] In contrast to the working-group leads, the ministers, chief negotiators, deputy chief negotiators, and top lawyers were in perpetual motion trying to resolve outstanding issues.

Two U.S. leads reported that Ambassador Hills was twice prepared to excuse the Canadians from the negotiations during the end game. One occasion was Ottawa's rhetorical efforts to scrap its "security of supply" obligation under the CFTA when Mexico turned thumbs down on a similar provision in NAFTA. Security of supply (or "offer of supply," as Ottawa prefers to call it) was Canada's controversial commitment, in the event of a crisis, to cut proffered oil and gas exports to the United States by no greater a percentage than energy supplies were reduced to its domestic market. The other occurred when the Canadians balked at a U.S. proposal, backed by Mexico, to permit suspension of panel review and resort to a national court in subsidy and countervailing duty disputes. According to senior U.S. officials, the team heads confused Hills' forceful negotiating style with a threat to banish the Canadians, who eventually won on this point. She seemed prepared to take extreme action because of her determination to wring yet one more concession from the other side. "U.S.-Canadian trade relations," said one insider, "are like a good marriage in which the spouses occasionally contemplate murder but never divorce."

Deals were finally struck across-the-board, including such sensitive areas as antidumping and countervailing duties, textiles, and energy—the last issues to be concluded. With respect to Chapter-19 items (antidumping and countervailing duties), the Canadians attributed the tardiness of an agreement to an unsuccessful last ditch "chiseling" effort by the U.S. Department of Commerce to weaken the standards of review under the CFTA. Ultimately, accommodations among the parties permitted President Bush to declaim the completion of a NAFTA accord at an early morning ceremony held in the White House's Rose Garden on 12 August, just before the Republican party convened its national convention in Houston. The White House never tried to accelerate the conclusion of negotiations for political reasons; still, NAFTA became a theme of this GOP gathering and even Hills, who had endeavored to keep the parleys out of the 1992 presidential campaign, weighed in with a highly partisan speech to the delegates.

Post-End Game

Following the White House ceremony, the principal lawyers for the three countries—Aguilar (Mexico), J. T. Fried (Canada), Kenneth P. Freiberg (U.S.)—took just four days off before returning to the Watergate. There they spent three seven-day weeks of 14-hour days seeking to produce a text that could be submitted to Congress in early September. The August text embraced the essence of what the country teams had agreed to, often condensed into several pages whose language was sometimes ambiguous. It remained for the attorneys to fill in gaps, flesh out the material into full-blown chapters—and, in some cases, agree upon common definitions of crucial concepts. In pursuit of these objectives, Aguilar, Fried, and Freiberg relentlessly interrogated and cross-examined the negotiators. Although represented to the public as mere fine-tuning or "legal scrubbing," the highly intelligent and aggressive country representatives continued to wrestle over substantive matters, especially when ambiguities and inconsistencies existed.

Among the issues resolved in this "post-end game" were the devising of formulas for phasing out Mexican restrictions on auto imports, clarification of the breadth of the government procurement coverage, and reaffirmation of the inclusion of oil field services in the energy chapter. With respect to the latter, the Mexicans apparently sought to "claw back," or renege on, services that they had originally agreed to include in the pact. Meanwhile, the Americans presented a new text for the energy chapter, which the Mexicans perceived as an attempt to attenuate the five "noes," particularly the prohibition on foreign firms engaging in exploration and production of Mexican oil. So subtle and apparently inoffensive was this material that the Mexicans believed that Washington had prepared it months before and that it was not an effort simply to refine language agreed upon at Watergate. "While the Canadians were straightforward, the Americans were Machiavellians . . . chess players whose next move couldn't be predicted," observed a member of Mexico's energy working group. Such maneuvers notwithstanding, Mexico's deputy chief negotiator insisted that "not a single issue was renegotiated in the post-August 12 period."[147] Katz vehemently denied any effort to procure a change in the energy provisions of the Mexican Constitution or attain equity ownership of the country's oil resources. Rather, he insisted, the U.S. team had, throughout the negotiations, merely searched for some *"yeses"* to complement Serra Puche's five noes. Specifically, they sought the opportunity for Pemex to confer incentives on service contractors, direct negotiations between U.S. natural gas suppliers and Mexican customers, and assured supplies of Mexican crude in the event of an oil crisis.

During this period, the private sector and labor advisory groups were also given an opportunity, as required by the U.S. Trade Act, to review the text and submit reports. Meanwhile, Canadian officials continued to consult with the International Trade Advisory Commission and various sectoral advisory groups in their country.

In late August, Katz took a five-day vacation at his cottage in Bethany Beach, Delaware. Still up in the air was final language on autos, investment, financial services, and government procurement. Although supposedly relaxing, Katz spent up to 10 hours one day in communication by facsimile and telephone with Blanco and Weekes. On one call about the final language on marking a party's goods exported to a NAFTA member, he reached Blanco—who was in Bogota to sign a Mexican-Colombian free-trade agreement. "You haven't finished this one yet," thundered Katz into the telephone, and he threatened to cancel the upcoming initialing of texts in San Antonio if the Mexican minister failed to give NAFTA his immediate attention.[148] The even-tempered Blanco did not oblige, and no agreement was reached on the subject.

On 7 October, in what appeared to be a "photo opportunity" for GOP candidate Bush, the trade ministers of the United States, Mexico, and Canada gathered in San Antonio to initial the agreement with their chief executives looking on as witnesses. Clearly, the Republican president was using the Mexican and Canadian leaders to bolster his sagging campaign. Mulroney was eager to give whatever lift he could to "my good friend, George." Salinas could not easily turn down the invitation. Without the American leader there would have been no NAFTA, and as late as 1 November, the Mexican president believed that Bush had a fighting chance to win.[149]

Retrospectives on the negotiations varied among the participants. Americans in the Government Procurement Working Group complained that the Mexican team, headed by Héctor Olea, occasionally reneged on commitments. "We got their word on a difficult issue at one meeting only to see them welsh at the next," according to a key player in the process. For their part, the Mexicans viewed as inconsistent Washington's desire that its equipment and service companies be given full access to Pemex, the Federal Electricity Commission, and other national enterprises, while insisting that it could eliminate neither its own minority and small business "set-asides" nor the states' preferment of goods produced within their borders.

Ottawa had its own bone to pick with Mexico City. The Canadians thought they had an understanding with the Mexicans on two key issues: rules of origin and dispute resolution. The Canadians believed, perhaps erroneously in this case, that their interests were served by moderate rules of origin that would attract investment from outside firms anxious to sell within the NAFTA area. In contrast, the "Big Three" producers, the auto-parts manufacturers, and the United Auto Workers lobbied for a high rule of origin to prevent Japanese companies from establishing beachheads in Mexico or Canada, where they could assemble vehicles from imported components for shipment to the United States. The CFTA's rule of origin for autos, though calculated differently, was 50 percent; for NAFTA the Americans urged at least 65 or 75 percent, while the Canadians believed they had Mexican support for holding the line at 60 percent. Without consulting the Canadians, the Mexicans agreed to 65 percent—a move perceived as capitulation in Ottawa. Ultimately, the parties opted for a 62.5 percent rule of origin for autos and panel trucks.

The Canadians also believed that Mexico shared their opposition to a U.S. proposal on resolving disputes arising under NAFTA, itself one of the most controversial subjects in the negotiations. Washington proposed that if a country disagreed with the decision rendered by a NAFTA-established panel in a dumping or countervailing duty case, it would be allowed to transfer the controversy to a national tribunal. Ottawa strenuously objected on the grounds that such action would frustrate the dispute resolution mechanism. The Mexicans, who appeared to oppose such unilateral withdrawal, wound up aligning with the Americans. Ultimately, the persistent Canadians gained agreement on an adjudicatory process that satisfied their interests. This episode convinced Ottawa that Mexico was so anxious to inscribe its name on a document bearing the magic words "Free Trade Agreement" that it would make sweeping concessions sought by Washington. In terms of earning the trust of their U.S. and Canadian counterparts, "these [Mexican] chaps just didn't get it," said one first-hand Canadian observer. In all fairness to the Mexicans, Washington and Ottawa were themselves not above reproach. As noted, American negotiators pushed for greater access to Mexican petroleum than Serra Puche had anticipated at the beginning of the talks. Working-group participants also dealt with such minor complaints as the holding of most sessions in Washington (done for the convenience of all parties, despite some objections) and limitations on USTR's budget, which meant that the Mexicans and Canadians had to chip in to pay the huge Watergate Hotel bill.

Occasional contretemps aside, civility permeated the deliberations, and the participants exhibited respect for each other at the conclusion of the talks. Deputy Chief Negotiator Roh, for instance, praised the "good rapport and mounting confidence that developed among the participants as the talks progressed." Continued Roh, "The Mexicans were honorable, intelligent, dedicated patriots, who were committed to trade liberalization."[150] An exchange of gifts betokened the bonhomie that had developed among the negotiators. (The American team, for instance, distributed T-shirts emblazoned with the dates and venues of the 24 major meetings comprising the "NAFTA Continental Tour 1991-92." At the bottom of the itinerary was the hyperbolic inscription: 2,710,465 phone calls!! 389,672 faxes!! 218,241 working group meetings!! Endless legal scrubbing!![151]) Another U.S. official contrasted NAFTA negotiations with those involving the Japanese. In the latter, he said, "there is no trust, the parties continually operate at cross-purposes, and there is protracted haggling over every dotting of an *i*, crossing of a *t*, or placement of a comma." A senior Treasury Department official praised the Mexicans as "wanting to achieve the greatest market opening possible, while recognizing the political constraints under which the negotiators operated."[152]

The Deal[153]

Key provisions of the 2,000-page accord include:

- *Agriculture:* In recent years, the Mexican government has imposed import permits on one-quarter of U.S. agricultural goods entering its country, as well as tariffs, ranging from 15 to 20 percent, on vegetable oils, processed meats, tree nuts, and other commodities. NAFTA converts nontariff barriers to tariffs through a process called "tariffication" and phases out, over 15 years, these levies on orange juice, melons, certain vegetables, and other sensitive items. A special "safeguard" provision will provide additional protection to U.S. imports of onions, tomatoes, eggplant, chili peppers, squash, and water-

101

melon. The USTR anticipates that annual U.S. agricultural exports to Mexico will rise from $3 billion (1991) to $5 billion (2009)—with meat, livestock, and grains accounting for much of the increase.

- *Automobiles:* Mexico has applied a combination of nontariff barriers and tariffs of up to 20 percent to virtually prohibit imports of parts and assembled vehicles into the world's fastest growing auto market. NAFTA will immediately halve Mexican tariffs and eliminate them over five years for light trucks and over ten years for cars. It further stipulates that these vehicles must contain at least half North American content—rising to 62.5 percent over eight years—to qualify for duty-free treatment. Roh described the opening of this previously closed economic sector as a "slam-dunk for the U.S."

- *Dispute Resolution:* NAFTA employs a three-tiered mechanism for resolving most disputes within ten months: (1) consultation; (2) review by a Trade Commission composed of the top trade officials from each country; and, if necessary, (3) a decision made by a binational five-member panel of private sector experts from the countries involved.

- *Energy:* The accord opens most petrochemicals in Mexico to foreign investment, permits private electricity production, authorizes direct sales of natural gas between U.S. and Canadian suppliers and Mexican customers, and allows Pemex to pay "performance" bonuses to successful oil exploration firms. The agreement still bars foreign ownership of Mexican oil reserves. Observers in the Texas-focused oil patch view the performance language as an important step toward Mexico's entering into "risk-contracts" in a few years, despite contravening one of Serra Puche's five noes. An important breakthrough lies in greater opportunities for U.S. and Canadian companies to increase sales to Pemex and the Federal Electricity Commission (CFE), which have followed a "buy-Mexico" policy. These two energy monopolies, whose purchases exceed $8 billion annually, must expose 50 percent of their acquisitions to open bidding by North American suppliers in 1994. The percentage jumps to 70 percent in the fifth year of the accord before reaching almost 100 percent after ten years. Tariffs on oil-field equipment will also be phased out. Trade associations believe that sales of goods and services to Mexico's energy sector will increase by $1 billion or more the first year that NAFTA takes effect.

- *Financial Services:* The provisions on financial services constitute a slam-dunk and a three-point shot, to embellish Roh's basketball metaphor on the auto chapter. With one exception, Mexico's $330 billion financial services market has been closed for more than 50 years to U.S. and Canadian firms that carry out banking, securities, and similar activities. Under NAFTA, virtually all limitations on establishing Mexican subsidiaries will be eliminated by 1 January 2000. Furthermore, North Americans involved in joint ventures can increase their ownership of insurance firms to up to 100 percent by 1996. Finally, the accord eliminates all equity and market-share restrictions by the year 2000, when this $3.5 billion sector too will be completely opened.

- *Government Procurement:* With a handful of exceptions, U.S., Canadian, and Mexican firms will have an equal chance to win most of the $18 billion in contracts that the Mexican government now awards, including those let by Pemex and CFE. NAFTA preserves small-business and minority set-asides in all three nations while establishing a procedure to inform small businesses about Mexican procurement rules and regulations.

- *Intellectual Property:* NAFTA vouchsafes a higher standard of protection for patents, copyrights, trademarks, and trade secrets than any other bilateral or international pact. The three signatories must provide rigorous protection of intellectual property rights based on national treatment. They are committed to enforcing rights effectively against infringement, both domestically and at the border. The U.S. International Trade Commission estimates that U.S. holders of intellectual property lost approximately $533 million in Canada and $367 million in Mexico in 1986 alone. As in the CFTA, Canada has retained its "cultural exception" to free trade in films, books, recordings, and other cultural industries.

- *Investment:* The agreement expands the definition of investment to encompass not only subsidiaries, but property owned in one of the NAFTA countries by the national(s) of another, as well as investment-related services conducted in that country. The accord grants national treatment to North American firms in any of the three nations. Should a host country breach the agreement's investment rules, a NAFTA investor, at his option, may pursue either remedies available in the host nation's courts or monetary damages through binding investor-state arbitration. Such arbitration is the first ever agreed to by two developed countries. U.S. investment in Mexico, which surged from $5.5 billion in 1988 to $16 billion in 1991, should expand even more when Americans gain an even footing with their Mexican counterparts.

- *Standards:* The accord sets as its goal achieving compatibility in health, safety, and industrial standards at the most rigorous levels found in any of the three countries. The signatories also agreed that unreasonable standards would not be used to thwart trade.

- *Tariffs:* NAFTA provides for the progressive elimination of all tariffs on goods meeting the pact's rules-of-origin criteria. For most items, existing customs duties will either be removed at once or phased out in five or ten equal annual stages. For certain sensitive products, tariffs will be gradually eliminated over a period of up to 15 years. No change was made in the CFTA, under which the tariffs on affected items traded between the United States and Canada will be phased out by 1998.

- *Textiles:* The accord eliminates in six years or less Mexican tariffs (10 to 20 percent) on more than 80 percent of U.S. exports of textile and apparel. A rigorous rule of origin ensures that Mexico will not be used as an "export platform" for third countries anxious to export into the United States.

During the 10-year phase-out period, a special safeguard mechanism will apply to textile products. During that period quotas may be imposed on imports of non-NAFTA goods in the event of import surges. There is also a tariff "snap-back" provision to redress surges in imports of NAFTA-produced apparel.

- *Transportation:* Nearly 90 percent of U.S. trade with its neighbors—$210 billion worth of goods—travels overland. Mexico and the United States have impeded such transport by requiring that trucks and buses transfer their cargoes and passengers at the border. Canadian carriers have faced similar obstacles. NAFTA provides open roads within a few years for railroads (1994), buses (1996), and trucks (1999). This provision should prove lucrative for U.S. firms because of their superior equipment, intermodal terminals, and warehousing facilities. All parties will benefit from moving goods faster, cheaper, and with fewer problems.

NAFTA and the CFTA

NAFTA differs from but improves upon the CFTA in several important ways. To begin with, it is much broader, covering such items as intellectual property and land transport that were not addressed in the U.S.-Canadian accord, as well as financial services that were inadequately treated in the CFTA. By the time the NAFTA negotiations began, Washington and Ottawa had three years of experience with the bilateral agreement, and therefore were in a position to identify areas for possible improvement in the trilateral context. For example, while the CFTA addressed government procurement, its provisions extended only to goods purchased by certain federal entities. NAFTA applies to goods, services, and construction undertaken by virtually all federal government agencies in the three nations. Although Canada and Mexico wanted to cover subfederal governments, the U.S. negotiators, sensing the congressional uproar that would occur, refused to liberalize the Buy America Act, the Intermodal Surface

Transportation Efficiency Act, and small business set-asides, which constituted major Canadian and Mexican demands in this area. In addition, unlike the CFTA, the North American pact contemplates the "tariffication" of import permits and other nontariff barriers to U.S.-Mexican agricultural trade (Canada has a separate agreement with Mexico, and the United States and Canada agreed to incorporate Chapter 7 of CFTA into NAFTA to complete the third side of the triangle). The result is to make levies on these items more transparent, invest far less discretion in bureaucrats, and ensure that revenues will go to the nation imposing the tariff rather than to the beneficiary of the import permit. As mentioned above, NAFTA also institutes the first arbitration mechanism for the settlement of disputes between a party and an investor of another party in an international trade agreement. Indeed, NAFTA's dispute resolution process is more comprehensive than that found in the CFTA. Moreover, the signatories enhanced the practical administration of NAFTA by involving customs officials in a working group from the outset; in the CFTA process, negotiators brought them in only near the termination of discussions. Even more important, the negotiators spelled out in much greater detail the procedures for administering NAFTA's provisions. They also agreed to develop Uniform Customs Regulations among the three participants. In so doing, they reduced bureaucratic discretion and minimized the likelihood of Honda-type conflicts in which the Americans claimed that Honda imports had not satisfied the CFTA's rule-of-origin requirement. Above all, NAFTA—even though freighted with legalisms and suffused with dependent clauses that make it less "reader friendly" than the CFTA—embodies a more modern agreement because of its emphasis on breadth and inclusiveness, the likely adherence of additional parties, and the ambitious removal of barriers to the exchange of goods, services, capital, and technology among the signatories. The CFTA, the first international trade accord to address trade in services, did so by listing those activities covered; in contrast, NAFTA sets forth only those services that are excluded. The latter approach, which also contrasts with that adopted in the Uruguay Round, is much more transparent and liberalizing, particularly when the new services are developed as technological advances make their mark in telecommunications, computing, engineering, and other areas. Although the language is often forbidding to laypeople, the document's length and detail should clear up many of the ambiguities that have sparked disputes under the CFTA. For instance, the provisions are infinitely clearer in such areas as rules of origin and customs administration. Finally, the Americans and Canadians waited for CFTA's formal approval before conferring benefits on the United States. In key sectors such as petrochemicals, the Mexicans unilaterally implemented NAFTA provisions to catch the attention (and dollars) of investors and to emphasize their enthusiasm for trade liberalization.

CHAPTER FIVE

NAFTA and the 1992 Presidential Campaign

Introduction

Inevitably, NAFTA became an issue in the 1992 presidential campaign. Above all, this contest provided a referendum on the U.S. economy. One poll after another taken during the campaign indicated that most Americans felt insecure about the nation's economic future.[154] These surveys, moreover, showed the economy to be the primary issue concerning voters and motivating their presidential preferences.[155] Such facts were not lost on the candidates, especially the Democratic nominee. As Clinton's campaign staff continually reminded him (and each other), "It's the economy, stupid!" The Bush camp worked hard to overcome the perception that the chief executive's foreign policy accomplishments eclipsed his concern for the nation's economic woes. Perhaps most significantly, fears about the economy spawned the most successful third-party candidacy since Teddy Roosevelt's Bull Moose campaign in 1912—that of Texas billionaire H. Ross Perot.

This concern about the economy had many strands: from the federal deficit, to high unemployment, to issues of trade—including the trade deficit and the decline of America's competitiveness abroad. During the 1992 campaign, no trade question assumed greater importance than did NAFTA. In fact, this was the first time since the bitter 1888 contest between tariff-cutter Grover Cleveland

and protectionist Benjamin Harrison that a trade issue attracted sustained scrutiny in a presidential race. The agreement became an issue because of its implications for the economy and because of the interplay of powerful forces both for and against the proposed pact. How each of the candidates dealt with these NAFTA-generated interest groups and issues reveals much about their campaign strategies and provides an insight into NAFTA's role in the election.

Clinton during the Primaries

Bill Clinton's handling of NAFTA spoke volumes about his presidential bid. Central to his strategy was an effort to cast himself as a "New Democrat," not beholden to old, shopworn liberal values and their constituencies. Instead, he presented himself as open to fresh ideas that transcended traditional liberal and conservative labels. Such an approach was necessary, it was thought, to win back moderate Democrats who had voted Republican during the 1980s. But this plan required a delicate balancing act. If Clinton moved too far to the center, he risked alienating remnants of the New Deal coalition—namely, organized labor, civil rights groups, and liberals in consumer and environmental organizations. Throughout the campaign, Clinton sought both to galvanize the Democratic base and reach out to the center—an approach exemplified in his handling of NAFTA.

Clinton's background furnishes a perspective on his attitude toward the free-trade agreement. Despite later campaign barbs about his being a "bubba" from Arkansas, Clinton had worked on the staff of the Senate Foreign Relations Committee and was disposed to support the continental accord well before launching his presidential campaign.[156] He had embraced the principle of free trade throughout his years as governor of Arkansas, and for good reason. Exports of manufactured goods and agricultural products generate 10 percent of the Razorback State's gross state product. One 1992 estimate put the number of export-dependent jobs in Arkansas, in industries ranging from rice farming to poultry, at 40,000. In addition, WalMart, the state's biggest corporation, had embarked upon a joint venture with Cifra S. A. to open retail outlets in Mexico—a project whose success depended on the market access and improved transport logistics assured by NAFTA.[157]

Governor Clinton's enthusiasm for the idea of developing foreign markets became clear at a Washington meeting of supporters convened by Mickey Kantor in mid-1991. When some in attendance expressed concern over the problems that backing free trade might generate, Clinton declared: "If you guys want me to run as an isolationist or a protectionist, you need another candidate. I'm not going to do it."[158]

Clinton was also a founding member of the Democratic Leadership Council (DLC). Formed in the wake of the 1984 Mondale debacle, the DLC described itself as "an idea center, catalyst, and national voice for a reform movement" that would reshape American politics, set the agenda for progressive government, and turn the Democratic party away from its tainted McGovernist past. The council emphasized "progressive ideals, mainstream values, and innovative, nonbureaucratic solutions."[159] Jesse Jackson predictably derided it as a "Southern White Boys' Caucus,"[160] while the director of the liberal Coalition for Democratic Values commented scornfully, "We do not need two Republican parties."[161] In 1990–91, Clinton served as chairman of the organization, which would soon include more than 800 elected officials in 33 state chapters, with a disproportionately large number of members in the South and Midwest. The DLC prided itself on emphasizing moderate issues and working with public officials attuned by the reality of competitive elections to the everyday concerns of the American people—as opposed to anointed and appointed special-interest group leaders and their out-of-touch political minions, often ensconced in safe seats. As a result, it hoped to attract centrist voters and dispel the Democratic party's image as a collection of tax-and-spend liberals. This posture placed them in competition for influence with organized labor, Black leaders, and other liberal constituencies within the party. The DLC spawned both a think-tank (the Progressive Policy Institute) and a magazine (*The New Democrat*) to develop and disseminate ideas.

More than two months before Clinton announced his bid for the White House, the DLC passed a resolution entitled, "The New

Choice in American Politics." The text of this document contained a ringing endorsement of NAFTA:

> The United States must use its enormous market power to expand fair and free trade around the world. We urge Congress to extend "fast track" negotiating authority for a free trade pact with Mexico that will lead to higher incomes and employment in both countries.[162]

Given his mainstream foreign-policy thinking and free-trade background, it is no wonder that Clinton's support for NAFTA predated his August 1991 entry into the presidential race. Once the campaign started in earnest, however, Clinton began to adjust his stance to accommodate the political realities of the primary season. He continued to voice support for free trade and fast track. In so doing, he hoped to establish his "New Democratic" credentials early and distinguish himself form such populist critics of NAFTA as Senator Tom Harkin (D-Iowa), former California Governor Jerry Brown, and Virginia Governor L. Douglas Wilder. But as the nomination fight tightened, Clinton amended his position to avoid offending organized labor—an interest group that exerted disproportionate influence in Democratic primaries, especially in industrial states.

In March this strategy faced its toughest test in the Michigan primary. Brown's vocal opposition to NAFTA in this trade-sensitive Rust Belt state threatened to slow Clinton's momentum, possibly stopping the Arkansan in his tracks. As the former California governor gained strength in the polls, Clinton considered criticizing NAFTA more forcefully. Ultimately, he decided against such a move, and instead opted for a risky alternative: He defended his free-trade and fast-track positions before an audience of auto workers in Flint; at the same time, he expressed distrust of Bush's ability to negotiate a fair agreement. The implication was, of course, that as president, Clinton would be more likely than Bush to protect the well-being of American workers and the quality of the environment in negotiating with Mexico and Canada. This strategy worked, as Clinton garnered 51 percent of the ballots cast in the Michigan primary. His formula for political success—complementing appeals to the center with overtures to the party's core—enabled him to eliminate from the contest his anti-NAFTA populist competitors for the Democratic nomination.

The Perot Threat

NAFTA's most persistent and strident opponent proved to be Perot. The origins of his candidacy are vague. There is, however, little doubt that the billionaire had at least contemplated a presidential bid well before his famed February 1992 appearance on CNN's "Larry King Live." Political activists and admirers had long urged him to enter politics. One had even started a "Draft Ross Perot for President" campaign and discussed it extensively with the Texas maverick himself a full eight months before the Perot phenomenon began to take shape.[163] These factors cast doubt on Perot's claim that the draft was a spontaneous, grass-roots movement without significant forethought or direction from above.

Nevertheless, the likelihood of an independent candidacy first received national attention on 20 February 1992. On that night, Perot told Larry King that if "the people" were to draft him by getting his name on the ballot in all 50 states, he would run a "world class" campaign for president.[164]

Perot's comments sparked a nationwide campaign to recruit the Texan as an independent. Droves of volunteers came forward in most states. Coordinated by a largely unpaid staff working out of Perot-leased office space in Dallas, these activists soon began collecting signatures to get their paladin's name inscribed on every state's ballot—a sine qua non for Perot's commitment to the race. Despite this disclaimer, the signs of a serious presidential bid by the Texas dissenter became unmistakable. He expanded the offices of his volunteer coordinators, stepped up his talk-show appearances, disseminated a toll-free number for potential volunteers, and hired as his chief political adviser Tom Luce, a long-time associate and one-time Texas gubernatorial candidate.

Although formerly a NAFTA enthusiast, Perot decried the agreement in early 1992. Even before his CNN appearance, he had excoriated the pact in a Dallas radio interview. "When the Mexican free-trade agreement was announced," Perot told KLIV listeners,

> I called a Who's Who of manufacturing and asked, "When will you build your next plant in the U.S."? They said, "Ross, we won't." Mexican labor, bad luck, is $1.55 an hour; good luck is 75 cents, average is about a dollar. Hire a young work force down there, build a new plant, pay off the local police chief. It's a rotten place to do business. I won't go to Mexico—I've told'em, they've been after me—I told them when the police chief in Mexico City doesn't live in the biggest house in town, call me. They haven't called me yet.[165]

Apparently, Perot's friends in the business community never did phone. Even while avowing a commitment to free trade and friendship with the Mexican people, he continued to lash out at NAFTA, portraying the pact in conspiratorial terms and Mexicans in stereotypes. Among the conspirators were "huge corporations," "myopic bureaucrats," "Washington insiders," "furtive negotiators," "PAC-influenced congressmen," and "foreign lobbyists." The latter were actually U.S. citizens, many of whom had left USTR and other federal agencies for the private sector. Their dastardly deed was to work for Mexico, a country long criticized—as described in chapter 7—for failing to lobby effectively in Washington. He characterized Mexican laborers as dirt poor victims of an authoritarian system who lived as ragamuffins and toiled for sweatshop wages. "The typical Mexican worker," he said, "is a 25-year-old with little or no health care expense working for a dollar an hour. You can't compete with that in the U.S.A., period."[166] He dismissed the argument that additional high-wage jobs generated by the agreement would offset the loss in low-paying manufacturing employment. Even if true, he stated, the new jobs would not help laid-off blue-collar workers. Their relative lack of education would impede their ability to take advantage of high-skilled opportunities, he averred.[167] "Perot recast the standard terms of trade debate: free-traders were now out-of-touch ideologues who passively accepted

America's decline, and protectionists were simply can-do patriots out to rebuild the national industrial base."[168]

In June, Perot's NAFTA-bashing and the reaction to it jolted the *Bolsa*, Mexico's new, glassy stock exchange. In press interviews, the Texas billionaire continued to criticize NAFTA sharply, still insisting that he genuinely backed free trade. Early in the month, he told the *New Republic*:

> Philosophically I am for fair and free trade . . . I am not a protectionist, but pragmatically as a guy who understands business, if I can build a factory in Mexico, pay my labor a dollar an hour, hire a 25-year-old work force, have little or no health care, little or no retirement, have no pollution or environmental controls, then if you are the greatest businessman in the world, if you are Einstein in business trying to compete with me in the United States, you can't even get into the ring with those numbers.[169]

Perot went on to warn that wrongheaded trade policy could cause hard-working Americans to lose "the equity in their homes, their kids can't go to college, they can't support their families, you've got chaos in America, because all the jobs went to Mexico."[170] The *Wall Street Journal*, a powerful, relentless NAFTA advocate, took Perot to task for his "idle comments." In a 15 June editorial, the *Journal* admonished him that "part of being a real candidate is that people and markets take you seriously."[171] In partial response to Perot's fulmination and the *Journal*'s rebuke, the *Bolsa* plummeted more than 300 points in June, losing 20 percent of its value between 1 June and late July.[172] As much as $2 billion may have fled the country late in the month.[173]

Nervousness about Perot's free-swinging protectionism was not confined to Mexican investors. The Democrats feared that the immensely rich Texan would attract blue-collar workers who had supported Harkin and Brown in the primaries; the Republicans were afraid that he would garner support from isolationists, nativists, and others who had resonated to Pat Buchanan. In fact, a 5-7 July *Wall Street Journal*/NBC News Poll showed Perot (33 percent) leading both Bush (31 percent) and Clinton (28 percent). An overwhelming majority of respondents found Perot (37 percent) the candidate "most able to deal with the economy" compared to Bush (16 percent) and Clinton (16 percent). More people also found Perot (37 percent) the candidate "most able to protect America's interests on trade issues" compared to Bush (27 percent) and Clinton (9 percent).[174]

To the relief of both parties, Perot withdrew from the race in mid-July, in the midst of the Democratic Convention. Having "just rationally looked at the facts" and determined that "the Democratic party has revitalized itself," Perot said that his continuance in the race would only "disrupt the political process." Asserted the mercurial billionaire, "I have concluded that we can't win in November and that the election will be decided in the House of Representatives"—where, he felt, he would have little chance of prevailing.[175] Other observers attributed Perot's decision to the increasingly close examination to which his campaign was being subjected. Mounting press scrutiny and attacks by the White House, along with positive publicity for Clinton during the convention, had led to a significant decline in Perot's popular standing.[176] By 15 July, the day before his withdrawal, his support had fallen to 20 percent from a high of 36 percent on 7 June.[177] These factors had also taken a toll on Perot personally. He had long been viewed favorably by the public, and his waning popularity was difficult for him to accept. He believed that he was doing his country a favor by running for president and could not understand why so many people were abandoning him. Part of the problem, as he saw it, was the "Republican dirty-tricks committee," which he repeatedly accused of planting negative stories about him and his message in the press; the media, he complained after quitting the race, had "created an image of a person in the last few months that is not the person I am at all."[178] Perot subsequently offered another reason for leaving the race—namely, that the Bush campaign had planned to discredit his daughter, Carolyn, with a doctored photograph and disrupt her August wedding. This bizarre allegation, one in a long line of peculiar charges made by Perot throughout his public life, led White House Press Secretary Marlin Fitzwater to call him "a paranoid person who has delusions."[179] Chimed in *Time* magazine,

"[Ross Perot is] an incurable conspiracy monger who espies plotters in every thicket and easily persuades himself that some of his wildest suspicions are true."[180]

The Nomination and Fall Campaign

As Clinton's nomination became more probable, the free-trade talks entered their final stage. As a result, the Arkansas governor changed his campaign dynamics with respect to NAFTA. Elements of the Democratic coalition who strongly opposed the pact, notably organized labor that had little love lost for Clinton and some environmentalists, were forced to accept the prospect of a pro-NAFTA nominee. This fact, along with the progress made on the accord during the spring and summer, prompted Clinton to give the issue greater attention. Although more vocally supporting free trade, he did not fully discard his cautious approach. Not only did he reiterate his doubts about "Bush's NAFTA," he also declared that he would have to see the details of the completed deal before endorsing it. He urged skeptical voters to trust him to protect American workers and the environment. In so doing, he contrasted himself with the floundering incumbent who had allowed the recession-afflicted economy to weaken while failing to make good on his promise to safeguard the environment.

Predictably, this approach also appeared in the Democratic platform, approved during the party's July convention in New York City. The platform language implied both support for the basic tenets of NAFTA and concern about protecting workers and the environment. The text read:

> Multilateral trade agreements can advance our economic interests by expanding the global economy. Whether negotiating the North American Free Trade Area (NAFTA) or completing GATT (General Agreement on Tariffs and Trade) negotiations, our government must assure that our legitimate concerns about the environmental, health and safety, and labor standards are included. Those American workers whose jobs are

117

affected must have the benefit of effective adjustment assistance.[181]

The selection of Al Gore as Clinton's running mate sent a less ambiguous signal to NAFTA supporters. Gore had been one of only 23 Democratic senators to vote for fast-track authority. He also complemented support for free trade with a commitment to environmental protection, as articulated in his book *Earth in the Balance: Ecology and the Human Spirit.*[182] In addition to Gore, Clinton recruited other NAFTA supporters to his campaign team: Robert Reich, an academic champion of America's need to specialize in "knowledge-intensive" industries; Robert Rubin, co-chairman of Goldman, Sachs & Co., which had helped achieve the privatization of Teléfonos de México; Joseph O'Neill, a lobbyist for Mexico who had served as a key aide to Senator Bentsen; Richard Feinberg, a distinguished Latin American expert; and Bruce Babbitt, a former Arizona governor and strong advocate of closer U.S.-Mexican relations.[183]

Other key members of Clinton's entourage were less bullish on NAFTA. Included in this camp were Mrs. Clinton, campaign manager David Wilhelm, and political adviser Paul Begala. Pollster Stanley Greenberg produced surveys indicating that a pro-free trade stance could cost Clinton the race in Michigan and Ohio. Greenberg himself, however, favored backing the trade pact to reinforce the "new Democrat" image.[184]

The campaign calculus changed again when the president proclaimed the completion of negotiations at the 12 August Rose Garden ceremony. Almost immediately Bush pressed Clinton to take a stand on the agreement and attacked the Democrat when he declined to do so.[185] Instead of endorsing NAFTA categorically, Clinton announced that he would withhold final judgment until he had studied the 2,000-page accord and Congress had finished conducting hearings on it.

More than time to study, the Democratic standard-bearer needed breathing room to devise a NAFTA strategy for the fall campaign. He decided to revive the balancing act that had served him so well during the primaries. In the face of escalating Republican attacks, Clinton planned to burnish his image as a "New

Democrat," while rallying the traditional party-faithful by issuing a four-year "putting people first" plan for the economy. He pledged to spend $200 billion to spur growth, revitalize cities, and rebuild the country's infrastructure. Yet the final phase of the campaign raised the stakes on every issue and forced the Clinton camp to scrutinize every decision. The strategy now employed included insisting that congressional hearings and further review of the agreement were imperative, while using congressional leaders like Senator Bentsen to highlight Bush's "politicization" of the trade pact.[186] This course allowed Clinton to keep both sides at bay, appear true to his pledge to ensure the best possible NAFTA, and perhaps score some political points as well.

Although Bush had proclaimed NAFTA to be a "done deal" in mid-August, many observers were suspicious of the timing: The White House ceremony was conducted just days before the beginning of the Republican National Convention in Houston, thus allowing Bush to display a trophy to the delegates before a national audience.[187] Opponents nourished the perception that the president had an incomplete agreement, despite Ambassador Hills' assertion that all that remained was "legal scrubbing" to put NAFTA in its final form. In fact, as described in chapter 4, substantive matters were discussed during the period between 12 August "conclusion of negotiations" and the initialing of the pact on 7 October.

In enlisting congressional Democrats to criticize Bush's apparent politicization of the accord, Clinton sought political cover while he delayed his own announcement on NAFTA. The Democrats launched this strategy on 8 September, when Carla Hills presented the lengthy document to the Senate Finance Committee, chaired by Bentsen. The courtly Texan forced Hills to admit that the text was not yet in final form and chastised the Bush administration for criticizing Clinton's delay. He accused the White House of "deliberately trying to politicize this agreement,"[188] adding that:

> This agreement is enormously complex. . . . The draft you have finally provided us is 2,000 pages long. It covers everything from corn to computers. Governor Clinton

did not even have that text. Yet the president thought Governor Clinton should sign on.[189]

In emphasizing the accord's shortcomings, Bentsen claimed that Bush was pressing Clinton to "sign on the dotted line when there wasn't even a dotted line to sign."[190] Reinforcing this orchestrated attack on the administration was the announcement that several other influential pro-trade Democrats planned to withhold their support until Congress completed hearings on the pact. Legislators such as Rostenkowski and Max Baucus, chairman of the Trade Subcommittee of the Senate Finance Committee, joined Bentsen in publicly castigating the White House's politicization of the issue.[191] "The Bush administration," argued Baucus, "appears more concerned with using NAFTA for partisan political advantage rather than getting the best possible market-opening for the United States."[192]

Toward a NAFTA Stand

Such gamesmanship gave Clinton the time he wanted on NAFTA. Eventually the Democratic nominee and his aides had to hammer out their formal position. In late September, the candidate met with 25 advisers in a suburban Washington hotel suite to craft a position. Not surprisingly, the Clinton camp was evenly split, reflecting long-standing divisions on the issue. Campaign Chairman Wilhelm opposed NAFTA because endorsing it could lead to the loss of key states' electoral votes. Echoing this primary-season warning, pollster Greenberg argued that in signing on to the agreement, Clinton risked forfeiting enough votes to Perot in Michigan to swing the state into the Bush column. Predictably, Reich, Rubin, and Feinberg weighed in on behalf of the accord. Communications Director George Stephanopoulos, Campaign Manager James Carville, and other insiders also urged Clinton to back the agreement for several reasons. For starters, endorsing NAFTA would neutralize the issue and take it away from Bush. No longer would Clinton be subjected to the criticism that his reservations about NAFTA sprang from his being indentured to the

AFL-CIO and other special interests. Also, endorsing NAFTA would enhance Clinton's reputation as "a different kind of Democrat," thus helping to convince still skeptical voters of his moderation and pragmatism. Finally, by supporting the agreement, Clinton would show himself to be a world-class statesman rather than a provincial politician.[193] The public, after all, expects its president to be visionary and expansive about the economy, rather than a doomsayer.

Though Clinton listened carefully to the many views, he himself made the final decision. He would embrace the existing accord but call for parallel arrangements on labor and the environment. "I'm for open markets, I'm for increasing our exports," said the candidate, according to one participant. "I just want to do it in a way that doesn't hurt people."[194] He secretly asked former San Antonio Mayor Henry G. Cisneros, later secretary of housing and urban development, to convey personally to President Salinas Clinton's commitment to NAFTA.[195]

On the eve of the agreement's initialing by the U.S., Mexican, and Canadian trade ministers, the Democratic nominee offered his qualified support of the accord. Yet the morning that he was to announce his endorsement, the exact text of his remarks had not been completed. Clinton screamed and yelled at Stephanopoulos about the draft.[196] His tirades, to which his young aide had become accustomed, may have been simply a way to release steam in the last weeks of a grueling campaign. The outburst also may have betokened the conflict that the candidate felt between presenting himself as a New Democrat, on the one hand, and realizing that he was offending Old Democrats, on the other, by placing his tentative imprimatur on a Bush initiative detested by the AFL-CIO. In any case, he delivered a 19-page speech at North Carolina State University on 4 October. In his presentation he stated that if elected, he would not renegotiate the pact but would improve upon the text through supplemental agreements. Calling its omissions "serious," he declared that he could not sign the accord in its present form. His reservations centered on his belief that NAFTA should be part of a "larger economic strategy" aimed at better preparing the U.S. economy and work force for the challenges of the future. "The issue," he declared, "is not whether we should support free trade or open markets. Of course we should. The real question is whether or not we will have a national economic strategy to make sure we reap its benefits."[197]

Clinton thus reached his ultimate stand on NAFTA in the same manner that he had crafted earlier, less comprehensive positions—that is, by balancing his "New Democratic" tendencies with an effort to propitiate the party's core constituencies. Just as Clinton's final stance reflected this key facet of his campaign strategy, so Bush's criticism of that stance underscored an important element in the president's own election plan.

Bush: The Globalist

Bush responded to Clinton's NAFTA speech by employing a familiar campaign tactic: he labeled the statement yet another example of Clinton's penchant to "waffle," taking both sides of an issue rather than choosing one position and sticking to it. This criticism betrayed a key aspect of the Republican campaign's strategy. The GOP not only employed NAFTA in the "positive" sense to highlight Bush's strengths, it also used the pact negatively to illuminate Clinton's weaknesses. Of course, the risks of making the free-trade accord a campaign issue at all had not been lost on the White House. Bush's advisers had vigorously debated the proper handling of NAFTA even before the primary season had begun. By late 1991, Desert Shield/Desert Storm seemed a distant memory, and the growing isolationist mood in the country made the Bush administration wary of actively pursuing a trade agreement during an election year.[198] A January 1992 Gallup poll revealed that 82 percent of Americans wanted the United States to focus on issues at home and scale back efforts abroad.[199] Also, in light of the NAFTA timetable, pushing the negotiations too fast meant risking a bitter fight with Congress during the heat of a campaign season. At the time, there was simply no way to predict who, if anyone, might benefit from such a political battle so many months in the future.[200]

Why, then, did Bush continue to impel negotiations with Mexico and Canada and declaim NAFTA's virtues to an increasingly angry and cantankerous electorate? A December 1991 ABC News/*Washington Post* poll, for example, showed that 75 percent of respondents believed that the president "spends too much time on foreign problems and not enough on problems in this country."[201] Still, Bush himself seemed to thrive on international affairs while manifesting indifference—or even outright boredom—toward domestic concerns. The economy was clearly Bush's short suit. With relatively little to show in this area, the president's camp sought to translate the incumbent's foreign policy expertise into a home-front advantage. NAFTA seemed to offer a perfect vehicle for achieving this objective.

The chief executive aimed to depict NAFTA as proof that his foreign policy successes could create jobs at home, where unemployment remained well above 7 percent throughout 1992.[202] For example, the Rose Garden ceremony announcing the agreement focused on how NAFTA would put Americans to work. "Open markets in Mexico and Canada," promised Bush, "mean more American jobs."[203] This event was the culmination of the White House's efforts to complete the agreement before the GOP convention so that the president could highlight NAFTA as a jobs-creator. Bush persistently hammered away at this theme following the announcement. In a Georgia factory town, the beleaguered chief executive declared enthusiastically, "I am going to fight for these open markets because that means more jobs in this country— every city and state of our country."[204]

The Bush team was especially hopeful that the agreement would catalyze victories in Texas and California. These Sun Belt states, which led the nation in exports to Mexico, embraced 86 of the 270 electoral votes required for victory in November.[205]

Yet the chief executive wanted to do more than simply champion NAFTA as an employment generator. He also sought to use NAFTA to portray himself as an economic leader who could guide the nation to security in the post-Cold War global economy. The early October ceremony in San Antonio, where Hills and her counterparts initialed the agreement, was meant to reinforce this image. The initialing, which could have been done—and, in a non-election year, probably would have been carried out—in the sober confines of Hills' Washington office, was instead elevated into a full-fledged international media event, replete with pomp and pageantry. Bush appeared alongside the glowing duo of Salinas and Mulroney, who, being political creatures themselves, understood the American president's need to make the ceremony look more important than it actually was. Mulroney, a close personal friend of Bush, made a point of praising the president's "compelling vision of the Americas as a hemisphere built on cooperation," and contended that the trade agreement would have been impossible without him. Not surprisingly, even though the White House maintained that the San Antonio trip was purely nonpolitical in nature, it was Bush's campaign that picked up the tab.[206] The highly publicized event, after all, unfolded in a key electoral state, allowing Bush to trumpet his mastery of international economic affairs for maximum political advantage.

Bush built on this theme in a speech at the port of New Orleans the day after the ceremony. There he underscored NAFTA's domestic potential and sought to bolster his image as a visionary by stating:

> You know, in the Cold War, we used our military might to force alliances, to push them together all across the Atlantic and the Pacific. Today, we can use our economic strength to forge new alliances, push them together. NAFTA is only the first. I see other trade agreements with nations in Europe and Latin America and Asia. As we tear down barriers, we create good, high-paying jobs for American workers, and that is what this Nation desperately needs. . . . Now we must build on our accomplishment and meet the challenge of a global economy. America cannot be timid, we cannot be uncertain. That is not our nature. We must be aggressive. We must lead. We must keep our eyes fixed on the future, for that is where our opportunity lies. This is the kind of leadership I've given America. As we've changed the world the past four years, this is the kind of leadership that I offer for the next four years, as we create jobs and renew this country.[207]

Bush not only took advantage of NAFTA to focus attention on his foresight and leadership, he also used it to castigate Clinton. To begin with, he depicted the Democratic standard-bearer as the captive of labor unions, environmental organizations, and other special interests. This portrayal conflicted with Clinton's attempts to use the trade issue to underscore his status as a "New Democrat." Bush also sought to contrast his opponent's vacillation with the president's purported record of decisiveness.

These attacks mounted in intensity after the pact was unveiled. Following the 12 August announcement, Clinton blunted Bush's offensive by pointing to the agreement's incompleteness. Bush had no persuasive or compelling rejoinder to this response, as evidenced by the Hills-Bentsen exchanges at the Senate Finance Committee hearings. The timing of Clinton's North Carolina State speech and the initialing ceremony sparked a more lively discussion. The Bush camp immediately leapt on Clinton's qualified NAFTA endorsement as another example of the Democrat's fence-straddling. They dismissed as unfounded his reservations about the agreement's lack of safeguards on the environment and worker protection. Meanwhile, they reiterated the charge that it was enthrallment to the AFL-CIO that prevented his fully endorsing the trade pact. Bush, Hills, and Mary Matalin, the president's acid-tongued deputy campaign manager, voiced these criticisms forcefully and repeatedly. Matalin, characterizing Bill Clinton as "an elusive character, unwilling to give straight answers to simple questions,"[208] expressed the campaign's view that Clinton "can't be on both sides of the [NAFTA] issue"[209] and charged that "Bill Clinton is trying to pawn himself off as a free trader when in fact he's just another protectionist pawn of big labor."[210] In response to Clinton's specific objections to NAFTA, Hills said, "The qualifiers sound to me like he is being held back by the labor unions who are opposed to the agreement."[211] Bush himself weighed in with the strongest critique of Clinton's position. In the same New Orleans speech in which the president employed the trade accord to accentuate his own strengths, he lambasted Clinton's NAFTA stance. Bush argued that Clinton's free-trade position had fluctuated during the year, depending on the strength of organized labor in the various primary states, finally culminating in a hedged endorsement. Such indecisiveness could not be tolerated in the White House, he declared. Bush insisted that Clinton's specific criticisms of the pact had already been adequately addressed. He cited the National Wildlife Federation's endorsement of NAFTA as proof that Clinton's skepticism toward the accord's environmental protection was unfounded.[212]

Perot Returns

The October segment of the Perot campaign was, like the earlier period, long on rhetoric but short on details regarding NAFTA. Perot's platform, entitled "United We Stand: How We Can Take Back Our Country," constituted a vague outline of policy prescriptions. The document embraced four paragraphs on U.S.-Latin American trade, but was fuzzy on NAFTA. Perot expressed support for stepping up commerce with other nations of the Hemisphere, acknowledged the desire of the U.S. Hispanic community for improved economic ties with Mexico, praised Mexico and President Salinas for recent efforts to revitalize the nation, and even wrote of the "exciting opportunity" that the free-trade agreement afforded the United States and its Spanish-speaking neighbor. Yet the same section also included familiar references to the cheap Mexican labor available to U.S. firms and Mexico's lax record on environmental regulation. Argued Perot:

> The challenge is to create a trade agreement that helps Mexico to continue to pull itself up but that does not pull us down. I do not want a trade agreement that trades away jobs. I want a trade agreement that creates good paying permanent jobs on both sides of the border.[213]

Such moderate writings contrasted with Perot's verbal bombasts, and his presence in the race provided voters with a distinct perspective on NAFTA. While Bush wrapped himself in the accord and Clinton accepted it with reservations, the self-styled Texas outsider escalated his attacks on the agreement. He reiterated his belief that "We have got to stop sending jobs

126

overseas," and continued berating "foreign lobbyists" who "make $30,000 a month, then take a leave, work on presidential campaigns, make sure [they]'ve got good contacts and then go back out." NAFTA, he argued at the 15 October debate in Richmond, Virginia, would result in a situation where "[Mexican] jobs come up from a dollar an hour to $6 an hour, and ours go down to $6 an hour." Then, he said, the playing field would indeed be level, "but in the meantime you've wrecked the country. . . . We got to cut it out."[214] In fact, the most memorable sound bite to emerge from the 1992 presidential debates was Perot's allusion to "a giant sucking sound going south"—a reference to the presumed rush of jobs to Mexico should NAFTA win approval. The more press attention NAFTA received, the fewer people backed it. By election day, only 21 percent of voters supported the initiative, and exit polls showed that a majority opposed NAFTA in Texas and Southern California, where Bush had particularly played up the accord.[215]

Conclusion

To some members of the Clinton camp, the results of the November election implied that the new administration should concentrate on jobs, health care, and other domestic issues rather than NAFTA and other international concerns. Bush, after all, who had emphatically and vigorously championed "global leadership" and the trade pact, saw his popularity plummet during the campaign. On 3 November 1991, he enjoyed a 59 percent approval rating,[216] but captured just 38 percent of the popular vote a year later. Meanwhile, Clinton (43 percent) and Perot (19 percent), who had both concentrated on domestic issues, won more than six out of every ten votes cast. Although the Democratic nominee (55 percent) had done as well as Dukakis (57 percent) and Mondale (53 percent) in attracting union voters,[217] NAFTA was still a potential "wedge" issue that could divide New Democrats from the party's Old Guard. Giving too much attention to Hemispheric trade, in sum, appeared a risky proposition. Besides, after 40-plus years of a Cold War, did not the people, as in 1920, yearn for normalcy over nostrums? Wasn't the electorate in a mood for retreat and not entanglements?

Advocates of international activism, on the other hand, could take some comfort from the 1992 election. The most rabid "American firsters" had attracted little (Wilder) or modest (Buchanan) support within their respective parties. At the same time, NAFTA critic Harkin was forced from the race soon after finishing fourth in the New Hampshire primary. Brown, who made it all the way to the Democratic Convention thanks to low-budget campaigning and federal matching funds, received only 13.9 percent of the votes at the New York conclave. Clinton, moreover, while issuing disclaimers and caveats, endorsed the NAFTA concept and rejected reopening the corpus of the agreement to fresh negotiations. Ironically, his very reluctance to propose bold international initiatives eventually enhanced the attractiveness of NAFTA as a prepackaged venture that could produce a foreign policy success. By the fall of 1993, Clinton's speeches, ringing with phrases about competing in a rapidly expanding global marketplace, evoked memories of Bush's rhetoric a year before.

CHAPTER SIX

The Side Deals

Introduction

Critics condemned Clinton's NAFTA speech as one of the worst of the campaign. The presentation was long, rambling, poorly organized, often vague, and marred with downright errors. Clinton, for instance, rehashed the myth, promoted by the AFL-CIO, that Canadian nurses had served as strike-breakers in New England. He also warned about the need to shield the U.S. economy from "surges" of Mexican imports, even though NAFTA's chapter 8 fully addressed this contingency. Such unfamiliarity with anti-surge safeguards belied his claim to have "read this agreement with some care."[218] In addition, the speech trumpeted a populist critique of Bush's trickle-down economics and the harm that it had inflicted on workers, farmers, and the environment. "He seems to be saying, so what if some workers get hurt or some farmers get hurt or some environmental damage is done," Clinton asserted. "So what? Sooner or later it will all come out in the wash. Well, a lot of Americans are being washed away by that economic philosophy."[219] The Democratic nominee also maligned the European Community and the Japanese for unfairly excluding U.S. manufactures and farm products from their markets and attacked the Republican administration for encouraging "American businesses to shut down here and move to Central America and the Caribbean."[220]

Yet juxtaposed to purple prose, erroneous statements, vague promises, and demagoguery was a profoundly astute economic analysis that explained in clear, compelling fashion the importance of international trade to the health of the U.S. economy in general and to the well-being of American workers in particular. Throughout the disjointed message, Clinton argued for a "new economic policy." Such a policy would promote improved education, more ambitious job training, better health care, greater investment in research, and energy conservation—with a view to forging a high-wage, high-growth economy.[221] Exports were central to achieving this goal. "Little more than a generation ago," Clinton said,

> the world was a far simpler place. We could support free trade and open markets and still maintain a high-wage economy because we were the only economic superpower and our capacity to control our destiny was largely totally within our own hands. Now, because money and management and production are mobile and can cross national borders quickly, we face unprecedented competition from developing countries as well as wealthy ones. You know that . . . a textile worker in Carolina has to compete against the textile worker in Singapore, perhaps to sell sweaters in Germany.[222]

If NAFTA were adopted in the context of "a serious economic policy at home, it could be a "very good thing for the United States," he added. "We simply cannot go backward when the rest of the world is going forward into a more integrated economy. We cannot go inward when our opportunities are so often outward."[223]

But NAFTA had to be "done right" to create jobs in the United States and in Mexico, he said. "If it is not done right, however, the blessings of the agreement are far less clear, and the burdens can be significant. I'm convinced that I will do it right. I am equally convinced that Mr. Bush won't."[224]

In accord with the NAFTA minuet that he had performed during the campaign, Clinton conditioned his support for the agreement on five unilateral steps and the negotiation of three

130

supplemental agreements. In other words, he would convert Bush's NAFTA into a pro-labor, pro-farmer, pro-environment accord that would benefit all Americans, not just big business. The unilateral steps were (1) job training and worker assistance, (2) environmental clean-up and infrastructure investment, presumably along the border, (3) strict application of pesticide laws to imported food, (4) public participation in defending any U.S. environmental laws applied against Mexican imports, and (5) the prevention of foreign professionals, such as the infamous Canadian nurses, from serving as replacement workers.[225]

More important, the Democratic candidate proposed three "supplemental agreements" to complement the NAFTA text. The first would establish an environmental protection commission with "substantial powers and resources," to prevent and clean up water pollution. This body would promote education about each nation's environmental laws, provide a forum for complaints, and apply monetary damages and other remedies to stop pollution. As a "last resort," a country could even withdraw from the agreement if a signatory failed to enforce its environmental statutes. The candidate asked Senator Gore to take charge of creating an effective commission.

Clinton proposed a second commission to safeguard worker standards and safety, emphasizing the enforcement of existing laws in each nation. Both the environmental and labor commissions would embrace such procedural safeguards as easy access to the courts, public hearings, the right to present evidence, and effective remedies. "I'll negotiate an agreement among the three parties that permits citizens of each country to bring suit in their own courts when they believe their domestic environmental protections and worker standards aren't being enforced," he stressed.[226] Finally, Clinton stated his intention to ask Congress for authority to take immediate action in the event of an "unexpected and overwhelming surge in imports into either country which would dislocate a whole sector of the economy so quickly that there's nothing we could [do] about it to overcome the economic impact."[227]

At their preinaugural meeting, Clinton and Salinas discussed the possibility of parallel accords. As with the NAFTA agreement itself, SECOFI and USTR were given primary responsibility for the requisite negotiations. The cast of characters on the Mexican side was the same as during the NAFTA talks—with Serra Puche and Blanco playing the key roles. With the change of administrations, Kantor succeeded Hills as U.S. trade representative and Deputy U.S. Trade Representative Rufus Yerxa replaced Katz as chief negotiator. Yerxa was a trade specialist who had served as chief of staff of the Ways and Means trade subcommittee before becoming U.S. ambassador to GATT. Michael Wilson remained as Canada's minister of international trade until midyear, while civil servant John Weekes continued as chief negotiator.

Side Deal on "Surges"[228]

The side deal on import surges was the least substantive of the parallel accords—with the drafting challenge arising out of the need to put something down on paper that would meet Clinton's commitment. As mentioned, the Raleigh speech's section on surges was the weakest part of the presentation and demonstrated that the Democratic nominee knew neither NAFTA's provisions nor U.S. laws that protect domestic sectors against the influx of foreign goods. Harrumphed Canadian and Mexican negotiators, "Doesn't the president understand what's in chapter 8?" This chapter defines surges and permits the reimposition of tariffs during the 15-year phase-out period (and the inclusion of Canadian or Mexican imports in a global emergency action) when increased imports cause or threaten injury of a domestic industry. Many U.S. officials also harbored misgivings about this side agreement. Some government specialists believed that Mexico would be more likely to employ trade restrictive measures against U.S. imports than vice-versa. There was even sentiment within USTR either to jettison a surge supplemental pact or trade it away for stronger environmental and labor agreements. Nevertheless, Kantor insisted on the side deal—in part because the president had enshrined it in his NAFTA speech, in part because the American sugar industry wanted an even higher comfort level vis-à-vis its Mexican competitors.

Why was the United States pushing for a deal that mirrored chapter 8?, asked the Canadians and Mexicans. They were, after all, more than a little paranoid about Kantor's resolute insistence on trade sanctions for violations of their domestic environmental and labor laws. Both Ottawa and Mexico City feared that USTR had a hidden agenda—namely, the crafting of yet one more device to add to countervailing duties, antidumping statutes, Section 301 of the trade act, and Super 301 legislation to impede their exports to the American market.[229]

Ultimately, the United States prevailed with respect to the side deal, though it was widely characterized in Washington as "window dressing," "cosmetic," and "a nothing." To appear to be doing something more about surges, the negotiators established a Working Group on Emergency Action, composed of one representative from each nation. This body, which reports to the Free Trade Commission established under NAFTA, convenes annually, unless the parties agree otherwise, and on the request of any signatory. The parallel agreement assigns four functions to the newly created tripartite group. First, it shall consider surge-related issues and make recommendations to the Free Trade Commission. Second, it shall weigh the possibility of invoking GATT's Article XIX (emergency actions) and serve as a consultative forum before or during any recourse to that article. Third, upon the request of any party, and with two-thirds concurrence, it shall examine trade, productivity, employment, and other economic factors with respect to any good. Any such discussions may not justify restricting or prohibiting trade in any manner inconsistent with chapter 8. Finally, it may recommend to the commission improvements in the chapter.

Environmental Side Deal

Even more contentious was the environmental side deal. To begin with, this negotiation involved more than a dozen agencies from the three countries. Although the USTR directed the negotiations, the U.S. working-group leads were Richard J. Smith, deputy assistant secretary of state,[230] and Alan Hecht, acting assistant administrator of the Environmental Protection Agency (EPA).[231] Also participating for the United States were the departments of Commerce, Justice, and Health and Human Services. In preliminary discussions, Mario Aguilar of SEDESOL and Raúl Urteaga-Trani of SECOFI's Washington office led the Mexican working group. Luis Miguel Díaz of the Secretariat of External Relations rounded out the delegation. In late May, Santiago Oñate Laborde, who had served as Mexican ambassador to the Organization of American States before becoming the attorney-general for SEDESOL, took over as the Mexican lead. The Canadian team was headed by Keith Christie, the director of policy coordination for NAFTA within the External Affairs Ministry. In addition, Brian Emmett, assistant deputy minister for policy, Environment Canada, took part in the parleys. In Ottawa, the Privy Council Office and the ministries of Finance, Industry, and Justice also participated in inter-agency activities related to the side agreement.

The Americans needed several months to forge a unified negotiating position. One point of disagreement was whether trade sanctions should be used to penalize violators of environmental laws. The USTR, EPA, and Treasury Department supported the use of such sanctions; the State Department did not. A draft paper that the State Department prepared for the National Economic Council (NEC), a Clinton-created supercommittee of Cabinet members and other senior officials modeled on the National Security Council, warned that supranational enforcement authority (as opposed to national enforcement) would "run up against serious Constitutional concerns in the United States."[232] This position was articulated by Joan E. Spero, undersecretary of state for economic and agricultural affairs, who argued against imposing trade sanctions for environmental law violations. Such a linkage, she contended, made little sense economically and would raise nationalist hackles in Ottawa and Mexico City. There was even the possibility that the Canadians, with difficult parliamentary elections on the horizon, might walk away from the bargaining table rather than submit to such an affront to national sovereignty. In contrast, Kantor stressed the need for a rigorous environmental side deal in order to muster political support for the pact. Apparently, Kantor also believed that, even though not spelled out in Clinton's October 1992 speech, trade sanctions were essential to fulfilling the new president's campaign pledge. A hallmark of Kantor's service at USTR has been his unflagging loyalty to the chief executive. As one observer stated, "If Clinton asked him to dismantle the Windner Building [USTR's 19th-century headquarters], Mickey would say, 'Mr. President, would you like that done brick-by-brick or floor-by-floor?'"

Environmentalists Reject "Minimalist" Approach

The most outspoken champion of Kantor's aggressive approach was the environmental community, which expressed hope that the U.S. negotiators would spurn a "minimalist" strategy. While Carla Hills had reluctantly sought out their views, the Clinton administration not only consulted environmental organizations, but encouraged them to submit suggestions on key issues. In addition, more Clinton appointees were personally sympathetic to environmentalism. The groups that participated ranged from the National Wildlife Federation and the World Wildlife Fund, which had backed fast track and approved much of the original NAFTA text, to Defenders of Wildlife, which had remained neutral, to the Sierra Club and Friends of the Earth, which had shrilly attacked the agreement. The groups, whose priorities varied, stressed their consensus on several objectives: establishing a trinational environmental commission with broad authority and an independent secretariat; preserving the integrity of federal and subfederal environmental laws, ensuring transparency and public participation in dispute settlement and other activities; earmarking adequate monies for environmental cleanup, such as through a regional development bank; allowing access to domestic courts so that private parties could seek compensation from individuals and companies rather than governments; and imposing trade remedies if inadequate enforcement gave rise to a competitive advantage, cross-boundary pollution, or contamination of the global commons.[233]

The environmentalists, particularly the National Audubon Society, Defenders of Wildlife, and the Sierra Club, also keyed on production and processing methods, a contentious issue strenuously opposed by the Mexicans. They proposed that a country have the right to exclude an import if it were manufactured in a way that harmed the environment. Tuna, for example, could be barred if Mexican fishermen killed dolphin while catching the tuna. The Canadians, in particular, opposed the initiative because it could have been used to restrict shipments of their Canadian timber. In any case, implementing this change would have required amending the NAFTA agreement itself, and none of the governments wanted to open what could have been a Pandora's Box.[234]

Environmentalists presented their ideas through multiple channels: the Office of the Vice President; the State Department, particularly through Richard Smith and Counselor Timothy Wirth; the White House's Office of Environmental Policy, headed by Katie McGinty; EPA Administrator Carol M. Browner; the National Security Council; the USTR; the office of Senator Max Baucus and equally sympathetic lawmakers; and other agencies at the negotiating sessions. "Not just the presidents but senior staff members of these NGOs could pick up the phone and call virtually anyone in the Clinton administration, with the exception of the president himself," said a State Department official.[235] Wirth, a former U.S. senator with an exceptional grasp of inside-the-beltway politics, was particularly anxious to involve the environmentalists. Not only was he sympathetic to most of their goals, but he hoped that involving them in the side-deal bargaining would smash their "blue-green alliance" with the AFL-CIO.

Negotiations Begin

On 17 March the negotiations began in Washington. Besides endorsing general principles of environmental protection, the three delegations reaffirmed their support for a continental environmental commission. The concept of a commission or an independent secretariat that lacked the authority to impose trade sanctions had been considered in discussions held the previous fall. At that time, the State Department had sought to lay the issue to rest with an agreement; the Mexicans, however, balked at the idea of concluding any accord during the waning days of the Bush administration. They had talked to members of the Clinton transition team and concluded that any deal struck with the Republicans would have to be renegotiated once the Democrats entered the White House.

Neither in the fall nor spring did Ottawa or Mexico City favor a trilateral mechanism to enforce domestic environmental laws. The Americans did not raise trade sanctions at the March 1993 meeting; still, the Mexican and Canadian representatives made no bones about their hostility to measures that would contravene their sovereignty. The U.S. team expressed support for a relatively independent secretariat for the environmental commission, but the U.S. agencies had yet to agree upon the limits of that independence. According to Kantor, the Clinton administration had not determined which environmental activities should be addressed unilaterally by Washington, bilaterally with Mexico, or trilaterally through a North American environmental commission.[236]

Just before the 13-15 April talks in Mexico City, Yerxa reported, perhaps with some exaggeration, that a "strong consensus" had emerged among all U.S. executive-branch agencies concerning the structure and authority of the commissions on the environment and labor. "They are not going to provide an excuse for trade protection," he said, "but they are going to ensure that there is some element of oversight and scrutiny" about domestic law enforcement and public access to legal systems to make sure that "laws are being carried out."[237] Canadian and Mexican authorities must understand, he added, that failure to agree to "credible and sound commissions and obligations" could mean that NAFTA "will not stand the scrutiny of the U.S. Congress."[238]

These arguments failed to convince the Canadians and Mexicans. The Ottawa session got off to a prickly beginning when Yerxa disagreed vehemently with his Canadian and Mexican counterparts at the 19 May opening dinner.[239] The substance of their dispute became evident in texts exchanged at this meeting. The documents showed the United States and Mexico at loggerheads on key issues, with the Canadians generally siding with the Mexicans. For instance, the United States supported (and the Mexicans opposed) applying trade sanctions to penalize non-enforcement of domestic environmental laws, bestowing substantial powers and independence on a trinational commission responsible for enforcing the supplemental accord, and permitting nongovernmental organizations (NGOs) to bring alleged enforcement failures directly to the commission.[240] Mexico agreed with the United States that the regional environmental commission should be composed of three elements: the environment ministers, a secretariat, and an advisory committee of nongovernmental representatives. Rather than the free-wheeling, quasi-independent, international secretariat envisioned by Washington, however, the Mexicans proposed that the secretariat be constituted by national sections—an idea that the three countries had discussed the previous fall. Such sections, funded domestically, could be on a short leash controlled by each country's environmental minister.[241] While the United States advocated allowing private individuals and NGOs to petition the secretariat directly to commence an inquiry, the Mexicans wanted to limit the participation of nonpublic entities to the advisory group. It also sought a two-thirds vote before a government, accused of an enforcement violation, would be required to respond to the charge.[242] Throughout the negotiations, SRE and SEDESOL representatives assumed more nationalistically assertive positions than SECOFI officials, who were under increasing pressure to cut a deal. For his part, Canadian Chief Negotiator Weekes called the U.S. proposals for inquiries by a secretariat and for dispute resolution with potential trade sanctions "too adversarial and too prosecutorial."[243] His analysis coincided with that of House Minority Leader Robert H. Michel R-Ill.) and Minority Whip Newt Gingrich (R-Ga.). In a 24 May letter to the White House, they warned that they would not back a NAFTA implementing bill that erects "multilateral environmental and labor bureaucracies with little accountability and sweeping mandates."[244] At the outset, the United States had hoped to wrap up the negotiations by 1 June; yet so discouraging were the results of the Ottawa session that no date was set for future talks until the chief negotiators consulted with their "political bosses."[245]

In fact, one political boss, Bill Clinton, made a conscious decision to allow the side agreements talks to drift.[246] To begin with, the White House was gearing up for the midsummer budget-bill battle and did not want its top personnel distracted by trade issues. The health care plan—the Clintons' highest priority—also required enormous attention. Reportedly, as late as the latter part of July, presidential adviser Stephanopoulos was urging that the parallel agreements be allowed to bog down so that NAFTA might be quietly abandoned by Clinton. Newly appointed presidential counselor David R. Gergen, among others, successfully argued against such a strategy, but as seen in chapter 9, the strength of Clinton's commitment to NAFTA was still in doubt.

Although major political issues were hanging fire, the U.S. side had encouraged their Canadian and Mexican counterparts to work on relatively nonpolitical questions. At the extremely discouraging Ottawa session, Smith, Hecht, Christie, and Oñate did form a technical working group to concentrate on nuts-and-bolts items. They knew that the political heavyweights would have to grapple with the tough issues. "Their goal was to keep paring down the undergrowth until everything was solved but the question of sanctions."[247] This working group addressed such items as the objectives of the supplemental accord and the functions and work program of the trilateral commission, which had been christened the Commission for Environmental Cooperation (CEC).[248] Smith and his team made headway on these questions in Ottawa and, a few weeks later, in Cocoyoc, Mexico. In the words of the Mexican participant: "We actually saw progress in our work. We began to feel good about our accomplishments."

Yet even as these technical discussions proceeded, Canadian Counsellor for Trade Policy Claude Carrière told European industry groups on 16 June that applying trade sanctions for the lax enforcement of environmental and labor laws would encourage "procedural harassment" by "wolves in sheep's clothing." The U.S. proposal, he said, would amount to "least-favored-nation treatment" for Canada and Mexico because they would be the only two nations subjected to such penalties. He reiterated Canada's opposition to an autonomous, international secretariat that could launch investigations, hold hearings, and issue reports "without any accountability to governments."[249] Ottawa feared that trade sanctions and an activist secretariat could have a chilling effect on present and prospective investors in Canada's troubled economy. Senator Jesse Helms (R-N.C.) amplified Carrière's concerns. The conservative lawmaker warned that regional commissions with authority both to investigate the nonenforcement of U.S. laws and impose trade sanctions might create "an international environmental gestapo."[250]

In early summer, the controversial question of trade sanctions reemerged at a meeting of National Economic Council principals. This Tuesday session, presided over by the president, brings 18 or more high-level officials to the Oval Office to discuss major economic issues. Christopher calmly but strongly expounded the State Department's opposition to sanctions. By then, this view enjoyed broad support within the business community. In fact, the U.S. Chamber of Commerce called trade sanctions for environmental noncompliance a step with "profound, and as yet incalculable consequences as a precedent for all future trade agreements."[251] Undaunted, the bulldog-like Kantor reiterated his opinion on the subject. Following a discussion of the pros and cons of both positions, President Clinton asked for Secretary Bentsen's advice. Although no enthusiast of sanctions, the courtly treasury head, who shares with Kantor the reputation as the most politically astute Cabinet member, sided with the U.S. trade representative. At that point, the president agreed, telling Kantor in so many words, "Mickey, you know what I want; now go out and get it." That one sentence clarified the administration's position, and Christopher, along with doubters in other agencies, began to work wholeheartedly toward achieving the goal that Kantor had so persistently advocated.

A flurry of activity took place in July. Kantor and Yerxa were involved in direct talks with their counterparts in SECOFI. As the pressure to conclude negotiations mounted, the so-called "trade boys" in both countries began to dominate decision making—with the nontrade agencies (DOS, EPA, SRE, SEDESOL, etc.) relegated to supporting roles. Although still present at the parleys, the Canadians emphasized that they would not permit the CEC to inflict trade sanctions on their country.

The chief negotiators met in Cocoyoc (8-9 July) to hammer out the final structure and powers of the regional environmental and labor secretariats and other technical matters. Later in Ottawa (22 July), they prepared a unified bracketed text that would be presented to the trade ministers when they met in Washington at the end of the month.

Commission for Environmental Cooperation (CEC)

The Washington endgame, held at the ornate Madison Hotel, lasted two weeks. At these sessions, the Mexicans agreed on a fairly rigorous environmental side deal (a relatively strong secretariat, an active role for NGOs, the ability of nonpublic entities to file complaints, and a largely symbolic trade sanction as an ultimate penalty) in return for a weak supplementary accord on labor. Insiders claim that the Mexicans reluctantly dropped their opposition to trade sanctions several days after Serra Puche met with Representative Gephardt on 6 August. Reportedly, the majority leader emphasized that the sanctions were a *sine qua non* for congressional approval.[252] Despite an eleventh-hour phone conversation with Clinton, Prime Minister Kim Campbell emphatically refused to yield on this issue. Instead, the Canadian team, now led by Tom Hockin who had replaced Wilson as international trade minister in June, emerged from the Madison with a separate penalty procedure. The enforcement of any environmental or labor fines would be accomplished by Canadian courts rather than by trade sanctions decreed by the newly minted CEC. The provinces, moreover, would be encouraged—but not required—to abide by the provisions of the environmental side deal. Ontario, British Columbia, and Quebec declined to take part; the seven other provinces affirmed a willingness to participate.

Commission for Environmental Cooperation (CEC)[253]

A council, composed of the environmental ministers of the three countries (the EPA administrator for the United States), governs the Commission for Environmental Cooperation. This council, which meets at least once a year, supervises the implementation of the supplemental agreement, provides a forum for discussing environmental matters, promotes cooperation among the parties, oversees the Secretariat, and addresses questions and disputes that may arise concerning the application of the side deals.

The Secretariat is responsible for furnishing technical, administrative, and operational support to the council, as well as to committees and groups that the council creates. In addition, the Secretariat must prepare an annual budget and program, including proposed cooperative activities. The Secretariat will also draft reports on matters within the scope of the annual program.

The Secretariat considers complaints from any person or nongovernmental organization or association alleging a signatory's failure to enforce its environmental statutes. Provided that the submission satisfies the criteria specified in the agreement, the Secretariat may propose that a factual record be developed. In preparing this record, the Secretariat can seek information from interested persons and independent experts. In a conciliatory gesture to Hockin, Kantor reportedly recommended locating the CEC Secretariat in Canada.

A Joint Public Advisory Committee includes five members from each country. This body's annual meeting coincides with the regular session of the council. The advisory committee, which boasts NGO representatives as members, advises the council and provides scientific, technical, and other information to the Secretariat. It also offers suggestions on the annual program, report, and budget of the council.

Dispute Resolution

If the council cannot resolve a dispute involving a member's alleged "persistent pattern of failure to effectively enforce an environmental law" involving the production of goods and services traded between the parties, any country may request an arbitration panel. Two out of three council members must concur before a panel is established.

Panelists, as a rule, will be chosen from a previously agreed roster of environmental specialists and other experts. With the disputing member's approval, a panel may seek technical advice and information from any person or body that it deems appropriate. The panel's report will be made public five days after it is communicated to the disputants.

If the panel finds that a member has failed to enforce its environmental law, the parties may—within 60 days—agree upon a mutually satisfactory action plan to remedy the nonenforcement.

If there is no consensus on an action plan, between 60 and 120 days after the final panel report, the panel may be reconvened to consider an action plan proposed by the party complained against or to draft its own plan. The panel will also decide whether to impose a "monetary enforcement assessment"—euphemism for a fine—on the target of the complaint.

The panel may be reconvened at any time to determine if an action plan is being applied fully. If it is not being implemented appropriately, the panel will impose a fine on the party against which the complaint has been lodged. The fine could reach a maximum of $20 million per offense in 1994 but would grow as trade expanded in subsequent years.

In the extremely unlikely event that the subject of a complaint fails to pay its fine or still refuses to enforce its environmental law, other remedies will be available. In a dispute between Mexico and the United States, the complaining party or parties can suspend NAFTA benefits based on the amount of the assessment. Most likely, the sanction would involve "snapping back" tariffs to their pre-NAFTA levels.

In the case of Canada, the Commission—at the request of the complainant—collects the fine and enforces an action plan in summary proceedings, without reconsidering the merits of the case, before a Canadian court of competent jurisdiction. In 132 years, Canadian courts have never failed to enforce such an order, according to senior government officials.[254]

BECC and NADBank

Negotiations that proceeded in tandem with the environmental supplemental accord gave rise to a Border Environment Cooperation Commission (BECC) designed to address environmental problems in the U.S.-Mexico border region. Both the United States and Mexico have five members on the BECC's board of directors. These men and women include the nation's senior environmental official, the commissioner of the International Boundary and Water Commission, a representative from a border state, a representative from a locality in the border region, and a public member who resides in the area. Representatives from state and local governments and NGOs dominate an 18-member advisory council, made up of nine Mexicans and nine Americans. The commission encourages widespread participation in its activities, including public comments on applications for the certification of projects.

The BECC assists border states and local communities in coordinating, designing, and financing environmental infrastructure projects with a transborder impact. The organization mobilizes capital from the private sector, from federal, state, and local governments, and from the North American Development Bank (NADBank). To be eligible for funding, projects must observe applicable environmental laws.

The bank is capitalized and governed by the United States and Mexico. Each country will provide $225 million in paid-in capital over a four-year period to leverage financing. Ten percent of the U.S. and Mexican shares of the NADBank will be available for community adjustment and investment. The State Department estimates that the U.S. shares will generate at least $200 million in financing for community adjustment and investment by complementing existing rural and small-business assistance programs. A six-member board, composed of three Mexicans and three Americans, governs the NADBank. The bank evaluates the financial feasibility of projects certified by the BECC and provides financing as appropriate.[255]

Labor Side Deal

The three parties negotiated the parallel accord on labor in concert with the environmental side deal. The trade ministers and chief negotiators took prime responsibility for the labor negotiations. There were, however, separate working groups that handled many of the technical issues. In contrast to the environmental working group, there were far fewer participants in the labor negotiations. The U.S. team included Lawrence Katz, a boyish-looking Massachusetts Institute of Technology professor, who serves as the Department of Labor's chief economist. Near the end of the negotiations, he was replaced by Jack Otero, the newly confirmed undersecretary of labor for international affairs. Donna J. Hrinak, deputy assistant secretary of state for inter-American affairs, also participated actively in the negotiations. Mexico's team was co-chaired by Norma Samaniego de Villareal, undersecretary of labor, and Israel Gutiérrez of SECOFI, who had been Mexico's lead negotiator in the NAFTA working group on textiles. Jim Lahey, who began as head of the Canadian working group, was replaced by John McKennirey from the Department of Labour. Also present were May Mopaw from Labour and Danièle Ayotte from External Affairs.

The American negotiators lacked direction at the outset of the talks. Yerxa, Katz, and Hrinak reviewed Clinton's Raleigh speech for clues to an appropriate position. They also studied an options paper prepared by an NEC interagency subgroup chaired by Jorge Pérez-López, the highly respected director of the Department of Labor's International Economic Affairs office, who was a key member of the U.S. working group. This draft document endeavored to "meet President Clinton's commitments and transform the perception of the agreement from one that benefits Mexicans at the expense of U.S. workers to one that benefits workers in both countries and assists the United States in its path toward a high-wage/high-skill strategy."[256] Pérez-López's team set forth three alternatives. Option A proposed an "unobtrusive" commission, buttressed by a small staff, that would promote a limited social charter. This charter would include only worker rights that were already incorporated in U.S. trade law—specifically, freedom of association, freedom to organize and bargain collectively, a ban on forced or child labor, standards for minimum wage and work hours, and health and safety regulations. To illuminate lapses in such standards, the commission would employ only "weak moral suasion." Otherwise, enforcement would be left to national institutions.

Option B called for a commission with greater independence, more staff, and a mandate to promote activities beyond those spelled out in option A. A more ambitious social charter would embrace "commitments linked to a high productivity North American development strategy." Contemplated here were: encouraging worker participation and representation, tying wages to productivity, investing in human capital, guarding against the "downward harmonization" of social security, combatting discrimination, and reversing trends toward inequality. These concepts sprang from Article 123 of the Mexican Constitution, the Salinas administration's Accord on Productivity and Growth, the social elements of the Canadian draft constitution that failed to win approval in 1992, and the European Social Charter.[257] This alternative proposed fostering a trilateral dialogue on labor standards in such key sectors as autos, apparel, and electronics. Remedies ranged from weak moral suasion to strong moral pressure—with "negotiated economic remedies where ambiguity over standards had decreased over time."

Option C, which picked up all of option B's features, permitted stronger enforcement. In an extreme situation, a tripartite dispute settlement panel appointed by the labor commission would even levy trade sanctions and unspecified "border measures."[258]

At the initial meeting on 17 March, Yerxa insisted that the labor standards pact have "real teeth," but stopped short of calling for the possible imposition of trade sanctions. Drawing on the NEC draft paper, the United States urged four main elements in a labor side accord: a charter of principles, a trinational commission, the promotion of labor standards and their improvement over time, and measures to ensure enforcement.[259]

Their mid-April proposal to employ trade sanctions to penalize violations of domestic labor laws ran into a firestorm of opposition. McKennirey patiently explained that some 90 percent of Canada's labor force was under provincial jurisdiction and that it might not be possible to obtain the concurrence of the 10 provinces to implement a labor agreement by 1 January 1994, when NAFTA was supposed to take effect. Moreover, the Canadian negotiating position itself would need to be developed in conjunction with the provinces. What he neglected to add was that anti-NAFTA, opposition-party premiers in Ontario and British Columbia would greet any suggestion that they modify provincial practices to accommodate Washington as a bad joke. Nor did the Mexicans welcome the creation of a supranational body, analogous to the Commission on Environmental Cooperation, that could publicize, and impose penalties for, the failure of countries to enforce their labor laws.

Labor Side Deal

At the Ottawa session in May, the United States proposed that trade sanctions be used for persistent failures to enforce the gamut of internal labor law. The Mexican government objected to such broad coverage. After all, the Mexican Confederation of Workers (CTM), the country's quasi-official labor movement, is a hierarchical, centralized organization that uses its close ties to the governing Institutional Revolutionary Party (PRI) and heavy-handed methods to maintain dominance over its members. With a presidential election scheduled for August 1994, neither the Salinas administration nor the PRI wanted to alienate the CTM and its crusty, 93-year-old leader, Fidel Velázquez Sánchez. Indeed, Velázquez dispatched labor representatives to the venues of the last several parleys to emphasize his hostility to the discussion of such issues as freedom of association, collective bargaining practices, and the encouragement of autonomous unions. When Samaniego met with Don Fidel's emissaries, she was said to be "visiting Jurassic Park," a reference to organized labor's reputation as "dinosaurs" in Mexico's semiauthoritarian political system.

Ultimately, the United States accepted a side deal, including a Canadian suggestion for different structures for the environmental and labor commissions, that was greatly watered down from the proposals submitted in May. Although officials in the Department of Labor would have preferred a stronger accord, there was no private sector pressure to attain one. Corporate America, which rejoices in the fact that American labor laws are among the most conservative in the developed world, was loathe to see management-labor relations raised as an issue. And, unlike the NGOs that often drove the environmental negotiations, the AFL-CIO spurned invitations to play an active role in devising the parallel agreements. Until July, the AFL-CIO's Mark Anderson attended sessions of the Labor Advisory Committee,[260] which monitored the negotiations, but he demonstrated no interest in crafting a supplemental deal acceptable either to the three governments or to the business community.

Labor Commission

The three countries created a Commission for Labor Cooperation (CLC). The governing body of the commission is the Ministerial Council, constituted by the labor ministers of each nation. They supervise the implementation of the side accord, including the activities of the International Coordinating Secretariat (ICS). They may also establish working groups and committees as deemed appropriate.

The International Coordinating Secretariat conducts the day-to-day work of the commission. It assists the council, gathers and publishes information on labor matters in Canada, Mexico, and the United States, plans and coordinates cooperative activities, and provides support for any working groups or evaluation committees established by the Ministerial Council. The three governments agreed that the North American Labor Secretariat would be located in Dallas.

In lieu of an NGO-infested, international advisory commission that might allege wrongdoing in workplaces throughout the continent, National Administrative Offices (NAOs) were established by each party. These offices serve as a point of contact for other members and provide information on domestic law and practice; receive public communications; conduct preliminary reviews; and promote the exchange of information relevant to the supplemental accords. Each party will have broad discretion in designing its own NAO. Therefore, Fidel Velázquez or his successor will have a powerful voice with respect to the personnel and activities of the Mexican office. Still, the NAOs do not focus on domestic situations, but on the labor conditions in the other countries. As a result, they provide a highly independent and critically minded source of information to the home government concerning matters it may wish to pursue with the other nations.

Consultations and Dispute Resolution

Compared to the environmental parallel accord, the labor agreement is much more limited in scope, even though the enforcement mechanisms are the same. The emphasis is on

148

exchanging information, discussing issues, and resolving problems through several consultative mechanisms. As mentioned above, NAOs may engage in cooperative consultations to supply data, clarify or explain labor laws, and answer questions about labor market conditions.

At the Madison, endgame negotiators decided to organize labor laws under three rubrics. The first covers workplace health and safety, minimum wage, and child labor. In these three areas, alleged nonenforcement can activate ministerial consultations, scrutiny by an ad hoc Evaluation Committee of Experts (ECEs), and full dispute settlement, including the imposition of trade sanctions on the United States and Mexico. The second group embraces the prohibition of forced labor, equal pay for men and women, compensation for occupational injuries, protection of migrant workers, and the elimination of discrimination based on race, religion, age, sex, and other grounds as determined in each nation. In these five "technical" areas, the ministers may consult and even direct an expert panel to write reports. Dispute resolution is barred. The third category involves the controversial issues of the right to strike, bargain collectively, associate freely, and organize. Here, only ministerial consultations may take place; no expert evaluation or dispute-settling action is allowed.[261]

Dispute resolution applies only to an alleged "persistent pattern of failure to effectively enforce" domestic labor laws. The dispute must be "trade-related"—that is, when workers produce goods and services that are traded between the parties. This provision, moreover, applies only to a "mutually recognized labor law"; that is, one country cannot insist on the enforcement of a labor law of another nation unless it has a similar law on the books. The rules for the functioning of labor panels mirror those for environmental panels, including the same fines and trade sanctions. As in the environmental side accord, the final enforcement step against Canada is carried out by Canadian courts.

Conclusion

The negotiation of the side deals differed from the NAFTA accord in several ways. To begin with, the environmental and labor accords broke new ground in trade discussions. In addition, Washington precipitated the 1993 discussions in which the Mexicans reluctantly took part. Political factors, moreover, loomed larger in crafting the side deals, and they were characterized by much more posturing at the outset of the talks—with virtually all key issues postponed until the endgame. Furthermore, the side deals gave rise to self-contained chapters approved by executive agreements. In contrast, NAFTA's chapters were interrelated and the accord itself was passed by legislative bodies.

Described as a "historic agreement" by Kantor, the side deals achieved five goals. First, they enabled Clinton to fulfill—in part, at least—his campaign pledge to make sure that NAFTA was "done right," while placing his imprint on the continental pact. Second, they supplied evidence to congressional Doubting Thomases that the White House had attempted to address concerns about import surges, the environment, and labor. In fact, the parallel accords won few votes—possibly only those of five House members, including Ron Wyden (D-Ore.)—but they provided political cover for lawmakers who needed some grounds for assuring labor and environmental groups in their districts that they had protected their interests. Third, they generated pro-NAFTA lobbying support on Capitol Hill. Particularly active were the six environmental groups, which supported the pact once it was fortified by the parallel agreements. These groups alone embrace some 80 percent of America's organized environmentalists. Fourth, they provided structures—the commissions, their secretariats, and other bodies—for continual consultation and cooperation on two sensitive issues. The annual ministers' meeting, for example, furnishes a powerful incentive for lower-level officials to resolve outstanding problems lest their principals (and governments) suffer embarrassment at the highly publicized continent-wide sessions. As for the negotiated enforcement mechanisms, cooperative ventures rather than fines or trade sanctions offer the best hope for improving environmental and labor conditions throughout North America. Finally, the environmental provision in particular strengthened NAFTA and enhanced the protection, conservation, and management of natural resources throughout the region in a manner that would set the standard for future international agreements.

CHAPTER SEVEN

Evolution of Mexican Lobbying in the United States[262]

Introduction

Soon after taking office, President Salinas realized that an active, astute presence in the United States was crucial to advancing Mexico's interests in general and to obtaining passage of a North American Free Trade Agreement in particular. Until recently, Mexican diplomats had tiptoed around Washington, D.C., as if they were intruders in the night. While making pro forma visits to the State Department and graciously receiving visitors who requested meetings, Mexican envoys seldom traveled the 20 blocks from their Hispanic-style, mural-adorned embassy on Sixteenth Street to Capitol Hill. Only occasionally did the ambassador and his staff seek to cultivate key members of Congress and luminaries in the press corps.

Mexico's Low-key Approach

What accounted for the low-key approach pursued by the Mexicans as late as the mid-1980s, when Canada, Korea, Taiwan, Israel, and other middle-sized countries were aggressively attempting to win friends and influence people with the help of expensive, high-powered public relations, law, and lobbying firms?

151

To begin with, lobbying meant intruding into the affairs of another country, and as such, flew in the face of Mexico's ballyhooed commitment to nonintervention. A variation on this theme was the Mexican government's antipathy toward justifying its policies to anyone, especially to a powerful neighbor with which it traditionally had a love-hate relationship. Even more troubling to some Mexicans was the possibility that efforts to influence Washington decisionmakers might open the door to even greater U.S. involvement in Mexico. John Gavin, U.S. ambassador to Mexico from 1981 to 1986, had raised hackles by speaking out on his host's trade, investment, immigration, and Central American policies, and Mexico City did not look forward to more of the same.

Obviously, appearing to kowtow to Uncle Sam meant political suicide for the Mexican officials involved. An irony of bilateral relations was that close association with the neighboring country—deemed highly advantageous by U.S. politicians anxious to court ever more numerous Hispanic-American voters—was considered the kiss of death to their Mexican counterparts.

Limited resources and cautious envoys contributed to Mexico's unobtrusiveness in the pre-NAFTA period. For instance, Ambassador Jorge Espinosa de los Reyes, who served from 1983 to 1988, graciously complied with requests for interviews but seldom sought meetings with influential Americans. The ambassador, a banker by profession, set the tone for the embassy's inertia. This posture met with approval in the Foreign Relations Secretariat (SRE), where advocacy for Third World causes, anti-U.S. nationalism, and suspicion toward politically appointed ambassadors to Washington thrived. Also discouraging Mexican lobbying was a fatalistic view that little could be done to prevent the Mexico-bashing that periodically burst forth in the United States.

As recently as 1989, only 5.6 percent of pro-Mexican lobbying expenditures in the United States were designated for political and quasi-political purposes, compared to 86.8 percent for tourist promotion. In the same year, the Canadians, who also moved cautiously around Washington until the early 1980s, earmarked almost 43 percent of their lobbying outlays to political and quasi-political objectives and 36.1 percent to tourism.[263] Although still lavishing resources on tourism, Mexico's politically related spending rose sharply with Salinas's overtures to Washington.

TABLE 2

EXPENDITURES ON PRO-MEXICAN LOBBYING ACTIVITIES IN THE UNITED STATES, 1978-1992 (in U.S. dollars)

Year	Business Promotion[1]	%	Legal Financial[2]	%	Tourism Travel[3]	%	Trade and Countervailing Duties[4]	%	Political[5]	%	Miscellaneous[6]	%	Total
1992	--	0	2,217,643	7.1	19,272,682	61.5	146,372	.5	9,518,971	30.4	176,138	.6	31,331,806
1991	433,587	1.2	1,826,612	4.9	27,227,860	72.6	197,930	.5	7,837,374	20.9	229,705	.6	37,523,363
1990	1,066,617	3.2	656,727	2.0	28,246,343	85.9	279,343	.8	2,584,668	7.9	66,142	.2	32,899,837
1989	1,050,718	4.5	699,033	3.0	20,089,844	86.8	265,607	1.1	1,037,905	4.5	4,740	0	23,147,847
1988	--	0	19,878	.1	13,757,470	93.9	455,122	3.1	412,419	2.8	--	0	14,644,879
1987	202,832	1.4	135,069	.9	13,428,342	92.5	224,645	1.5	528,817	3.6	--	0	13,428,342
1986	--	0	163,208	.8	19,159,388	94.2	231,042	1.1	788,269	3.9	7,550	0	20,349,457
1985	--	0	107,615	.8	13,424,285	96.6	45,375	.3	306,368	2.3	10,729	0	13,894,372
1984	--	0	253,208	3.5	6,517,595	90.0	142,284	2.0	322,383	4.4	8,083	.1	7,243,553
1983	--	0	304,439	4.5	6,014,011	90.0	331,947	5.0	42,288	.5	2,210	0	6,694,894
1982	--	0	63,927	.6	9,723,164	98.8	23,671	.2	54,462	.4	--	0	9,845,223
1981	--	0	176,688	1.4	12,301,090	95.5	202,194	1.6	110,009	.8	90,000	.7	12,879,981
1980	--	0	34,804	.3	11,855,793	93.4	442,071	3.5	308,403	2.4	45,623	.4	12,686,694
1979	10,394	.1	11,133	.1	7,694,452	88.6	236,909	2.7	621,461	7.2	111,250	1.3	8,685,599
1978	--	0	17,607	.2	7,991,968	95.4	52,940	.6	216,602	2.6	100,619	1.2	8,379,735

Source: Reports submitted to the Registration Unit, Internal Security Section, U.S. Department of Justice, Criminal Division, under the Foreign Agents Registration Act of 1938, as amended.

[1]Includes attempts to encourage both U.S. investment in Mexico and joint ventures between U.S. and Mexican firms.

[2]Involves advising the client on legal questions and/or financial matters, such as the issuance of bonds.

[3]Efforts to stimulate U.S. tourism in Mexico.

[4]Trade promotion and the representation of Mexican clients in countervailing duty suits before administrative and judicial agencies of the U.S. government.

[5]Attempting to influence members of the legislative and executive branches on public policy issues, including bills pending before the U.S. Congress.

[6]Promotion of cultural activities, collection of information, etc.

TABLE 3

EXPENDITURES ON PRO-CANADIAN LOBBYING ACTIVITIES IN THE UNITED STATES, 1978–1992 (in U.S. dollars)

Year	Business Promotion[1]	%	Legal Financial[2]	%	Tourism Travel[3]	%	Trade & Countervailing duties[4]	%	Political[5]	%	Misc[6]	%	Total
1992	1,001,673	5.4	915,391	4.9	4,631,326	24.8	7,079,933	37.8	4,967,145	26.5	116,465	0.6	18,711,933
1991	4,827,012	19.6	1,023,356	4.1	7,920,516	32.1	5,071,058	24.7	5,373,878	21.8	460,147	1.7	24,675,987
1990	3,577,473	16.3	658,470	3.0	8,351,071	38.1	2,287,321	10.4	6,974,604	31.8	84,772	0.4	21,933,711
1989	3,791,505	16.9	924,154	4.1	8,108,620	36.1	3,174,032	14.1	6,456,649	28.7	35,228	0.2	22,490,188
1988	3,107,084	15.6	2,201,792	11.1	6,794,480	34.2	3,536,354	17.8	4,130,362	20.8	90,346	0.5	19,860,418
1987	2,690,379	16.0	1,124,598	6.7	3,600,018	21.4	3,404,032	20.2	4,839,341	28.7	1,182,564	7.0	16,840,932
1986	2,009,777	13.4	671,451	4.5	2,678,240	17.9	2,025,434	13.5	6,210,300	41.4	1,395,919	9.3	14,991,121
1985	2,294,651	16.1	1,269,691	8.9	2,594,423	18.2	2,902,392	20.3	4,033,315	28.2	1,183,315	8.3	14,277,787
1984	2,856,530	17.8	1,429,138	8.9	3,663,292	22.8	3,208,279	20.8	2,959,909	18.4	1,925,973	12.1	16,043,122
1983	2,203,247	15.5	1,376,097	9.7	2,684,507	18.9	4,115,242	29.0	1,512,867	10.7	2,287,359	16.2	14,179,319
1982	1,950,181	15.9	2,020,285	16.5	2,286,769	18.5	1,984,157	16.2	2,069,495	16.9	1,980,218	16.0	12,273,123
1981	1,766,720	25.1	367,611	5.2	1,997,775	28.3	1,533,410	21.7	360,495	5.1	1,025,379	14.6	7,051,390
1980	1,803,218	19.1	838,174	8.8	3,044,498	32.1	1,837,599	19.4	216,053	2.3	1,746,727	18.4	9,486,268
1979	1,392,914	15.0	444,771	4.8	5,147,137	55.6	1,240,306	13.4	476,872	5.1	559,456	6.1	9,261,456
1978	1,414,828	16.3	180,320	2.1	5,054,598	58.1	1,227,155	14.1	142,927	1.6	678,892	7.8	8,698,721

Source: Reports submitted to the Registration Unit, Internal Security Section, U.S. Department of Justice, Criminal Division, under the Foreign Agents Registration Act of 1938, as amended.

[1] Includes attempts to encourage both U.S. investment in Canada and joint ventures between U.S. and Canadian firms.

[2] Involves attempts to encourage both U.S. investment in Canada and joint ventures between U.S. and Canadian firms.

[3] Efforts to stimulate U.S. tourism in Canada.

[4] Trade promotion and the representation of Canadian clients in countervailing duty suits before administrative and judicial agencies of the U.S. government.

[5] Attempting to influence members of the legislative and executive branches on public policy issues, including bills pending before the U.S. Congress.

Salinas's New Chapter in Mexican Lobbying

Salinas's December 1988 inauguration ushered in a sea-change in Mexican diplomacy toward the United States. To begin with, Salinas dispatched Gustavo Petricioli as Mexico's ambassador to the United States in early 1989, where he served until replaced by Jorge Montaño four years later. A Yale graduate, confidant of ex-President de la Madrid, the man who had succeeded Silva Herzog as finance secretary, and a gregarious individual who skillfully used entertainment as a diplomatic tool, the 61-year-old "Gus" Petricioli became a familiar figure in official Washington. He did not confine himself to "inside the beltway" contacts. As early as September 1990, Petricioli participated with Representative Kika de la Garza (D-Tex.), chairman of the House Agriculture Committee, in a West Coast forum on U.S.-Mexican relations that endorsed both NAFTA and a "new era" of bilateral cooperation.[264]

The new ambassador selected Walter Astié Burgos, an adroit career diplomat, as his deputy chief of mission. Astié's previous position had been on the acutely nationalistic U.S. desk at the Foreign Relations Secretariat, an agency whose involvement in policy-making had diminished greatly since Mexico's chief executives began rejecting statism in favor of market-focused policies. On SRE's U.S. desk, Astié had not been particularly helpful in expanding the role of the Mexican Embassy in Washington. Traditionally, tensions beset the relationship between the ministry, whose personnel march to their own ideologically charged, institutional drumbeat, and Mexico's ambassador to Washington, a presidential designee who is often unenthusiastic about SRE's gringo-baiting agenda. In Astié, Petricioli recruited an SRE insider who could deal with the Foreign Relations bureaucracy and thus free the ambassador to promote President Salinas's broader goals in the United States.

To fill other senior posts, Petricioli went outside SRE to choose competent pragmatists who knew the United States well but exhibited none of the anti-Yankee sentiment associated with the secretariat. The embassy established a congressional liaison office, first headed by Joaquín González Casanova, a lawyer with extensive experience in the United States. Too, the press and public affairs office was expanded from a director and three secretaries to a director, three attachés, and three secretaries. In 1986 the embassy had 50 diplomats and support personnel. Between late 1988 and early 1992, the number rose from 65 to 85. Four additional governmental agencies established representation in Washington, raising the number to ten.[265] Not only were the embassy's personnel more specialized, but they were better prepared, as evidenced by their holding more advanced academic degrees than their predecessors.[266]

A new embassy, opened in late 1989 just three blocks from the White House, epitomized Mexico's diplomatic élan. The $16 million complex not only betokened a move toward the center of power, but it enabled the Mexican government to place most of its agencies under one roof, thus improving coordination and the flow of information.

SECOFI's Washington Beachhead

Changes in the embassy and the expertise and enthusiasm of its officials aside, the Commerce Ministry established its own Washington office to coordinate NAFTA activities in the U.S. capital. Petricioli concurred in this decision, even though it relegated the embassy to a supportive rather than a starring role in the trade negotiations. The ambassador knew that Alan Gotlieb, Canada's dynamic envoy to the United States during the early CFTA negotiations, had alienated many U.S. officials by concentrating on the free-trade pact to the detriment of other bilateral questions. Consequently, Petricioli focused on broader Mexico-U.S. issues while SECOFI took the lead in NAFTA, just as in 1988-1989 when Mexican Treasury officials, accompanied by their own legal team, had spearheaded negotiations in Washington on their country's debt with the United States and other creditors.

The embassy did, however, contribute to the pro-NAFTA campaign. Ambassador Petricioli frequently appeared on Capitol Hill, delivered speeches throughout the country, and cultivated close, productive ties with Secretary Baker, General Scowcroft,

Senator Bentsen, Representative Bill Richardson (D-N.M.), and other border state lawmakers. Meanwhile, Javier Treviño, the embassy's adroit minister-counselor for press and public affairs, took advantage of contacts arranged by media specialists. In addition to traveling to large cities, Treviño carried Mexico's message to the editorial boards of some 40 newspapers in small- and medium-sized cities, many of which were represented by influential members of Congress. This approach paid rich dividends in terms of endorsements, even by the *Cleveland Plain Dealer*, the *Milwaukee Sentinel*, the *Detroit News and Free Press*, and 10 other newspapers in the Rust Belt. For his part, Dr. Manuel Suárez-Mier, a University of Chicago–trained economist and the embassy's highly respected minister-counselor for economic affairs, logged some 400,000 miles as he made 500 speeches for the agreement in 39 states. Embassy personnel who assisted the working groups were Miguel Leaman, minister-counselor for commercial affairs (textiles, safeguards, tariffs, standards), Yvonne Stinson (dispute settlement), Alma Alfaro (textiles), Arturo Jessel (tariffs and standards), and Eugenio Salinas (investment and government procurement).[267]

Despite the presence of a number of Washington hands in the embassy, Blanco chose his former professor, Herman Von Bertrab, to head the SECOFI NAFTA office in the United States. Von Bertrab was born in Tampico, where his German father's construction company drilled oil wells. During World War II, he studied first at a German high school and then at a French high school before entering the Society of Jesus. He concentrated on Latin, Greek, philosophy, and theology at a Jesuit seminary in Innsbrook, Austria, and later earned master's (MIT) and doctoral degrees (U. of Texas) in the United States. When the Jesuits sought members of their order to study economics and social sciences, Von Bertrab volunteered. This background prepared him for the teaching appointment at the Technical Institute of Monterrey, where he met Blanco. In 1972 Von Bertrab left the Jesuits to devote himself to private business. The companies with which he is involved train securities brokers, ship cut flowers to Canada, and supply sesame seeds to McDonald's restaurants.[268]

Von Bertrab arrived in Washington in December 1990 to organize the NAFTA office. He thought in terms of a "platoon" of talented individuals rather than a cumbersome, hierarchical structure. To this end, he recruited U.S.-trained young men, some of whom had worked for the IMF, World Bank, OAS, and other international organizations, men whose intelligence overshadowed their lack of experience in trade issues. His team included Luis de la Calle (media contacts, relations with Hispanic groups), Ildefonso Guajardo (liaison with USA*NAFTA and state and local governments), Félix Aguilar (contact with lobbying firms, congressional vote-counting), Rodolfo Balmaceda (organization of speaking engagements and pro-NAFTA "roadshows"), José Treviño Botti (materials production, contracts with consultants), José Navarette (research), Raúl Urteaga-Trani (environmental issues), Eduardo Wallentín (labor and environmental issues), and José A. Canela-Cacho (research).[269]

As indicated by the functions performed by its personnel, SECOFI's NAFTA office in Washington engaged in a number of activities. It disseminated material on Mexico and NAFTA, supplied information to Mexico City about developments in the United States, provided speakers who could preach the gospel of continental free trade throughout the United States, took the pulse of Congress for Serra Puche and Blanco, helped to organize the visits of high-ranking SECOFI officials to Washington, and dispatched staff members to observe NAFTA working groups held in the United States. Those men involved in working groups were de la Calle (financial services), Guajardo (agriculture), Canela-Cacho (automobiles), and Urteaga-Trani (environmental supplemental agreement).

The most important function of this office was to recruit a Who's Who of political insiders adept at swaying legislators and the media. The Mexicans signed up two dozen prominent allies to help attract support for NAFTA.[270] They also hired Burson-Marsteller, a public relations firm whose clients range from the American Paper Institute to the U.S. Olympic Committee, to burnish Mexico's image. B-M, as it is known within the "K Street canyon" inhabited by Washington lobbyists, cultivated editorial writers, wrote speeches for Mexican dignitaries, and prepared and published pro-NAFTA materials. In 1993 alone some 100,000 brochures, fact sheets, and press kits were disseminated.[271]

In addition to Burson-Marsteller, SECOFI hired at least 32 other American lobbyists, legal advisers, and publicists to sing Mexico's praises on Capitol Hill and in the executive branch. "We tried to have a balanced team to give us a reading of the whole Congress," said Von Bertrab. "This was all new to us. It's been learning how to adapt to all-American conditions."[272]

SECOFI and Von Bertrab hired marquee players who boasted excellent ties with Republicans and Democrats. To key on the GOP, they recruited Charls E. Walker, an expatriate Texan who was deputy secretary of the treasury under President Nixon and who had become a dean, if not *the* dean, of the lobbyists corps. As a child, he sometimes slept on the porch of his family hotel in Graham, Texas, so that his parents could rent out his room. But large Washington lobbying and speaking fees had converted him into "a very diminutive millionaire," by his own admission, who served on corporate boards, traveled in a large black limousine, and hobnobbed with Washington's power-elite.[273] Years before he told acquaintances that he viewed capital investment the way Mark Twain viewed good bourbon: "Too much is barely enough."[274] In view of the handsome fees received from the Mexicans, Walker could say the same of free trade in the early 1990s. A less flamboyant "heavy hitter" with guaranteed entrée to GOP stalwarts was William E. Brock, principal of the Brock Group. He is a former senator, Republican party chairman, and U.S. trade representative. Also hired for its Republican ties was the firm of Gold & Liebengood. One of its partners, Howard S. Liebengood, served as sergeant-at-arms of the Senate when Republicans controlled the upper body in the early 1980s.

Although there were more potential GOP than Democratic votes for NAFTA, SECOFI officials could not afford to ignore the latter party's House and Senate majorities. Joseph P. O'Neill, a former staff member for Senator Bentsen, was retained as a link to Senate Democrats.[275] Once Clinton was elected, SECOFI hired Christopher R. "Kip" O'Neill, whose father, Thomas P. "Tip" O'Neill Jr. (D-Mass.) had been an immensely popular Speaker of the House. Other notable players included TKC International Ltd., Public Strategies Washington, Inc., and Manchester Trade Ltd. While not an integral part of SECOFI's team, SJS Advanced

Strategies gathered information, conducted research, and lobbied for COECE, the umbrella group for Mexico's private sector.

Heavily involved in "Team Mexico" was Robert E. Herzstein, whom colleagues fondly refer to as "Mr. Mexico" and "Mexico Central." Following graduation from Harvard Law School, the soft-spoken Westerner had practiced law in Washington for more than 30 years, advising U.S. and foreign companies, trade associations, and governments on international trade, foreign investment, and government regulation of business. A Democrat, he served as the first undersecretary of international trade in the Commerce Department during the Carter administration and, subsequently, advised Canada and Israel on their negotiations of free-trade agreements with the United States. Herzstein, a member of the Council on Foreign Relations, is a partner in the Washington office of Shearman & Sterling, the only firm responsible for both legal work and lobbying in behalf of NAFTA. A Herzstein colleague, Daniel Tarullo, who played a marginal role in advising Mexico during the negotiations, was named by President Clinton as the State Department's assistant undersecretary for economic affairs.[276] Herzstein's formal link to SECOFI was through Guillermo Aguilar, the ministry's brilliant chief legal officer, who held the same rank as Von Bertrab.

Regular meetings—first monthly, later weekly—helped to focus the Mexican lobbying effort. On Friday mornings, usually at the embassy, Von Bertrab and Petricioli (later Montaño) would preside over a meeting of 15-to-20 key actors. Usually present were Herzstein, Anita Epstein (also of Shearman & Sterling), the O'Neills (Kip and Joe), a representative of Gold & Liebengood, Phil Potter, and a Hispanic lobbyist such as Gabriel Guerra-Mondragon. Tom Bell, a Burson-Marsteller vice president, would attend these sessions, as would Serra Puche, Blanco, Zabludovsky, and other SECOFI decisionmakers from Mexico City if they were in town. No representative of the Clinton administration took part in these strategy sessions; in fact, William Daley, whose role as the White House's point man on NAFTA is analyzed in chapter 9, discouraged joint ventures between U.S. officials and SECOFI personnel.

On Mondays the main players' lieutenants would gather to implement decisions made the previous Friday and concentrate on nuts-and-bolts issues. Von Bertrab or Félix Aguilar, who quickly became an expert on U.S. legislative politics, chaired these meetings, while Gary Springer or Anita Epstein represented Shearman and Sterling. Who was going to contact whom about a particular issue constituted a typical agenda item.

A mounting concern among Mexico's advocates was the slowness of the United States Alliance for NAFTA, constituted in late 1992, to commit itself fully to gaining passage of the accord. Two factors militated against rapid action. Most important was the reluctance of the Fortune 500 firms that dominated USA*NAFTA to throw their resources into the battle until they knew the content of the side deals, whose negotiation was not completed until mid-August. Also significant was the mid-1993 removal of Kay R. Whitmore, head of USA*NAFTA, as the chief executive officer of the Eastman Kodak Co. His ouster left a vacuum in the organization's leadership, which had not been strong to begin with. Whitmore was preoccupied with his highly publicized corporate troubles, and Eastman-Kodak's director of international trade, Sandy Mazur—who served as USA*NAFTA's chief staff person— neither worked well with colleagues nor gave the organization clear, effective guidance. This deadlock and drift ended after Labor Day 1993 when Whitmore and Mazur were replaced, respectively, by Lawrence A. Bossidy, CEO of AlliedSignal, and Kenneth W. Cole, AlliedSignal's affable, Texas-born vice president for government affairs. The Bossidy-Cole team energized a vigorous lobbying effort complete with prime-time television commercials, half-page advertisements in major newspapers, the dispatch of lobbyists to Capitol Hill, and the designation of corporate captains in each state—a process begun in the fall of 1991—to generate grass-roots business support. AT&T, for example, catalyzed the Florida campaign, Procter and Gamble took charge in Ohio, AIG was at the forefront in New York, and TRW Inc. spearheaded the Virginia initiative. In mobilizing local business communities, USA*NAFTA worked closely with the Wexler Group, a public relations-lobbying company with especially close links to congressional Democrats. Helping to design and simplify the group's message was the

Washington public relations firm of Grunwald, Eskew and Donilan, which extolled the free-trade pact as "Good for jobs. Good for U.S."[277] USA*NAFTA's most important contribution to the campaign was its cultivation of 85 Republican congressmen, with whom the White House team had no formal working relationship. Nick Calio, who had served as President Bush's legislative liaison, helped USA*NAFTA win GOP support for the trade pact.

SECOFI also opened an office in Ottawa, although on a much more modest scale. After all, Prime Minister Mulroney's Progressive Conservatives, despite low standing in public opinion polls, had the parliamentary majority that ensured NAFTA's approval in Canada.

Pursuit of Hispanic-Americans

SECOFI enlisted several prominent Mexican-Americans in the lobbying effort. Most important was Guerra-Mondragon, a Democratic fund-raiser who enjoyed a longtime relationship as a friend and campaign activist for Clinton. He concentrated on liberal Democratic and Hispanic members of Congress.[278] In addition, Von Bertrab recruited Abelardo L. Valdes, Carter's State Department protocol chief, Eduardo Hidalgo, an erstwhile secretary of navy, and two former New Mexico governors, Toney Anaya and Jerry Apodaca, all Democrats. Besides working Capitol Hill, these men attempted to drum up support for NAFTA among Hispanic-Americans, especially in the Sun Belt. In the past, Chicanos, concerned with improving their situation north of the Rio Grande, had failed to serve as advocates for Mexico in the United States the way that Jews backed Israel and Greek-Americans supported Greece. Meanwhile, Mexican elites tended to disparage Mexican-Americans for social and political reasons. Although far from united, Chicanos have begun recently to play a modest role in bilateral affairs—in part because of their pride in the Salinas administration, in part because of impetus from the Mexican government, and in part because of the development of their own political agenda.

SECOFI and the embassy took other steps to activate Mexican-Americans. First, pursuant to a broader effort to coordinate the efforts of Mexican diplomats in North America, Petricioli convened the first of what has become an annual meeting of Mexico's 40 consuls in the United States, along with his country's attachés for trade and tourism. At this August 1990 session in Chicago, the ambassador and Blanco urged the group to spread the word of the benefits of the free-trade agreement to the Mexican-American communities with which they worked, as well as to local Anglo leaders. The second meeting, held in New York in August 1991, also included Ambassador Jorge de la Vega Domínguez, Mexico's envoy to Canada, and the Mexican consuls general in Canada (from Montreal, Toronto, and Vancouver).

Second, 150 leaders of the Hispanic-American Alliance for Free Trade (HAAFT) were invited to Washington in March 1991. This organization—founded earlier in the year with the encouragement of SECOFI's NAFTA office, headquartered in Washington, and headed by Elaine Coronado—is composed largely of owners of small- and medium-sized businesses from El Paso, Chicago, Los Angeles, San Diego, and other cities with large Hispanic populations. Following briefings by President Bush, Hills, Mosbacher, Petricioli, and others, members of the group fanned out across Capitol Hill to visit their congressmen. In addition, SECOFI sponsored trade missions to Mexico for HAAFT activists and other representatives of the Hispanic business community.

Third, Mexican diplomats disseminated information about NAFTA through the Presidential Program for Service to Overseas Mexican Communities. Salinas began this initiative after an October 1989 meeting in Washington with Chicano leaders, who sought closer ties with Mexico. Lodged within the SRE, the program cooperates closely with Mexican consulates in Chicago, Houston, Los Angeles, Miami, and San Diego. Its director, Roger Díaz de Cossio, has traveled frequently to the United States to promote Mexico-Chicano relations.

Fourth, on the heels of their 1989 meeting with Salinas, leaders of organizations such as the National Council of La Raza, an umbrella group of 134 Hispanic community affiliates, and the League of United Latin American Citizens (LULAC) began to lobby in behalf of NAFTA in hopes of currying favor with the Bush administration for their own goals. La Raza, for example, sought a ban on guest-workers and increased funding for border infrastructure. Meanwhile, Cuban-American activists, long critical of Mexico's unswerving friendship with the Castro regime, joined the effort "to mend fences and extend a gesture of good will."[279] Puerto Rican Governor Rafael Hernández Colón even dispatched a vaguely worded letter to congressional leaders declaiming the "benefits of open markets."[280]

Finally, in July 1992, Nacional Financiera (NAFIN), Mexico's development bank, and the Mexican Investment Board announced their readiness to promote joint ventures between Mexicans and Hispanic-Americans. This program, in which NAFIN provides up to one-fourth of the risk capital, applies to investments in small businesses in both Mexico and the United States.[281]

In the final analysis, Mexico's best lobbyist proved to be Salinas himself. He knew the United States better than any of his predecessors, having earned three advanced degrees from Harvard University. A month before taking office, he met with President-elect Bush in Houston. Their initial warm rapport improved as the two chief executives joined forces to wage the free-trade "battle." By late-1993, Salinas had met eight times with his U.S. counterpart, more than any previous Mexican chief executive.[282] Invariably, the presidents used these sessions to promote NAFTA.

After an April 1991 bilateral meeting in Houston, Salinas made a whirlwind tour of Ottawa, Boston, Chicago, and San Antonio to drum up support for the agreement. On 12 April, he became the first Mexican leader to address the Texas legislature. "Our economies are certainly different," he argued. "But in their very differences lie sources of exchange and the possibility of creating the comparative advantages that will enable us to compete."[283] Throughout his travels, Salinas emphasized that increased Mexican exports to the United States would give rise to jobs in Mexico and reduce the number of illegal workers who sought to cross the Rio Grande.

Mexico's heightened activity in Washington was reflected in the statement of a State Department official: "The Mexicans used to be invisible here. Now they're all over the place."[284] A writer for the *Wall Street Journal* went so far as to claim that Mexico had "suddenly upstaged Japan as the foreign government with the most visible lobbying muscle."[285] One Mexican official summarized his government's spurt of activism by saying: "When in Rome do as the Romans do. When in Washington, do as people inside the beltway do."[286]

By the end of the campaign, Mexico's estimated expenditures on NAFTA reached $45 million[287]—with upwards of $15 million expended in 1993 alone.[288] Such substantial outlays, which constitute a normal part of influencing decisions in Washington, handed a sword to NAFTA's opponents to wield against the pact. Charles Lewis, executive director of the Center for Public Integrity, a watchdog of initiatives to influence government, suggested that Mexico's foreign lobbying campaign may have been the biggest in history. "With Mexico hiring a large number of former officials," he said, "it can look like they're trying to buy the treaty."[289] Perot went even further to condemn efforts to pressure Washington decisionmakers. "Mexico is a good neighbor and a friend of the United States," he wrote, "but the U.S. should not be subjected to foreign political campaigns and foreign lobbying."[290]

Conclusion

Did Mexico get its money's worth in the NAFTA struggle? The answer depends on what payoff was expected. Undoubtedly, Salinas and his colleagues benefited from the legal advice rendered by Shearman & Sterling and other law firms. Also helpful was the enormous amount of intelligence about the U.S. political process gathered and analyzed by Mexico's NAFTA advisers. Where these advisers fell short was failing to alert Mexico City to the possibility that Bush, with whom the Salinas regime was identified, might lose in 1992. Indeed, Clinton's victory persuaded Petricioli, whose nonlegislative contacts were largely with Republicans, to return home so that a new envoy could start afresh with the Democratic administration. Montaño, his replacement, enjoyed some rapport with the new administration inasmuch as he, as Mexico's U.N.

ambassador, had hosted a cocktail party for Clinton during the 1992 Democratic Convention in New York.

In terms of lobbying, however, Mexico City officials quickly learned that U.S. lawmakers resonate to contacts from constituents, not to visits, calls, press releases, and brochures—no matter how professionally prepared—from foreign governments and their agents. As will be demonstrated, NAFTA passed because the President of the United States, albeit belatedly, committed the enormous resources of the executive branch to achieving victory. In this effort, USA*NAFTA's activities, because they reflected the interest of American corporations, proved more effective than the several dozen K Street firms that SECOFI had mobilized. What the campaign did do for Mexico was to provide a crash course in how the U.S. political system operates, while developing and honing its own lobbying skills.

Even though their pro-NAFTA pursuits were focused on Washington, Mexico developed a network of supporters that includes Hispanic-American civic, business, and professional organizations. These groups could help influence future U.S. policy on NAFTA-related conflicts, narcotics, law enforcement, immigration, and other sensitive subjects managed carefully by Washington and Mexico City during the free-trade talks.

CHAPTER EIGHT

Congress: The Last Best Hope for Victory

Introduction

Congress provided the battleground where Mexico's newly crafted war machine and other antagonists marshalled their troops—with the main conflict centered in the deeply divided House of Representatives. From Smoot-Hawley until the 1970s, Congress had played a passive role as the executive branch, often justifying its actions as crucial to the Cold War struggle against the Soviet Union, worked to liberalize trade.[291] Some protectionist, domestically oriented legislators sought to exert influence, but usually only at the margins of trade policy. They would insert escape clauses in trade bills, limit the percentage of tariff cuts, place restrictions on executive authority, demand greater USTR consultations with Congress, and—when possible—safeguard hometown industries.[292] More important than the foreign dimension of trade legislation was the lawmakers' concern about its domestic consequences. They sometimes weighed in with measures to assist workers disadvantaged by imports. Such relative passivity diminished as trade, as a portion of GNP, climbed from 7 percent in 1965 to 16.5 percent by 1992. Even more of a "wake-up call" to once largely indifferent representatives and senators was the emergence of a trade deficit in the 1970s. At that point, Representative *X* began to view import-export policy not as the esoteric province of executive-branch gurus

167

whose actions he might try to modify, but as a politically sensitive factor as to why an increasing number of factories were shutting down in his congressional district.

The Administration's Case for NAFTA

Through testimony and lobbying, NAFTA's proponents knew that they had to make their case on Capitol Hill—with Clinton administration officials and representatives of USA*NAFTA spearheading the effort. Indeed, Kantor, who appeared to have doubts about NAFTA during the campaign and transition, became increasingly passionate in promoting the accord each time he appeared before a congressional committee. First, USTR officials and their cohorts argued that NAFTA would reinforce certain healthy U.S. economic trends. Secretary of State Warren Christopher asserted, for example, that "Mexico is America's fastest-growing major export market, and we have a vital stake in its future growth and openness."[293] Since 1988, exports had powered 70 percent of America's growth, and its trade account with Mexico had swung from a $5.7 billion deficit in 1987 to a $5.4 billion-plus surplus in 1992—a figure that fell below $2 billion in 1993 because of a sluggish Mexican economy. Second, the accord would stimulate trade and investment while creating employment throughout North America. USTR observed that exports to Mexico already supported more than 600,000 American jobs—a figure that would exceed one million with NAFTA's implementation. Third, by raising Mexico's wages and living standards, the accord would diminish pressure for illegal immigrants to seek employment north of the Rio Grande. "NAFTA is the best hope for reducing illegal immigration in the long haul," argued Attorney General Janet Reno. If it were allowed to fail, she warned, "stopping the flow of illegal immigrants will be much, much more difficult, if not impossible."[294] Fourth, the pact would make U.S. exports more competitive with trading rivals by giving American producers access to cheap labor in Mexico, just as the Germans benefit from low wages in Eastern Europe and the Japanese profit from cheap labor in Malaysia, the Philippines, Thailand, and other Pacific rim countries.

Fifth, passage of NAFTA would spur Mexico's economic development, institutionalize the local version of perestroika accomplished by de la Madrid and Salinas, and thereby enhance stability in a contiguous country. Sixth, Mexico would serve as a bridge to closer U.S. ties with other Latin American countries through the "Enterprise for the Americas Initiative," proposed by President Bush and discussed in chapter 10. Christopher believed that it was vitally important for the United States to encourage economic and political liberalization both in Mexico and throughout the region. "In this hemisphere," he declared, "democracy is ascendant. Markets are opening. Conflicts are being resolved peacefully. By approving NAFTA, the United States sends a powerful signal that we support these favorable developments."[295] Seventh, closer cross-border cooperation was essential to breaking the back of the illegal narcotics trade; the secretary of state called it a "shared problem" that would be much more troublesome if NAFTA were rejected. Eighth, with GATT talks entering their "final crucial days," as Christopher warned, "there could be no worse time" to defeat NAFTA—an act that could fatally compromise the "maximum leverage" and "maximum leadership" the United States needed to maintain at the Uruguay Round.[296] Finally, Mexico's development would expand the size of its middle class and generate more political pressure for pollution control. As journalist David R. Gergen expressed it (long before accepting a White House post in mid-1993), "The developing nations that have joined the world's marketplace are those with the cleanest air and water. Doubters need only compare the skies over Singapore with those over Beijing."[297]

While agreeing that the effects on the U.S. economy "would be small for many years," 300 professional economists signed a letter to President Clinton supporting the North American Free Trade Agreement.[298] Not only did conservatives (James M. Buchanan and Milton Friedman) join their liberal brethren (Paul A. Samuelson and James Tobin) in endorsing the continental trade pact, but all eight living American Nobel laureates in economics gave NAFTA their seal of approval.[299]

Meanwhile, the middle-of-the-road Brookings Institution, the nonpartisan Congressional Budget Office, and the International

Trade Commission (a federal agency independent of the White House) reviewed all available trade-agreement studies available. They found that, in the worst of circumstances, NAFTA would have but a tangential impact on the United States.[300] This conclusion sprang from the fact that the U.S. economy dwarfs that of its Spanish-speaking neighbor. In 1993, for instance, America's Gross Domestic Product ($6.328 trillion) was 18 times greater than Mexico's $349 billion).[301] The North American situation offered a contrast to that of post-World War II Europe. Then, American and European leaders championed European unification to thwart Communist expansion and obviate the emergence of a Fourth Reich. Ultimately, corporations took advantage of the ever more lucrative European Community, but it was the politicians who had laid the groundwork for unification. In contrast, it was business interests on both sides of the border that seized upon the de la Madrid-Salinas liberalization to impel bilateral contacts. So abundant were the complementarities and economies of scale to be garnered from U.S.-Mexican integration that there was relatively little politicians could do to accelerate or impede the process. NAFTA did furnish a mechanism for resolving conflicts, phasing out tariffs and quotas, providing "snap-back" remedies for surge-afflicted economic sectors, protecting intellectual property, and assuring national treatment to investors from the three countries. As indicated by the several measures of integration cited below, the two economies were amalgamating; NAFTA would only ensure that the process occurred in a relatively incremental and orderly manner rather than in an ad hoc, willy-nilly fashion. In addition, U.S. governmental and nongovernmental influence over pollution, labor relations, and other delicate subjects in Mexico was likely to be greater in the context of a trade accord than if the Congress killed the capstone of Salinas's administration.

TABLE 4

BILATERAL ECONOMIC RELATIONS:
U.S.-MEXICAN TRADE, 1970-1994

Year	Mexican Exports to U.S. ($ millions)	% of all Mexican Exports	Mexican Imports from U.S. ($ millions)	% of all Mexican Imports
1994 (proj.)	45,100	83.5	47,600	71.3
1993	39,600	83.0	41,400	71.1
1992	35,200	71.0	40,600	71.2
1991	31,200	69.6	33,300	62.0
1990	30,900	69.8	28,400	64.6
1989	27,200	65.5	25,000	70.8
1988	23,500	65.5	20,600	66.7
1987	20,500	66.6	14,600	61.9
1986	17,600	61.7	12,400	61.9
1985	15,029	68.6	11,132	69.1
1984	14,612	60.4	6,695	59.3
1983	13,034	n.a.	4,958	n.a.
1982	11,887	52.0	8,921	59.9
1981	10,716	55.3	15,398	63.8
1980	10,072	63.2	11,979	65.6
1979	6,252	69.6	7,563	62.6
1978	4,057	68.1	4,564	60.4
1977	2,738	59.5	3,493	58.2
1976	2,111	60.9	3,774	62.5
1975	1,668	53.8	4,113	57.9
1974	1,703	58.7	3,779	62.2
1973	1,318	58.8	2,277	54.2
1972	1,288	75.8	1,745	58.2
1971	911	65.1	1,479	61.6
1970	839	65.3	1,568	62.7

Source: U.S. Department of Commerce (1970-1985) and U.S. Department of Treasury (1986-1994).

TABLE 5

BILATERAL ECONOMIC RELATIONS:
U.S. DIRECT INVESTMENT IN MEXICO, 1970–1992

Year	Investment in Mexico ($ millions)	Investment in All Countries ($ millions)	% in Mexico	Investment in Developing Countries ($ millions)	% in Mexico
1992	13,330	486,670	2.7	n.a.	n.a.
1991	12,257	460,955	2.7	111,608	14.0
1990	10,255	426,958	2.4	102,360	9.2
1989	8,264	381,781	2.2	90,374	8.0
1988	5,712	335,893	2.0	80,060	7.0
1987	4,913	314,307	2.0	73,017	7.0
1986	4,826	259,980	1.9	60,609	8.0
1985	5,087	232,667	2.2	54,474	9.3
1984	4,568	212,994	2.1	54,474	9.1
1983	4,999	226,117	2.2	50,978	9.8
1982	5,544	221,512	2.5	52,441	10.6
1981	6,977	226,359	3.1	56,182	12.4
1980	5,989	215,578	2.8	53,277	11.2
1979	4,490	186,750	2.4	44,525	10.1
1978	3,690	167,804	2.2	40,339	9.1
1977	3,230	149,848	2.2	34,462	9.4
1976	2,984	137,224	2.2	29,050	10.3
1975	3,200	124,212	2.6	26,222	12.2
1974	2,825	118,613	2.4	28,479	9.9
1973	2,379	103,675	2.3	25,266	9.4
1972	2,025	94,337	2.1	25,235	8.0
1971	1,838	86,198	2.1	25,358	7.2
1970	1,786	78,178	2.3	21,448	8.3

Source: U.S. Department of Commerce, *Survey of Current Business* (Washington, D.C.: Government Printing Office, 1970–1992), and U.S. Department of State.

TABLE 6

LEGAL AND ILLEGAL MEXICAN MIGRATION
TO THE UNITED STATES, 1970–1993

Fiscal Year	Legal Mexican Immigrants	Illegal Aliens Apprehended Mexicans	Total	% Mexicans
1993	126,561	1,269,294	1,327,258	95.6
1992	213,802	1,205,817	1,258,481	95.8
1991	946,167	1,131,510	1,197,875	94.5
1990	679,068	1,092,258	1,169,939	93.0
1989	405,172	865,292	954,243	91.0
1988	95,039	949,722	1,008,145	94.0
1987	72,351	1,139,606	1,190,488	96.0
1986	66,533	1,671,458	1,767,400	95.0
1985	61,077	1,266,999	1,348,749	94.0
1984	57,557	1,170,769	1,246,981	93.9
1983	59,079	1,172,306	1,251,357	94.0
1982	56,106	887,457	970,246	91.5
1981	101,268	874,161	975,780	89.6
1980	56,680	817,381	910,361	89.8
1979	52,100	988,830	1,076,418	91.9
1978	92,400	976,667	1,057,977	92.3
1977	44,079	954,778	1,042,215	91.6
1976	57,863	781,474	857,915	89.7
1975	62,205	680,392	766,600	88.8
1974	71,586	709,823	788,145	90.1
1973	70,141	576,823	655,969	87.9
1972	64,040	430,213	505,949	95.0
1971	50,103	348,178	420,126	82.9
1970	44,469	277,377	345,353	80.3

Source: U.S. Department of Justice, Immigration and Naturalization Service, *Annual Statistical Yearbook* (Washington, D.C.: Government Printing Office, 1970–1993).

TABLE 7

BILATERAL ECONOMIC RELATIONS:
U.S.-MEXICAN TRAVELERS' EXPENDITURES, 1970–1993

Year	Mexican Travelers to the United States ($ millions)	U.S. Travelers to Mexico ($ millions)
1993	5,670	5,813
1992	6,223	5,795
1991	5,881	5,642
1990	5,572	5,444
1989	4,275	4,784
1988	3,212	4,046
1987	2,392	3,567
1986	2,188	2,939
1985	2,259	2,889
1984	2,153	3,233
1983	1,951	3,618
1982	3,098	3,324
1981	3,775	2,862
1980	2,522	2,564
1979	1,975	2,460
1978	1,456	2,121
1977	1,316	1,918
1976	1,364	1,723
1975	1,490	1,637
1974	1,142	1,475
1973	830	1,264
1972	620	1,135
1971	565	959
1970	583	778

Source: U.S. Department of Commerce, U.S. Travel and Tourism Administration, Bureau of Economic Analysis.

Note: Arrival figures exclude Mexican border crossings before 1984.

TABLE 8

BILATERAL COMMUNICATIONS:
U.S.-MEXICAN TELEPHONE CALLS (in millions), 1978–1992

Year	Mexico to United States		United States to Mexico	
	No. of Messages	Total Minutes	No. of Messages	Total Minutes
1992	137.4	608.6	190.0	1,277.2
1991	93.4	468.3	147.1	1,038.2
1990	91.6	457.2	129.8	934.4
1989	77.2	389.1	110.5	796.9
1988	62.0	310.9	88.0	642.3
1987	45.9	236.6	66.4	502.8
1986	39.4	214.2	56.2	422.9
1985	32.6	182.8	47.4	349.2
1984	24.9	147.1	41.7	307.0
1983	26.7	144.5	39.3	294.3
1982	25.8	155.6	36.4	251.8
1981	22.4	130.0	29.8	214.5
1980	18.4	107.0	26.1	187.7
1979	14.3	83.0	21.6	155.7
1978	10.7	62.3	17.0	122.8

Source: U.S. Federal Communications Commission, *Statistics of Communications: Common Carriers* (Washington, D.C.: Government Printing Office, 1971–1992).

TABLE 9

BILATERAL COMMUNICATIONS:
FOREIGN VISITORS TO THE UNITED STATES, 1970–1993

Year	Visitors From All Countries	Visitors From Mexico	% of Total
1993	37,560,478	9,824,000	26.2
1992	47,556,490	11,167,000[1]	23.5
1991	42,985,520	7,718,000	18.0
1990	39,539,010	7,217,000	18.3
1989	36,563,703	7,240,000	19.8
1988	34,095,212	7,883,000	23.1
1987	29,500,445	6,713,000	22.6
1986	26,007,748	6,355,000	24.4
1985	25,399,492	7,141,000	28.1
1984	26,933,616	8,515,000[2]	31.6
1983	21,512,680	1,846,000	8.6
1982	21,502,788	2,475,000	11.5
1981	23,475,024	3,568,000	15.2
1980	22,179,000	3,026,000	13.6
1979	20,310,068	2,570,000	12.7
1978	19,842,142	2,142,420	10.8
1977	18,609,715	2,029,745	10.9
1976	17,523,192	1,920,509	11.0
1975	15,698,054	2,155,651	13.7
1974	14,122,619	1,840,849	13.0
1973	13,995,134	1,619,451	11.6
1972	13,057,056	1,377,143	10.5
1971	12,738,935	1,170,583	9.2
1970	12,362,205	1,085,772	8.8

Source: U.S. Department of Commerce, Office of Research, U.S. Travel and Tourism Administration.

[1]The methodology for collecting Mexican data was changed in 1992; therefore, data are not comparable to previous years.

[2]After 1984, figures represent travelers whose length of stay was one night or longer; previous numbers underrepresented Mexican travel.

Anti-NAFTA Sturm und Drang

Such considerations aside, critics assailed NAFTA with a vehemence that transcended the pact's economic significance. Lane Kirkland, the 71-year-old president of the AFL-CIO who pledged to "go for broke" to kill the accord, excoriated the trade pact as "a poison pill left over from the previous administration." He dismissed the Clinton-negotiated side deals as a "bad joke . . . a Rube Goldberg structure of committees all leading nowhere."[302] Jesse Jackson called NAFTA an unjust agreement championed by big U.S. companies seeking "maximum profit with minimum concern for people," and pledged to hold anti-NAFTA demonstrations at boarded-up factories across the nation.[303]

Carl Pope, executive director of the Sierra Club, the only major environmental organization that endorsed Clinton in 1992, deplored NAFTA for using weak oversight and inadequate measures to attack Mexico's "pollution havens." "It doesn't meaningfully tackle the problem," charged Pope, "because it provides only minimal protection from toxic dumping and toxic hazards on the job. Mexico doesn't have a community right-to-know law that enables citizens to fight toxic emissions in their neighborhoods."[304]

Ralph Nader lent his voice to the anti–free-trade chorus, arguing that "[e]verything NAFTA touches becomes more autocratic and less democratic." The consumer advocate also complained that:

> From its morbidly secretive conception by corporate lobbyists and their Bush administration allies, to the fast-track procedural straitjacket that prohibits amendments to NAFTA, to the decisions by the inaccessible international tribunals that are alien to this country's jurisprudential practices, NAFTA diminishes U.S. democracy.[305]

Ross Perot, Pat Buchanan, and Jerry Brown—three unsuccessful 1992 presidential candidates whom House Minority Leader Michels ridiculed as the "Groucho, Chico, and Harpo of NAFTA politics"[306]—inveighed against the agreement throughout 1993.

177

Billionaire Perot kept up his attacks on the accord, which he said would eliminate hundreds of thousands of American jobs, pitting "American and Mexican workers in a race to the bottom."[307] Buchanan assailed NAFTA as "a leveraged buyout of American liberty." He also denounced a tentative U.S.-Mexican decision to spend $6 billion to attack border pollution, asking: "Why should the American people be responsible for cleaning up the pigpen that the Mexicans have made on their side of the border?"[308] Brown, for his part, blasted "Washington insiders" for promoting an agreement "negotiated in secret and written in arcane language," one that in his opinion would only further "wasteful production and frenetic global exchange."[309]

If NAFTA's impact on the United States was likely to be minimal and economic integration between the two countries inevitable, what accounted for the *sturm und drang* directed at the agreement? The detractors' rhetorical and lobbying overkill sprang less from NAFTA's substance than its symbolizing of Washington's readiness to participate fully in the post-Cold War world economy at a time when the American dream was under siege. The real wages of blue-collar "losers" started to stagnate during the 1970s; their white-collar counterparts, "winners" until the late 1980s, also began to suffer as their inflation-adjusted hourly wages declined from $16.40 to $16.10 between 1989 and 1993.[310] Moreover, recessions differed from previous ones inasmuch as laid-off workers—production-line employees, middle managers, and college-educated professionals alike—frequently failed to regain their old jobs once recovery began. A computer-driven technological revolution meant that firms with an increasingly global trajectory could achieve higher output with a reduced work force. The corporate argot of the 1990s—"outsourcing," "reengineering," "restructuring," "downsizing," and so forth—often meant the destruction of jobs, with 449,364 layoffs occurring during the first nine months of 1993 alone.[311] Men and women fortunate enough to regain full-time employment often worked at substantially lower wages. An influx of legal and illegal immigrants further depressed wages and sharpened resentment. Meanwhile, a soaring trade deficit evidenced the prosperity of Germany and Japan, countries that America had defeated during World War II and helped regain their economic footing after they surrendered. Finally, the 1990 collapse of the "evil empire" deprived Washington of the lodestar that had guided its foreign policy for two generations.

Complementing economic insecurity was the personal stress associated with mounting crime, homelessness, and incivility in towns and cities, as well as the crumbling of families. As one observer wrote:

> A central characteristic of the "have-not" or "loser" coalition that emerged full force in the NAFTA debate is that its members are experiencing family collapse and fatherlessness in far higher numbers than is the "winner" coalition.[312]

Amid this climate of change, uncertainty, and fear, a growing number of Americans searched eagerly for scapegoats and resonated readily to conspiracy theories. The North American Free Trade Agreement provided an inviting target for their wrath and frustration.

The AFL-CIO Weighs In

No group seemed more threatened by globalism than the AFL-CIO. The organization argued that a free-trade agreement would facilitate the relocation of U.S. factories to Mexico to take advantage of sweatshop conditions, depress wages north of the Rio Grande, and spark unfair competition with domestic manufacturers. Equally harsh was labor's criticism of the corruption and lax work standards springing from the Confederation of Mexican Workers' coziness with its government. "[CTM Secretary-General] Fidel Velázquez is the Al Capone of Mexico's labor relations," warned the spokesman for a U.S. worker rights group.[313]

Until the late 1960s, labor leaders viewed trade liberalization as a means to raise working people's standard of living around the globe. This idealism vanished as imports began to penetrate such manufacturing sectors as textiles, footwear, automobiles, steel, and electrical consumer goods. Former AFL-CIO President George

Meany believed that U.S. corporate investment abroad presaged the loss of domestic jobs and posed a threat to union members.[314]

Over the decades, the AFL-CIO watched union rosters shrink both in absolute terms and as a percentage of the work force. The number of unionized workers fell from a high of 22.2 million in 1975 to 16.6 million in 1991. Meanwhile, union cardholders as a portion of nonagricultural workers plummeted from 31.6 percent (1955) to 16.1 percent (1991).[315] In 1993 the AFL-CIO itself represented only 11 percent of American workers, down a third from 16.4 percent in 1975. This decrease took place despite the AFL-CIO's having absorbed the 1.3 million-member Teamsters union in the late 1980s. Some of the largest of the federation's 86 affiliates suffered the worst declines. Between 1975 and 1990, the number of Steelworkers dropped from 1.1 million to 421,000; International Ladies Garment Workers, from 363,000 to 133,000; Machinists and Aerospace Workers, from 780,000 to 474,000; and Carpenters and Joiners, from 700,000 to 408,000.[316]

Several considerations explain this free fall in membership. AFL-CIO officials pointed to 12 years of anti-union Republican presidents, outdated federal labor laws, and the readiness of U.S. plants to move to Mexico and other offshore venues to profit from rock-bottom wages. Scholars, on the other hand, attributed 65 percent of the loss in union members to reduced employment in unionized industries, 30 percent to increased employment in nonunionized fields, and 5 percent to ineffective organizing campaigns.[317]

The presence of a few younger, articulate union presidents aside, the AFL-CIO's leadership projects an image of old, mostly white, largely male leaders who seem more content to recall past glories and thunder at current devils than to introduce innovations or welcome into their ranks innovative young leaders. The federation's 35-member executive council presents a Rubenesque tableau, composed mostly of jowly old men with receding hairlines, prominent paunches, and pugnacious scowls. New ideas and fresh leaders might stem the slide in cardholders, whose number, if the current trend continues, could fall below five million by the year 2000. Significantly, the nine AFL-CIO unions that grew between 1985 and 1991—including public employees, teachers, service workers, teamsters, and professional athletes—boasted presidents who were, on average, more than five years younger (56.7 years) than the average AFL-CIO's executive council member (62 years) and appeared more dynamic than leaders of declining unions.[318]

Erosion in membership was only one indicator of labor's weakness. The AFL-CIO's role in presidential nominations had declined since the organization effectuated Walter F. Mondale's infelicitous nomination in 1984. In that year, the Democratic standard-bearer carried only his home state of Minnesota and the District of Columbia. Also distressing to union leaders was their inability to exert political control over rank-and-file members. Although Bill Clinton did capture a majority of union households in 1992 (55 percent), the GOP candidate ran almost as well among this constituency—the so-called "Reagan Democrats"—in 1980 (50 percent) and 1984 (52 percent).[319]

Lane Kirkland and his colleagues wanted NAFTA defeated because they believed, correctly, that free trade threatened to eliminate some unionized jobs while creating work for individuals who might not affiliate with a labor organization. At the same time, they sought to regain their influence within the Democratic party, on which Clinton was trying to paint a new face as he nudged it toward the center. A triumph on NAFTA would enhance labor's political prestige as well as boost its chances of winning on other issues such as a ban on striker replacements and an increase in the minimum wage. The unions set their face only against "this NAFTA," naively implying that hundreds of negotiators might return to the bargaining table to design a more politically intrusive and protectionist free-trade accord that they could endorse and that would pass muster in Mexico City and Ottawa.

NAFTA became an issue of labor solidarity. Although having nothing to fear from the initiative, the American Federation of State, County and Municipal Employees, the American Federation of Teachers, and other largely white-collar organizations participated fully in the anti-NAFTA drive to show that they were part of a cohesive union movement. On the other hand, some leaders of a local of the United Electrical, Radio and Machine Workers of America in Erie, Pennsylvania, backed the trade pact. After all, their members worked in a General Electric plant, which made locomotives for export to Mexico. The union officials in Erie were informed in no uncertain terms by Washington labor leaders that any public endorsement of NAFTA would lead to swift and massive retaliation against their local, according to former Congressman Bill Frenzel, who was drumming up support for the accord.[320]

Environmentalists and Consumer Allies

Though forming the most potent anti-NAFTA force and running its own anti-NAFTA campaign, the AFL-CIO aligned itself with environmental and consumer groups with which the trade unionists had often crossed swords on legislation in the past. Interestingly, it was organized labor that was responsible for focusing national attention on the link between pollution and U.S.-Mexican trade. In 1989 the AFL-CIO's Edward M. Feigen directed a special project that exposed the contamination produced by south-of-the-border, American-owned *maquiladoras*. He enlisted the National Toxics Campaign (NTC), a now-defunct environmental group, to assist with the testing of hazardous wastes found at industrial sites in northern Mexico. From this initiative was published *Rivers in Peril*, a book written by the NTC's Sanford Lewis, which helped make the issue salient to the NGO community in the United States.

The labor-environmental-consumer alliance against NAFTA served three purposes. It brought the labor movement a number of young, articulate allies. It also mobilized grass-roots organizations to complement labor's essentially "top-down" lobbying effort conducted from its Washington, D.C. headquarters.[321] Finally, union leaders realized that championing ecological protection had broader appeal than self-serving, employment-related issues alone. Numbers about employment varied wildly. Yet most think-tanks, including those receiving union contributions, concluded that NAFTA would generate more jobs in the United States than it would destroy. In any case, the number (several hundred thousand) frequently cited approximated the monthly rise or fall in U.S.

employment levels. This was hardly a figure that would make or break the American economy.

Evidence that union leaders were "wearing green" appeared in a virulent union newspaper advertisement warning that fast-track approval, because of the dearth of sewage treatment and other health precautions in Mexico, would worsen diseases arising from polluted water and food in border towns.

The environmental groups, consumer organizations, and foreign foes of the agreement with whom labor worked to defeat NAFTA could be classified loosely as (1) "constructive engagers," (2) "jaguars," and (3) "bitter-enders." Most active in the first category were the National Wildlife Federation, the Natural Resources Defense Council, and the Environmental Defense Fund. Sharing their pragmatic approach were such marginal players in the NAFTA controversy as the World Wildlife Fund, Conservation International, and the National Audubon Society. The constructive engagers believed that NAFTA negotiations, like GATT's Uruguay Round, were inevitable and thought it prudent to broaden the dialogue with the administration rather than stridently denounce its motives and proposals. As described in chapter 3, the 5.3-million-member National Wildlife Fund, headed by Jay Hair, helped President Bush attain fast-track passage.

Ultimately, the constructive engagers who collectively claim some 7.5 million members concluded that NAFTA, improved by side agreements, would have a positive impact on the environment. In mid-September 1993, six groups stood shoulder-to-shoulder with Vice President Gore and announced their support for the agreement.[322] After the photo opportunity, they began a vigorous lobbying effort in behalf of the pact.

More militant were practitioners of the "jaguar approach," a term applied by Robert F. Housman, an attorney with the Center for International Environmental Law (CIEL), another minor player in the NAFTA drama.[323] Housman's metaphor captured the popular perception of how jaguars hunt (though, in fact, these animals hunt alone): "One pursuer races to the head of the pack until he tires and is replaced by another, who in turn is succeeded at the lead when he falls back. This strategy wears out the prey." The environmental jaguars tend to see themselves as more idealistic than the Washington-centric constructive engagers who, they allege, have succumbed to cooptation and "Potomac fever." Symptoms of the latter, according to journalist Mark Dowie, are "a knee-jerk adherence to the legislative fix, an abiding faith in lobbying, and a reliance on ephemeral voting blocks to mitigate social and political problems. Like any addict with enough money to support his or her habit, the reform environmental movement has either denied its problem or explained it away."[324]

The less bellicose jaguars demanded three provisions in the final NAFTA package. First, they sought public participation in dispute resolution. Second, they insisted that increased trade benefits be conditioned upon improved enforcement of antipollution laws in Mexico and along the U.S.-Mexican border. And third, they urged adequate funding for cleaning up the environment and building waste-treatment plants and other infrastructure. These organizations favored the concept, first publicized by House Majority Leader Gephardt, of imposing a tariff on border trans-actions. "This is a small price to pay," said Housman, "to purchase the fork with which to eat a free meal."[325]

Some jaguars were more aggressive than others. The tamer ones, according to Housman, were his CIEL, Defenders of Wildlife, and the Humane Society of the U.S. The more ferocious were Public Citizen, Greenpeace USA, Friends of the Earth, and the Sierra Club, with the latter two having especially good contacts in official Washington when they choose to use them. These five organizations (along with the Humane Society and CIEL) expressed their concerns in a full-page *Washington Post* advertisement in mid-December 1992.[326] Entitled "George Bush and the Secret Side of 'Free' Trade," the piece condemned GATT, the Uruguay Round, and NAFTA as Orwellian. Specifically, the critics contended that U.S. laws could fall hostage to so-called free-trade commitments. As touched upon in chapter 6, Mexico, for example, had won a GATT ruling that the Marine Mammal Protection Act, designed to protect dolphins caught by tuna boats in the eastern tropical Pacific, was a "barrier to trade." (Subsequently, the United States and Mexico negotiated a phase-out of purse-seine fishing so threatening to dolphins.) Emboldened by the action of GATT—sometimes denounced as GATTzilla after the Japanese monster

Godzilla—Mexico would, it was argued, use a free-trade accord to attack other environmental legislation. Furthermore, in promoting the "harmonization" of health and safety practices, NAFTA could well harmonize "downward" U.S. standards against asbestos use and the presence of DDT and other poisonous residues on food. "The same fate probably awaits the California state initiative . . . that requires the labeling of products for carcinogens and toxics," the coalition declared. Faceless bureaucrats meeting in secret sessions, they warned, would usurp environmental policy from elected officials.[327]

Disenchantment over the side deals and philosophical hostility toward capitalism meant that many jaguars wound up as bitter-enders like the AFL-CIO, which continued to regard NAFTA as an abomination. Not content to be outspent, outmanned, and outmaneuvered by industrial giants and their political action committees, the bitter-enders complemented Capitol Hill lobbying and news conferences with strident challenges to corporations and government agencies. Their aggressiveness took the form of lawsuits against intransigent regulators, noisy demonstrations, consumer boycotts, shareholder suits, and nonviolent direct action against polluters (the NRDC, a constructive engager on NAFTA, has employed similar tactics on other issues).

Providing a link between environmentalists and trade unions were several grass-roots-oriented coalitions. These organizations, which further blurred the distinction between militant jaguars and bitter-enders, also embraced religious, consumer, agricultural, and human rights activists. They were the Ralph Nader-sponsored Citizen Trade Watch; the 50-member Mobilization on Development, Trade, Labor and the Environment, which stimulated cooperation with Mexican and Canadian foes of the trade pact; and the San Francisco-based Fair Trade Coalition. In addition to espousing "bread and butter" issues articulated by the AFL-CIO, these amalgams condemned NAFTA as undemocratic, claimed it would vitiate the Clean Air Act, the Clean Water Act, and other environmental legislation, and insisted that it would devastate Mexico's natural resources. Bitter-enders also decried torture, electoral fraud, and human rights abuses in Mexico.

Foreign Critics Bring Their Case to the U.S. Congress

These broad-based coalitions also forged links to constructive engagers and bitter-enders in Mexico and Canada, where only a handful of organizations occupied a middle-of-the-road position. Most conspicuous among Mexican constructive engagers was the Autonomous Institute of Ecological Research (INAINE). Headed by Luis Manuel Guerra and funded by public and private sources, this organization promotes compliance with Mexico's comprehensive environmental laws while emphasizing data collection and validation to determine the full extent of Mexico's ecological crisis. Another voice of moderation was the recently formed Mexican Environmental Law Center, which considers itself the nation's "environmental conscience." Gustavo Alanis Ortega, its president, also promotes stricter adherence to national statutes, enhanced public awareness of ecological problems, and greater citizen involvement in decision making. More assertive, but generally responsible on environmental issues, were the Group of a Hundred, the Ecological Association of Coyoacán, the Union of Environmental Groups, and Pronatura.

At the forefront of the bitter-enders was the Mexican Action Network on Free Trade (RMALC). RMALC embraced a collection of intellectuals, journalists, ecologists, activists from the Authentic Labor Front (FAT) and other small unions, and leaders of the nationalist, anti-U.S. Party of the Democratic Revolutionary.[328] Bertha Luján, a member of FAT who heads RMALC, argued that a trade agreement would bankrupt less efficient firms, exacerbate unemployment in a nation where one million young people enter the work force each year, compromise the nation's highly prized independence, and adversely affect health care, living standards, Mexican culture, and the environment. Sharing Luján's views on NAFTA's danger to the environment were the Mexican Ecological Movement, headed by Alfonso Cipres Villarreal, and the Valley of Mexico's Regional Ecological Forum. Forum spokesman Miguel Valencia chided Salinas for Mexico's "born-again greenness." In the same vein, the Mexican Ecological party, whose president Jorge González Torres was a presidential candidate in the August 1994 contest, characterized the trade pact as an opportunity to "establish

186

hazardous waste dumps in the border region" and a "national humiliation," one which will deepen Mexico's enslavement to the United States.[329] Sergio Aguayo Quezada, a distinguished academic and human rights activist, warned that under NAFTA, the United States might pressure Mexico to forge a military alliance, modify its nationalistic petroleum policy, and alter its treatment of foreign investment.[330] Meanwhile, Jorge G. Castañeda, an internationally known UNAM professor, insisted that the accord "may only exacerbate the country's already stark disparities and dislocations." In *Foreign Affairs* magazine, he wrote that "rather than speeding and facilitating Mexico's long-awaited and much-hoped-for democratic transition, the near-term effect may be to slow the momentum for political reform."[331]

Pollution Probe Canada was that country's most notable constructive-engager, and even it wound up opposing NAFTA. Bitter-enders abounded in the Canadian Labour Congress (CLC), the Council of Canadian Lawyers (CCL), and the Canadian Action Network (CAN).

Mexican and Canadian critics of the pact were confronted with strongly pro-NAFTA legislatures at home. Spokesmen for the RMALC and environmental groups faced a Mexican Senate composed almost entirely of PRI members. Similarly, Canadian opponents encountered a parliament dominated by Mulroney's Progressive Conservatives. These detractors consequently took their case to the United States, where lawmakers seemed more persuadable. Through speeches, news conferences, and participation in public forums, they tried to convince U.S. decisionmakers that the accord would exacerbate poverty, civil rights abuses, environmental degradation, and political corruption in Mexico. CLC and CAN representatives, for their part, averred that the U.S.-Canadian FTA had wiped out some 500,000 manufacturing jobs in Canada, a contention vigorously rejected by both the Mulroney and Bush administrations.[332]

Perot Again

Perot began the 1993 NAFTA season by recommending that Washington and Mexico City launch a free-trade pilot project because of the big wage gap between the two economies. Although short on details, he said that the partners subscribing to a trial run should "have a clear understanding that either nation may decide to cancel this agreement, if in that nation's judgment, the pilot program is not successful."[333] The Texan told the House Small Business Committee that a group of intelligent people could prepare a pact that safeguarded American workers in 30 days.[334]

By late summer 1993, Perot had sought to become the drum major of the anti-NAFTA parade. Rather than twirl a baton, he decided to wave a book before the public to swell the ranks of his procession. In September he—along with Pat Choate, a plump, bearded economist whose 1990 book *Agents of Influence* mordantly attacked American lobbyists hired by foreign countries—published a 142-page monograph. At the outset, they warned that "buried in the fine print [of NAFTA] are provisions that will give away American jobs and radically reduce the sovereignty of the United States."[335] The activists claimed that Washington had been "outtraded" by Mexico and Canada in a "secret deal" that would wreak havoc on the U.S. economy.[336] Among the allegations made by the co-authors was that NAFTA would extinguish as many as 5.9 million American jobs, that low wages would entice U.S. firms to relocate their plants in Mexico, that the free-trade accord would destroy America's manufacturing base, and that the pact was not really a free-trade agreement, but a mechanism "to assure foreign investors that their capital investments and plants will be safeguarded in Mexico."[337] In addition, they argued that NAFTA would turn Mexico into a "platform" that European and Asian countries could use to penetrate the U.S. market, that NAFTA would imperil U.S. agriculture, and that the agreement would enable "Northern Mexico . . . [to] replace Detroit as the car production center of North America."[338] As part of the web of conspiracy spun by the book, the authors claimed that fast-track authority allowed negotiation of the pact "in complete secrecy without the

188

participation of either Congress or the U.S. public."[339] Perot and Choate also alleged that NAFTA would undermine U.S. food safety and health regulations, promote drug smuggling, and spur illegal immigration. In a variant of "The Russians are Coming" or "The Yellow Peril Will Get Us," the authors erroneously claimed that, thanks to free trade, "Mexican truck drivers—qualified or not, fatigued or not, able to read English or not—and their Mexican trucks—overloaded or not, well-maintained or not—will soon be on U.S. highways."[340]

The Clinton administration responded at once to these charges. Within a week of the book's publication, the USTR released a 74-page statement rebutting Perot's conclusions and reaffirming support for the pact. Kantor asserted, as had several newspapers, that Perot's book was "riddled with inaccuracies, errors and misleading statements" and was thus a deeply flawed critique of NAFTA. The U.S. Trade Representative claimed that nearly 200 errors marred the publication.[341] Pro-NAFTA think tanks such as the Heritage Foundation also produced detailed, heavily documented critiques of the paperback philippic.[342]

Optimism of NAFTA Foes

Several factors emboldened NAFTA's opponents to believe that they could carry the day in the House of Representatives. First, two of the three top Democratic leaders—Majority Leader Gephardt and Majority Whip David E. Bonior (D-Mich.)—opposed the initiative and sought to recruit colleagues to their side. Of the two, Gephardt was, in the parlance of the Versailles Treaty battle, the "reservationist"—the proponent of a NAFTA improved by side deals—and Bonior the "irreconcilable." Yet when the side agreements proved unsatisfactory to him, Gephardt told the *Washington Post*: "We're losing all these jobs to free trade. We didn't take care of the environment, infrastructure wasn't built, there's no training for American workers and there isn't a darn thing going on with Mexican wages. . . . Can't we do better than that?"[343] In throwing his considerable weight against NAFTA, Gephardt, 52, signaled his desire to pursue the House speakership rather than the White House. Once a Clinton ally in the Democratic Leadership Council, the Missouri Democrat unsuccessfully pursued his party's presidential nomination as an angry, South Korea- and Japan-bashing protectionist in 1988—a role that he has continued to play. Historically, chief executives, as stewards of the national interest, have been internationalists. Gephardt's anti-NAFTA stance placed him on the other side of a divide that Clinton characterized as a debate between "whether we embrace [global economic] change and create the jobs of tomorrow or try to resist these changes, hoping we can preserve the economic structures of yesterday."[344]   At no point did Bonior, 48, who represents Macomb County, an upwardly mobile ethnic suburb north of Detroit, display the least sympathy for the accord. The well-liked populist showed the ardor of a former seminarian when, in a June 1993 floor speech, he denounced Mexico's long history of repression, electoral fraud, and human rights abuses. He even quoted slavery foe Frederick Douglass to the effect that "neither persons nor property" are safe in a repressive and corrupt system. Passing the trade pact, he insisted, would "reward" Mexico's authoritarian rulers and punish average Mexicans by locking in "a system that exploits its own people."[345]   As early as the spring of 1993, he began weekly televised attacks on the accord, orchestrated strategy meetings, and button-holed colleagues to join what was, for him, a crusade against tyranny and for working-class Americans whose unions formed a surviving pillar of Roosevelt's New Deal coalition.[346]

Second, Gephardt and Bonior's presence among the opponents left the president without a strong floor manager for NAFTA. Speaker Foley, a thoughtful, aloof aficionado of classical music, prefers conciliation to arm-twisting, and functions largely as a broker among a heterogenous array of House Democrats, ranging from Barney Frank (D-Mass.) on the left to Charles W. Stenholm (D-Tex.), head of the Conservative Democratic Forum, on the right. Lest he diminish his effectiveness with fractious colleagues, the 64-year-old speaker remained above the fray and did little proselytizing for the trade deal. The man who could have filled the leadership vacuum, Ways and Means Committee Chairman Rostenkowski, was preoccupied by a full-bore Justice Department probe of his financial dealings. Rostenkowski did help drum up support for NAFTA, but the possibility of an indictment, complemented by a difficult reelection race, limited the time and energy he could devote to the cause. Day-to-day responsibilities for the legislation devolved to Robert T. Matsui, a senior Ways and Means member, and Bill Richardson, one of four deputy majority whips and an activist within the 19-member Hispanic Caucus.[347]

Third, the presence of 100 freshmen House members, 63 of whom were Democrats, encouraged the anti-NAFTA forces to believe that they would prevail. After all, the first-term Democrats had depended more on contributions from labor political action committees (PACs) in their 1992 victories (44 percent) than did senior colleagues (31 percent) to raise the $239,800 spent by the average winning candidate.[348] Enhancing their need to curry trade unionists' favor was the difficulty many would face in seeking reelection. Since World War II, the president's party has lost an average of 26 House seats in "off-year" contests—with aspiring congressional sophomores representing the most endangered species.[349] No member relishes being turned out of office, but the 103rd Congress boasted a disproportionate number of new members for whom politics was a career, not an avocation. Almost three-quarters of the House freshmen (and two of the 11 new senators) were veteran politicians.[350]

Fourth, also encouraging to NAFTA's detractors was Perot's highly visible opposition to the accord. In the 1994 congressional races, he would have the option of endorsing anti-free-trade incumbents, supporting challengers against pact supporters, or running third-party candidates under the "United We Stand America" banner. At the very least, he could continue to lambaste the "mess in Washington," thereby souring the public on incumbents. Enhancing respect for the Texas billionaire on Capitol Hill was his having captured at least 20 percent of the vote in one-fourth of the country's 435 congressional districts. The significance of this figure was obvious because an unusually large number of congressmen (112 in the House alone) won their 1992 elections with less than 55 percent of the vote. Given this marked rise in electoral competi-tiveness, Frank Luntz, a former Perot pollster, estimated that 68 House and Senate lawmakers, including Speaker Foley, could lose their seats if Perot or his supporters launched a vigorous anti-incumbent campaign in 1994.[351]

Fifth, the Congressional Black Caucus (CBC) had voiced opposition to NAFTA, and the redrawing of legislative districts in 1991 had paved the way for a doubling, to 39, of the caucus's size.[352] Close ties to organized labor, whose PACs have contributed generously to African-American candidates, buttressed this opposition. Another consideration was the CBC-Gephardt bond, reinforced by the Majority Leader's friendship with fellow St. Louisian William L. "Bill" Clay (D-Mo.), 62, a House member since 1969, a founder and key political strategist of the CBC, and chairman of the Post Office and Civil Service Committee. Gephardt's unflinching support for Clay, who had had a number of confrontations with the House Ethics Committee (and recorded 328 overdrafts on the House bank), his passionate support for District of Columbia statehood (a proposal championed by African-American legislators), and his opposition to NAFTA should help him obtain CBC backing for the speakership when Foley retires.

Sixth, House Democrats understood that the president, afflicted by low popular approval, would need their votes desperately on health-care reform, just as their support had been crucial to passing his budget bill—won by a 218 to 216 largely party-line vote (51 to 50 in the Senate)—in August 1993. As a consequence, they believed that the White House, which was sending ambiguous messages about its enthusiasm for NAFTA, would give them a "bye" on the trade pact, with no hard feelings because of their importance to the enactment of its domestic agenda.

Finally, House incumbents were more attuned than statewide officials to the anti-NAFTA case. The representatives' smaller constituencies enhance their sensitivity to a limited number of interests, and possible NAFTA losers were more vocal than putative NAFTA winners. In contrast, a majority of senators and 41 governors announced early on that they favored the free-trade pact.[353] Not only do such officials enjoy longer terms—six years for senators and four years for most governors, compared to two years for representatives—but all states embrace multiple interests that check and balance each other, giving the senator or governor greater freedom of action on trade and other issues.

Conclusion

Pressures from all sides clearly abounded as lawmakers prepared to cast the NAFTA vote in November 1993. Though the opposition was by far the more vocal, the president and his allies shared a quieter, if equally determined, sense that on the free-trade pact, they were the stewards of progress. Each side of the debate featured strange bedfellows, and each side promoted its unusual crosspartisan coalition as proof of broad support "out there"—beyond the Beltway, on the Main Streets of America—for its position. Congress was approaching a fateful decision: to advance and engage in the international arena, as it had done after World War II with the establishment of the United Nations, or to retreat and turn inward, as it had done after World War I with the rejection of the Versailles Treaty. As a defining event, the final vote on NAFTA would determine America's course as it prepared to enter the 21st century. Key to NAFTA's fate would be an all-out campaign by Bill Clinton in behalf of the trade pact.

CHAPTER NINE

The Showdown Vote

Introduction

In his seminal work on executive decision making, Richard Neustadt emphasized the importance of clearly communicating presidential intentions to subordinates. Delivering ambiguous messages, he warned, could cost the White House political capital. General Douglas MacArthur, for example, may have felt emboldened to publicly propose policies on the conduct of the Korean War that conflicted with President Truman's goals because of the obscure means Washington used to transmit its objectives to the five-star martinet. Rather than explicitly forbidding him from making statements on foreign or military matters without prior clearance, the Pentagon sent him a message through an apparently routine communication addressed to all government departments. "The order was expressed in terms more easily construed as the concoction of press attachés to hush Assistant Secretaries than as Truman's word to his Supreme Commander," Neustadt wrote.[354]

Yet it was not simply a failure to communicate that haunted the White House as Clinton, in the words of commentators, "hit the ground stumbling" in 1993 under the weight of unanticipated problems with personnel, policies, and politics. His objectives were vague and he was a greenhorn at the poker table when it came to dealing with Washington. It took him three tries and nearly two months to appoint an attorney general, as his first two choices had "nanny" problems arising from their employment of illegal aliens. No sooner had cries of a "Nannygate" begun to subside when Senator Sam Nunn (D-Ga.) and other legislators turned thumbs down on the new government's proposal to abolish the ban on gays serving openly in the armed forces. To add insult to injury, in April the Senate filibustered to death the chief executive's $15.5 billion economic stimulus package. When queried on its priorities, a now-besieged administration pointed to the impending budget bill and health care reform. As a result, Clinton's intentions on NAFTA were about as clear as the Arkansas River after a gullywasher. Even though fond of quoting the classics, he ignored the Socratic admonition to "Know Thyself."

Also inviting doubts about the accord's prospects was U.S. District Court Judge Charles Richey's 30 June decision that the Bush administration had violated the 1970 National Environmental Policy Act by not preparing an environmental impact statement (EIS) on NAFTA's effect on the quality of the human environment. Agreeing with the complaint brought by Ralph Nader's Public Citizen, the Sierra Club, and Friends of the Earth, Richey ruled that such a statement would have to be developed before the trade pact's submission to Congress. Although Kantor declared that the ruling "will not alter [the NAFTA] schedule," an EIS requires costly and voluminous studies and therefore threatened to delay the sending of the accord to Capitol Hill.[355]

The Painfully Silent Summer

Pro forma endorsements of NAFTA notwithstanding, Clinton paid little attention to the accord throughout the summer. As mentioned previously, he did squelch suggestions from Stephano-poulos and others that deadlocked talks on the side deals might provide the White House an ideal excuse for abandoning NAFTA. "We are going forward," he told a Cabinet member. "I am for this."[356] Still, the chief executive's commitment seemed so tentative that Treasury Secretary Bentsen sought a tete-à-tete with Clinton to make certain that NAFTA would not die from neglect. The reassurance that he received conflicted with priorities established by Clinton's own staff. Their proposed fall schedule called for the president to devote more than a month drumming up support for health care reform and just one day promoting the North American accord. Bentsen again met privately with Clinton. "They were both priorities, health care and NAFTA, but once again the schedulers weren't setting the agenda," the former Texas senator said. "I spoke with him specifically about that, and some others did, too." The schedule was changed.[357]

Apart from the delays caused by the side deals, five institutional factors prevented NAFTA from obtaining more attention from the president earlier. First, W. Bowman "Bo" Cutter, the deputy director of the National Economic Council, failed to make maximum use of the admittedly unwieldy body to advance NAFTA's cause. He was asked to have the dozen or so agencies represented on the NEC report to him on their upcoming activities involving Mexico. If the Department of Housing and Urban Development, for example, were planning on opening low-income apartment units in the border region in January 1994, perhaps it could hold a well-publicized dedication ceremony before the NAFTA vote in Congress. Cutter did ask to be informed of pending events but set no deadlines for the agency heads. As a result, there was little or no coordination of photo-opportunities with the pro-NAFTA venture. Second, Clinton's populist campaign pledge to slash White House personnel by 25 percent meant that the nerve center of his new administration was understaffed, particularly in its first year when there was an overwhelming need for a remarkably young and inexperienced staff to learn how official Washington works.

Third, the White House lacked a chain of command conducive to making decisions. Thomas F. "Mack" McLarty, a Clinton friend since childhood, was a congenial, permissive chief of staff who failed to bring coherence and discipline to decision making. These weaknesses later led the president to replace him with Budget Director Leon E. Panetta, a Washington insider. McLarty's job was made harder by the chief executive's penchant for rambling, diffuse fraternity house-style discussions of issues, which often involved individuals with little expertise in the subject matter at hand. To the extent that a structure existed, the White House embraced three power centers: the president, the vice president, and the first lady.[358]

Fourth, a battle royal raged for control of the president's political soul. Secretary Bentsen, Panetta, Deputy Budget Director Alice M. Rivlin, Presidential Counselor Gergen, and members of the Council of Economic Advisers generally favored deficit reduction and a moderate version of Clinton's program. They believed that to govern it was necessary to win support in the business community and on both sides of the partisan divide. In contrast, the political "consultants"—Begala, Carville, Greenberg, and Mandy Grunwald (allied with Stephanopoulos)—championed middle-class tax cuts, job-creating investments, sweeping health care reform, and other issues they had promoted during the campaign. The sometimes arrogant and self-righteous consultants preferred to work with liberal Democrats and their constituencies, resisted compromises, and were ready to caustically attack opponents, sometimes employing populist, soak-the-rich rhetoric.[359]

Finally, Bentsen, Kantor, and other trade-pact proponents would have readily challenged fellow Cabinet officers or senior White House staff members for greater emphasis on NAFTA versus health care. Health care's chief advocate, however, was not a political appointee, but Hillary Rodham Clinton, considered at times "*de facto* chief of staff."[360] Even senior administration officials are reluctant to contest priorities set by the First Lady. Washington *cognoscente* remember all too well how Donald Regan lost his job as chief of staff after exciting Mrs. Reagan's fury over President Reagan's work schedule. In dealing with first ladies, Regan's successors and others close to the chief executive seem mindful of advice offered by one of Mrs. Reagan's speech writers—namely, that she was to be "treated with the kind of gingerly respect due a lioness: one admires its beauty, anticipates its desires, and never, never gets it angry."[361] Of Ms. Clinton, one journalist wrote, "The name *Hillary* invokes a certain respect, a tiny shiver of danger, a hint of the deference that might be owed, say, a Medici in sixteenth-century Florence."[362]

Daley Comes Aboard

   To give impetus to NAFTA, Clinton had to look beyond his personal entourage for assistance because, by late summer, the trade accord appeared to be not just a defining event for U.S. policy; it had become a test of Clinton's success as president as well. Except for a narrow victory on his budget bill, he boasted few major triumphs on Capitol Hill. In early June, Clinton had withdrawn the nomination of Lani Guinier to head the civil-rights division of the Justice Department. So controversial were the African-American professor's views on minority political representation that critics had derided her as a "quota queen." Two days later, Kay Bailey Hutchison trounced interim Senator Bob Krueger to fill Bentsen's vacated Texas U.S. Senate seat. And a national poll revealed that after 100 days in office, Clinton's approval rating stood at just 55 percent—the lowest for any elected president since the Gallup organization began collection this information in 1952.[363] By late August, Clinton's standing had dipped to 44 percent, with 47 percent disapproving his performance and 9 percent undecided.[364] Compounding the White House's problems was the tendency of the mass media—depicted as the "Bad News Bears" by researchers—to grossly distort economic news in a manner that would make viewers squeamish about NAFTA and other international initiatives.[365]

   While economics professors and editorial page writers were singing the praises of free trade, Congress was a long way from joining the choir. "It's a Mad Hatter's tea party," said Kantor. "We have won the intellectual arguments on this. The political argument is much tougher."[366] To take charge of the political game in hopes of gaining NAFTA's approval and, with it, the revival of a flagging presidency, Kantor successfully urged the appointment of William M. Daley as special counselor to the president for NAFTA. Two 30-something Chicagoans—Rahm Emanuel, Clinton's chief fund-raiser during the campaign, co-chairmen of the inauguration, and the White House's deputy communications director; and David Wilhelm, the president's choice for chairman of the Democratic National Committee—strongly supported the move. Like many

Midwest Democrats, they had been disappointed when Daley had not been named secretary of transportation.

Daley was no stranger to politics or command. His father was Richard J. Daley, who from 1955 to 1976 combined the roles of chairman of the Cook County Democratic Committee and mayor of Chicago to become one of the country's most influential politicians. In 1960 he delivered the votes that were crucial to John F. Kennedy's carrying of Illinois and, in turn, of the Electoral College. Eight years later, Robert F. Kennedy, then a candidate for the Democratic nomination himself, said, "Daley means the ballgame."[367] Upon graduating from law school, Bill Daley spurned public office in favor of helping his older brother Richard, Jr., climb the political ladder. After his brother reached the mayor's chair once occupied by their father, Bill practiced law, advised his brother, arbitrated disputes within the Cook County Democratic family, and served as Clinton's Illinois chairman in 1992.

Thus, he brought impressive assets to the NAFTA drama: shrewdness, diplomacy, a political pedigree, a Midwest background that he shared with many NAFTA doubters, his record as a major fundraiser for the Democratic party, and excellent Capitol Hill ties, particularly with the 20-member Illinois delegation. In a manner unusual for official, power-hungry Washington, the Chicago native avoided the limelight, eschewing the informal title of "NAFTA czar."

Not everyone was impressed by Daley and his mission, which was to raise the stakes so high for NAFTA that the mercurial president would have no alternative but to commit himself fully to the continental agreement. Upon reaching Washington, Daley received a chilly reception from activists in the health care "war room," including Ms. Clinton, Ira Magaziner, Bob Boorstin, Stephanopoulos, and several of the consultants. They regarded NAFTA as a policy competitor with health care, which—they insisted—had been delayed too long and should now be the administration's top priority. They had no sense of the importance of the free-trade pact in its own right, as well as an issue that, if successful, could build alliances for health reform and other social programs. And, as social liberals, they were ideologically unsympathetic to this Bush project, so adored by big business and so loathed by organized labor. The latter was, after all, a generous and influential ally in what had become their health care crusade. Besides, Daley was a "short-timer," a devoted family man who spent his weekends in Chicago to which he would return permanently in several months. While the *Wall Street Journal* identified more than 500 people in 30 working groups beavering away on the health issue, Daley found only three or four people involved with NAFTA in a White House where confusion reigned. At first, NAFTA's special counselor was assigned only a small office in the USTR building; he later moved to three small offices in the Executive Office Building (EOB) before gaining access in early October to his own war room (he called it the "trade room") consisting of one huge office and two large rooms in the EOB. The increasing presence of the 33-year-old Emanuel, a close Clinton adviser, in the trade room helped to legitimize and strengthen Daley's role in administration. Although Daley would return to Chicago, the brusque, often abrasive Emanuel would still be around to reward those who had contributed to the NAFTA effort.

Daley's operated in a low-key manner. "If NAFTA were an opera," Peter Behr wrote in the *Washington Post*, "Daley would certainly not be its tenor, nor even the conductor. As he describes his role, it is more like the prompter in the stage pit who saves the performers who forget their lines."[368]

Joining Daley in the trade room was Bill Frenzel, a former high-ranking Republican House member from Minnesota who also boasted Midwestern roots, excellent congressional links, and a pragmatic bent toward issues. The ex-lawmaker, who was then a guest scholar at the Brookings Institution, laid down four conditions for his pursuing passage of NAFTA—namely, that he receive no pay, that he be permitted to step aside discreetly if the House and Senate Republican leaders believed his work counterproductive, that he have access to whomever necessary—including the chief executive—to accomplish his objectives, and that he be convinced that Clinton was 100 percent in favor of the initiative. In late August, upon announcing Frenzel's appointment, the president told him: "You're going to see how much I want this [pact] and that I am ready to do everything that's reasonable to attain its passage."[369] Rather than camp in the Executive Office Building, which Frenzel visited only at night to thank volunteers, he worked from an intern's desk in the minority staff office of the Ways and Means Committee. His days were spent both in scheduled meetings with GOP members and "mainly in waylaying them as they went back and forth from their offices to the floor or committee sessions." He communicated regularly with congressmen Jim Kolbe (R-Ariz.) and David Dreier (R-Calif.), who were keeping tabs on Republican support for the free-trade accord. The fact that Frenzel had access to policy meetings on NAFTA, especially those concerning the White House's plans for financing the agreement, enabled him to assure the GOP's congressional leadership that not only was Clinton fully behind the pact but that he would generate the revenues required for its implementation in a responsible manner.[370]

Daley's team also included Paul Toback from White House Chief of Staff McLarty's office and Kurt Campbell, a White House Fellow on leave from Harvard's Kennedy School, who had been assigned to Secretary Bentsen's staff.

Although Daley's trade room involved itself in all aspects of the NAFTA campaign, there was a loose division of labor within the administration. Howard G. Paster, a 48-year-old Brooklyn-accented presidential assistant for legislative affairs who had formerly lobbied for big labor and big business, and his deputy, Susan Brophy, concentrated on political questions involving Congress. After the August 1993 congressional recess when members had been deluged with anti-NAFTA appeals, they began arranging regular meetings with pro-trade pact leaders on Capitol Hill. Executive branch participants in these sessions included Daley, Kantor, Frenzel, Paster, Brophy, Tom Nides (Kantor's chief-of-staff), and Nancy Leamond, the USTR's congressional affairs liaison. Among legislators who often attended were Minority Leader Michel, Kolbe, Dreier, Robert T. Matsui, and Bill Richardson, as well as a group of pro-NAFTA senators assembled by Senator Bill Bradley (D-N.J.). Besides keeping open the lines of communication between the Capitol and the White House, Paster and Brophy arranged contacts—phone calls, luncheons, dinners—between the president and lawmakers. They also made certain that Clinton knew precisely what themes to emphasize in speaking with a particular senator or representative. Paster's office devoted special attention to legislators whose probability of supporting NAFTA would be enhanced if they could be assured of assistance with fund-raising, a presidential visit to their districts, or help with projects ensnared in bureaucratic red tape.

Although ever mindful of the largely political needs of congressmen, Kantor met with dozens of legislators, including 50 undecided Democrats, to discuss their substantive concerns about the trade agreement. In what became—after the 1991-1992 main negotiations and the 1993 side deals—the third round of NAFTA bargaining, the U.S. Trade Representative explored bilateral understandings with Mexico that would make the accord more palatable to lawmakers and their constituents. Governor Lawton Chiles and the 23-person Florida delegation, for instance, made it clear that they would be better disposed toward NAFTA if greater protection were afforded to their state's citrus and sugar industries. Before granting such a concession at Mexico's expense, Kantor, Yerxa, or Roh had to obtain SECOFI's approval. These eleventh-hour maneuvers acutely irritated Serra Puche and Blanco, who spent the weeks before the final vote in Washington; still, they usually complied with USTR's request because of NAFTA's importance to their country and chief executive.

While helping to coordinate all NAFTA-related activities, Daley's office had its own agenda, subject to continual revision at the twice-weekly strategy sessions that he convened beginning in late August with 16 to 18 agency and Cabinet representatives. Daley's team devised a "message of the week" (they sometimes lasted several weeks) to be disseminated on Capitol Hill. The first appeal was defensive—that is, urging congressmen to avoid making anti-NAFTA commitments until they had heard the administration's story. Next, the trade room stressed job creation, with a state-by-state breakdown of NAFTA's employment benefits. Finally, they emphasized the trade pact's centrality to a credible, effective foreign policy.

Daley activated agencies in behalf of NAFTA in what became the most comprehensive lobbying venture by Cabinet members in history. Bentsen made the greatest personal commitment of time and energy to drumming up support for the accord. Laura D'Andrea Tyson, chairman of the Council of Economic Advisers,

203

called or visited virtually every female legislator. EPA Administrator Carol M. Browner was johnny-on-the-spot when individual representatives and senators had questions concerning the environment. Allegations that he had received illegal payments from a Vietnamese businessman preoccupied Commerce Secretary Ronald H. Brown and diminished his participation in the selling of NAFTA.

The Daley trade room preferred to have a Kissinger, Nixon, Scowcroft, Carter, or Baker make the foreign policy argument for NAFTA. The State Department, however, did become involved as a secondary player. From a command center in the department's sixth floor, Ambassador Charles "Tony" Gillespie, former envoy to Colombia and Chile, directed an operation that resembled the last six weeks of a political campaign. Gillespie and his 34-member task force, which drew on most of the department's area and functional bureaus, answered questions for congressmen, sent out pro-NAFTA literature, and mobilized ambassadors and other senior officials to make speeches throughout the country. Secretary Christopher, a veteran of the department's campaign for the Panama Canal treaties in the late 1970s, found time in a heavily committed schedule to meet personally with 57 congressmen and make four speeches on NAFTA, emphasizing the pact's salience to U.S. foreign policy objectives. So caught up was Christopher in the NAFTA enterprise that he phoned Gillespie at home on a Saturday evening, ten days before the 17 November vote, to underline the importance of checking back with House members originally placed in the "no" column.[371] All told, the State Department generated 214 speeches, 116 media interviews, visits by its representatives to 85 cities in 34 states, 63 briefings to members of Congress and the business community, and 21 visits by one or more lawmakers to Mexico. James R. Jones, the U.S. ambassador to Mexico who had spent 14 years in the House of Representatives and who had been approached by the White House to become the NAFTA czar, continually entertained, visited, phoned, or provided information to legislators in behalf of NAFTA. When some freshman members seemed apprehensive about visiting Mexico lest it appear that the trip would compromise their freedom of action, Jones conveyed the message: "I've been in your shoes and understand your feelings. I truly believe that your constituents will respect you for learning as much as possible, first-hand, about such an important issue."[372] When Representative John J. Lafalce (D-N.Y.) voiced concern for the professional and personal safety of Mexicans who had testified before his committee in opposition to NAFTA, the ambassador wrote him that "there is no reason to believe that the Mexican government, any more than our own, will look backward at who took what side in the debate instead of forward to implementation."[373] The overwhelming majority of legislators whom Jones briefed wound up voting for the pact. Even Democratic doyenne and fund-raiser *par excellence* Pamela Harriman, the multimillionairess who serves as ambassador to Paris, made calls to legislators urging support of NAFTA.

Daley's team also directed "hoopla" events in members' districts and in Washington to attract favorable publicity to NAFTA. President Clinton starred in the first pro-NAFTA production that Daley choreographed. This performance took place in the East Room of the White House on 14 September. On that date, the president signed the supplemental accords negotiated by the three countries. He delivered an impassioned speech—arguably, the best since his Inaugural Address—that promoted the NAFTA-cum-side deals, while dispelling allegations that he was a reluctant proponent of the pact. At the outset, Clinton conceded that NAFTA would be a "hard fight," but promised "to be there with all of you every step of the way." He then told how the post-World War II forging of "a system of global, expanded, freer trade . . . played a major role in creating the prosperity of the American middle class." Now, he admitted, most people were working harder for less, making them "vulnerable to the fear tactics and adverseness to change that is behind much of the opposition to NAFTA." "For two decades," he added,

> the winds of global competition have made these things clear to any American with eyes to see. The only way we can recover the fortunes of the middle class in this country so that people who work harder and smarter can at least prosper more, the only way we can pass on the American dream of the last 40 years to our children and

their children for the next 40 is to adapt to the changes which are occurring.

In addition to economic interests, the chief executive extolled NAFTA as "essential to our leadership in this hemisphere, in the world":

Having won the Cold War, we face the more subtle challenge of consolidating the victory of democracy and opportunity and freedom. For decades, we have preached and preached and preached greater democracy, greater respect for human rights, and more open markets for Latin America. NAFTA finally offers them the opportunity to reap the benefits of this.[374]

Joining Clinton at the elaborate ceremony were ex-Presidents George Bush, Gerald Ford, and Jimmy Carter. Reagan and Nixon, who had previously endorsed the accord, could not be present because of scheduling conflicts. Bush told the audience that NAFTA opponents were "taking the cheap and easy way out," and that if the free-trade package failed, "the biggest loser . . . would be the U.S." He repeated the assertion that the accord would institutionalize Salinas's economic and political reforms, thereby making Mexico a wealthier and more stable neighbor.[375] Ford agreed with Bush, adding that NAFTA would help stanch the flood of unlawful aliens entering the United States by generating new and better-paying jobs in Mexico. Carter took advantage of the occasion to excoriate Perot. Although never mentioning the mercurial Texas tycoon by name, the former president stated: "Unfortunately in our country now we have a demagogue who has unlimited resources and who is extremely careless with the truth, who is preying on the fears and the uncertainties of the American people."[376]

An audience of congressmen, governors, business executives, and present and former ranking executive-branch officials heartily cheered the presentations. "It was a revival, and I think NAFTA was born again today," said Representative J. J. Pickle (D-Tex.), an enthusiastic supporter of the agreement.[377] In the words of Barry Rogstad, president of the American Business Conference: "Those of us who support NAFTA cannot help but be impressed with the tone and quality of President Clinton's advocacy."[378] Daley and his cast of characters deserved multiple curtain calls for the show. Indeed, before the event, they worried that the signing of an Israeli-Palestinian peace accord in the Rose Garden on 13 September would upstage their event and diminish its interest for the media. As it turned out, the ex-presidents who had come to Washington for the Mideast ceremony agreed to stay over to take part in the NAFTA extravaganza.

Administration staff members working on health care might also have diverted media attention from the NAFTA event had not Rostenkowski intervened. When aides to Ms. Clinton asked him to bring the House Ways and Means Committee to the White House for a health-care briefing on 14 September, he exploded, "NAFTA is Billy's day," he told an acquaintance. "I'm not walking on it. Don't —— with Billy."[379]

Another major event brought "Great Americans for NAFTA" to Washington for a late October endorsement of the pact. This group included former secretaries of state, commerce, and treasury. Also present were all living American Novel laureates in economics. Men and women who agreed on little else demonstrated their support for the North American accord. The importance of this gathering was threefold. It attracted media attention. It also demonstrated to a wavering Congress and public that many of the nation's most respected individuals backed an ambitious role for their country in world affairs. Above all, the event showed the president that the establishment approved of his efforts in behalf of NAFTA. While at ease when backslapping and chitchatting with John and Jane Six-Pack in McDonalds and bowling alleys, the Georgetown- and Yale-educated former Rhodes Scholar also craves acceptance by the elite. The goal of this conclave was, in the words of one insider, "ensuring that Clinton, who had clearly signed on to the agreement, committed so much of his time to the pro-NAFTA campaign that the other guy [the opposition] would swerve first." "It became a game of chicken," he added, and Daley's efforts helped put the president behind the wheel, prepared to stake the presidency on the outcome of the contest.

Everyone seemed to admire the unassuming Daley, with the exception of union leaders who believed that he was working against labor's interests. Larry Penn, a retired Teamster-turned-songwriter, put this sentiment to music. He criticized the Chicagoan for abandoning his hometown roots to help Clinton push the free-trade pact through a reluctant Congress. Penn vented his rage in a song, "Won't You Come Home Bill Daley?" which became a hit at anti-NAFTA rallies around the Midwest. The lyrics begin:

> That NAFTA trade agreement
> Won't be fair
> Your daddy's rolling over in his grave
> Don't bring this shame, Baby,
> Down on your name, Baby
> Bill Daley, won't you please come home?[380]

Such ditties did not deter Daley from intensifying the vote search, as the president began preaching the merits of the accord like a Baptist minister exalting good works. Clinton took his message to ports, factory floors, business conventions, and university campuses. His return to a campaign mode energized the chief executive and enhanced his effectiveness. All told, he made 18 public appearances on behalf of the agreement. One of the few venues that he avoided was union halls. Clinton did not want to turn the NAFTA debate into a knock-down-drag-out contest between the White House and organized labor. He was mindful that powerful union chiefs could help him on health care and other issues and did accept an invitation to address the AFL-CIO's annual convention, held in San Francisco in early October. On that occasion, he believed that Lane Kirkland had agreed to disagree on NAFTA and that organized labor had pledged not to retaliate against lawmakers who voted for the continental pact. After all, despite their differences over free trade, Clinton had appointed a number of trade unionists to important positions.[381]

As the congressional vote neared, some labor officials sought to intimidate lawmakers. On 4 November, for example, the secretary-general of the San Francisco Labor Council of the AFL-CIO warned Representative Nancy Pelosi (D-Calif.) that her announced support for the agreement constituted "turncoat action." "Even though you are considered a safe district, we will not forget," wrote Walter Johnson. "Many other Democratic fence-riders do not have your assumed luxury. We intend to take this action against all Democrats who support this dastardly treaty."[382]

Clinton took advantage of a 7 November appearance on "Meet the Press" to express his anger at labor's intrusiveness. While acknowledging that the White House was about 30 votes short in the House of Representatives, he said that NAFTA's prospects had suffered because of "the vociferous, organized opposition of most of the unions telling these members [of Congress] in private they'll never give them any money again; they'll get them opponents in the primary." He condemned organized labor for "real rough-shod, muscle-bound tactics." He added that: "At least for the undecided Democrats, our big problem is the raw muscle, the sort of naked pressure that the labor forces have put on."[383]

AFL-CIO leaders flinched at his comments. Thomas R. Donahue, secretary-treasurer of the organization and the captain of the federation's anti-NAFTA drive, described the president's assertions as a "cheap shot." Claimed Donahue, "I think the Administration is behind right now in the vote and they're reaching desperately to get ahead."[384] Just as criticism of rapper Sister Souljah's hate lyrics had certified Clinton's independence of Jesse Jackson during the 1992 campaign, however, his "muscle-bound tactics" remark reinforced the president's image as a New Democrat willing to take issue with labor barons. Even more than political calculations, the remarks reflected Clinton's having been "riled" by the AFL-CIO's failure to keep its gentleman's agreement not to attack NAFTA's congressional supporters.

Gore-Perot Debate

Two days after the "Meet the Press" episode, another New Democrat clashed with a NAFTA opponent: Vice President Al Gore debated Ross Perot on "Larry King Live." Why did the White House risk a showdown with the feisty maverick, especially as the Harvard-educated Gore so often appeared more rigid and wooden than the Secret Service agents who protected him? Clinton explained the decision as an effort to counter the Texan's emotional appeal with a fact-based response. "Ross Perot is a master of the one-liner and the emotional retort," the president noted. "But I believe that the vice president has an unusual command of the facts and a real commitment, a profound commitment to this issue."[385] The more political answer was that the White House needed to energize the NAFTA debate; it was still two dozen or more votes short of the elusive 218 number needed for passage, and the Democrats had suffered stinging electoral defeats in New Jersey, Virginia, and New York City earlier in the month. Various ideas were floated to regain momentum. Bentsen, for example, suggested holding a televised North American "town meeting" at which Clinton and Salinas could field tough questions about the continental accord. Daley raised the possibility that former Chrysler President Lee Iacocca debate his friend Perot. Gore, whose office is next to the president's, dropped in and volunteered to debate the Texas billionaire. Without subjecting the proposal to analysis by Daley's team, Clinton embraced the idea—and proposed it to reporters one day while climbing out of his limousine. A confrontation with Perot, he believed, would demonstrate to wavering congressmen the administration's willingness to fight and take risks for a cause in which it believed. In addition, the debate would send an emphatic message to skittish Democrats: "They're not voting against NAFTA suddenly," said one official, "They're voting against Bill Clinton."[386] In responding to Perot's debate challenge, Daley and other presidential advisers were identifying opposition to NAFTA with an irascible, mercurial individual whose approval ratings had fallen from 47 percent in March to 30 percent at the time of the televised dust-up.[387] One national poll even reported that 51 percent of respondents found Perot "a little bit scary."[388] Organized labor and environmental foes of NAFTA deeply resented Perot's being selected to represent "their side," especially because he could not deliver a single vote in Congress.[389] The wisdom of a Gore-Perot confrontation eluded many observers. A Daley lieutenant in the trade room reported receiving dozens of phone calls from businessmen who exclaimed: "You guys are nuts; Perot is going to devour the vice president!"

210

Although viewers gained little new information about NAFTA during the 90-minute face-off, many saw Perot in a new light in the 11.2 million homes that received the program.[390] The Texan who had so often appeared avuncular, folksy, and likeable came across as crabby, churlish, and downright impolite. He alternated diatribes against NAFTA with a whining oratorio about being interrupted. Neither debater got all of his facts straight, but Perot seemed drawn to the absurd, such as claiming that all of Mexico's 80 million [sic] people lived in abject poverty and that American taxpayers would have to spend $55 billion to clean up the U.S.-Mexican border.[391] After railing against foreign-paid lobbyists, the billionaire equivocated on his having lobbied the Ways and Means Committee himself for preferential tax treatment in the mid-1970s.[392] Amid Perot's haranguing and heckling, the handsome, dapper vice president, who had prepared meticulously for the debate, never allowed himself to become flustered or shrill. At the beginning of the telecast, he gave Perot a framed picture of Representative Willis C. Hawley (R-Ore.) and Senator Reed O. Smoot (R-Utah), co-sponsors of the disastrous 1930 tariff act that bears their name. These crusty old men, with their clipped haircuts, sour-pickle countenances, and stodgy ideas, bore a striking resemblance to Perot. In contrast, Gore exuded youth, vigor, and the optimistic belief that America could excel in an ever more complex and competitive global economy.[393]

NAFTA's backers rejoiced at Gore's performance. "Hey, it's almost respectable to be for NAFTA," crowed Daley.[394] The debate "lower[ed] the fear factor" among House members worried about Perot's influence, said Stephanopoulos. It changed from "fear to a touch of embarrassment" to be aligned with the Texas populist, he added.[395] The polls validated these positive assessments. A *USA Today*/CNN survey indicated that 59 percent of viewers believed that Gore outperformed Perot, while only 22 percent of those interviewed awarded the contest to the Texan.[396] One week after the debate, a *Wall Street Journal*/NBC survey found that Americans favored NAFTA by a 36 to 31 percent margin (compared to 33 to 29 percent opposition the month before). Even more important, 11 percent of the respondents said they had changed their mind in the past few weeks—with 71 percent of those expressing support for the pact. Of respondents interviewed who had seen the entire Gore-Perot donnybrook, 50 percent stated a preference for NAFTA.[397] These figures helped to move undecided lawmakers toward the NAFTA camp. The debate also calmed jittery Mexican financial markets as the *Bolsa* jumped 81 points following Gore's strong showing.[398] As journalist Sidney Blumenthal wrote: "A house had landed on the Wicked Witch, and the Munchkins nervously came out of hiding: more than thirty representatives endorsed NAFTA the following week."[399]

The Clinton-Gingrich Show

Richardson and Matsui did yeoman's work among their colleagues; however, the aggressive anti-NAFTA efforts of Gephardt and Bonior persuaded Daley and his Capitol Hill allies of the importance of maximizing the number of Republican votes. At first, some Republican leaders were reluctant to activate their rank-and-file on behalf of the trade pact. They knew that Clinton, who had pushed through his budget package in a highly partisan manner, was losing ground with the public. Why should the GOP do any favors for a floundering president who seemed unable to deliver a critical mass of Democratic votes? By going out on a limb on an apparently doomed issue, reasoned many Republican strategists, they would only incur the wrath of Perot's "United We Stand America" movement, most of whose members had supported Reagan and Bush in the 1980s. "What the hell to we get out of this except the good government award?" asked one GOP notable.[400]

Democrats could count on House Minority Leader Michel to recruit GOP support for NAFTA because of his moderation and past involvement in bipartisan ventures. Skeptics, however, worried that Minority Whip Newt Gingrich, a skilled and acidic Democrat-basher, might try to sabotage the free-trade plan. Following the 1992 Democratic Convention, the sharp-tongued Georgian had compared the Democratic platform plank on family matters to Woody Allen's lifestyle, adding that Clinton himself "has a deep psychological need to pander to the worst instincts of whatever group he's in front of."[401] Was it possible that Gingrich might round up sufficient commitments to ensure a respectable Republican showing, but without just enough of his colleagues' votes to deny Clinton a victory?[402] Ex-congressman Frenzel, who was in constant contact with GOP lawmakers, assured Daley and the White House of Gingrich's loyalty to the cause.

Although committed to the fight, Gingrich proved a prickly ally of the pro-NAFTA movement. He, for example, repeatedly goaded the president to get involved personally in the NAFTA campaign. As late as October 1993, he described the administration's push for the pact as "pathetic,"[403] even though Daley and Clinton were, by then, accelerating their efforts.

Soon after uttering this barb, for which he later apologized, Gingrich began to see the chief executive's actions match the impressive rhetoric of the East Room speech. The turning point in the Republican leader's recruitment of NAFTA votes was the president's "Meet the Press" denunciation of organized labor. "It said to a lot of our guys that, if he's going to take that kind of a risk in taking on labor unions, how can I turn my back on him?" said Gingrich.[404]

The Gore-Perot debate provided additional cover to GOP lawmakers who had feared that the Texas billionaire would work to unseat them in 1994. In the course of an hour-and-a-half, Perot's image evolved from political powerhouse to petulant bully. Although Gingrich believed that both he and the administration should each round up 110 votes for the pact, everyone knew that the Democrats would be hard-pressed to muster 100 votes—and that the Republicans would have to come up with 120 to achieve success. "He's working hard," said Stephanopoulos of Gingrich several days before the vote. "He's putting in the hours. He's making the calls."[405] In addition to advancing free trade, Gingrich wanted to show that he could cooperate effectively in a bipartisan context.

Clinton complemented public appearances with active lobbying. First he made three telephone calls a day to undecided congressmen, then he began inviting groups of lawmakers to the White House for lunch and dinner, and finally, he started cutting deals to pull NAFTA opponents and fence-sitters to his side. He paid particular attention to the Florida delegation, most of whose 26 members remained undecided until the eleventh hour. A key element in gaining half of their votes was the administration's pledge to safeguard producers of sugar, citrus, tomatoes, asparagus, and sweet peppers as tariffs with Mexico were gradually eliminated.[406] In addition, the White House attracted ten votes from Southern textile-producing states by agreeing to phase out over 15 years, instead of 10, textile import quotas with the Philippines and some other developing nations.[407] Also negotiated were concessions involving flat glass, durum wheat, home appliances, wine, and peanuts, appeasing Democrats and Republicans in a variety of states.[408] Perhaps the most unusual request the administration received came from Representative Clay Shaw (R-Fla.). He sought not protection for specialty produce but the Mexican government's commitment to arrest and extradite a Mexican accused of sexually abusing the young niece of the congressman's secretary. President Salinas personally talked with Shaw by telephone to assure him that the requested action would be taken.[409] The pro-NAFTA forces garnered the five commitments that "put us over the top" at 1:30 p.m. on the day of the vote, according to an on-the-scene administration official who asked not to be named. He was referring to five Georgia congressmen, who sought protection for their state's peanut producers. "You might say," the official added tongue-in-cheek, "that we got the free-trade pact for peanuts."

One disappointment for Clinton administration horse traders was Esteban E. Torres (D-Calif.). A former official of the United Auto Workers and a prominent member of the Hispanic Caucus, Torres intimated that he could deliver between eight and 12 votes besides his own if a binational North America Development Bank were established to cushion the impact of the accord on workers and communities. Clinton phoned the legislator to say that he liked the idea. Bentsen set aides to work ironing out the details. Kantor, Reich, and Tyson also got involved. Yet Torres stood alone in the well of the House to announce his support, leading one House Democrat to quip "one man, one bank."[410] What Torres did not know was that a financial institution would have been created with or without his backing of the pact. Daley simply repackaged the institution and gave Torres credit for it in order to nail down his vote.

Throughout the weeks of intense lobbying, Daley's trade room had better intelligence about vote shifts than his adversaries. This accuracy sprang from a bipartisan whip system employed by NAFTA's advocates. Specifically, Richardson and Gingrich continually shared information and kept each other abreast of members' preferences. In contrast, NAFTA's foes relied upon separate Democratic and Republican nose-counting operations. After all, the extremely partisan Bonior, who was mobilizing anti-pact votes among Democrats, was his party's whip. As such, he could not bring himself to divulge information about individual Democratic lawmakers to the GOP. In the same vein, he did not scrutinize the figures furnished by Duncan Hunter (R-Calif.), who was rounding up Republican votes and keeping track of his colleagues' preferences. Throughout the process, Bonior's estimates were quite accurate, but those of the aggressive and impulsive Hunter were overly optimistic. Relying on Hunter's numbers, Bonior even announced in early November that his side was within several votes of winning. That the conservative California Republican's erroneous counts lulled the NAFTA opposition into a false sense of security may have cost them the victory that they believed was in the bag.

NAFTA's foes excoriated Clinton's vote-swapping actions. "They have practically given away the family silver," huffed Representative Olympia Snowe (R-Me.).[411] As indicated in table 10, two researchers tentatively concluded that the White House conferred almost $2 billion-worth of benefits on NAFTA supporters. In response to such "payoffs," Ralph Nader set up a "NAFTA Pork Patrol" to calculate the exact cost of these concessions to U.S. taxpayers.[412] The dispense of such largess infuriated organized labor. "Amid all the planes, trains and bridges and the protections for citrus, peanuts, sugar and wheat," AFL-CIO leader Kirkland said, "there was not one word about the right of workers on both sides of the border to obtain decent wages and safe working conditions or to defend themselves from gross exploitation."[413]

TABLE 10

ALLEGED BENEFITS CONFERRED BY THE CLINTON ADMINISTRATION ON NAFTA SUPPORTERS

Legislator	Project	Cost	Comment
Rep. E. B. Johnson (D-Tex.)	Construction of two C-17 military cargo planes	$1.4 billion	C-17 has a history of technical failure, including doors opening during test flights and wings buckling.
Rep. J. J. Pickle (D-Tex.)	Promise to locate Center for the Study of Trade in the Western Hemisphere in his district	$10 million	
Rep. Glenn English (D-Okla.) Rep. Bill Brewster (D-Okla.) Rep. Bill Sarpalius (D-Tex.) Rep. Larry Combest (R-Tex.)	Limits on Canadian shipments of durum wheat, used to make pasta		Unless Canada cuts back on its own wheat subsidies.
Rep. E. Clay Shaw (R-Fla.)	Administration pressure on Mexico to extradite a man suspected of raping Shaw's assistant's niece		
Rep. Esteban Torres (D-Calif.) Rep. Xavier Becerra (D-Calif.) Rep. Nancy Pelosi (D-Calif.) Rep. Lucille Roybal-Allard (D-Calif.) Rep. Ed Pastor (D-Ariz.) Rep. John Bryant (D-Tex.)	Funding the North American Development Bank intended for infrastructure projects	$250 million	No money was allocated for toxic cleanup, as originally claimed.
Rep. David Price (D-N.C.) Rep. Tim Valentine (D-N.C.) Rep. Bob Clement (D-Tenn.)	Awarding to American Airlines two international air routes to London		This airline serves major cities in their states.

TABLE 10

(Continued)

Legislator	Project	Cost	Comment
Rep. Bob. Smith (R-Ore.) Rep. Joel Hefley (R-Colo.) Rep. Wayne Allard (R-Colo.) Rep. Bob Stump (R-Ariz.)	Plan to raise grazing fees on federal lands abandoned by administration		Resulted in loss of millions of dollars for the federal treasury.
Rep. Lewis Payne (D-Va.)	Payne's district to be considered a potential site for the National Institute of Standards and Technology.	$500,000 to $3 million	Clinton's written promise to consider Payne's district as the site.
Rep. Fred Grandy (R-Ia.) Rep. Neal Smith (D-Ia.)	Administration pressure on Mexico to hasten tariff reduction on appliances		Move would benefit Iowa-based firms such as Amana and Maytag.
Rep. Porter Goss (R-Fla.) Rep. Dan Miller (R-Fla.) Rep. Tom Lewis (R-Fla.) Rep. Harry Johnston (D-Fla.) Rep. Jim Bacchus (D-Fla.) Rep. Carrie Meek (D-Fla.) Rep. Alcee Hastings (D-Fla.) Rep. Earl Hutto (D-Fla.) Rep. Tillie Fowler (R-Fla.) Rep. William Jefferson (D-La.)	Completion of agricultural research center in Ft. Pierce, Florida; and special protection for Louisiana and Florida citrus, sugar, and vegetable producers	$16 million	According to GAO, the sugar deal alone will cost consumers $1.4 billion annually.
Rep. Thomas Ewing (R-Ill.) Rep. Jennifer Dunn (R-Wash.) Rep. Ron Packard (R-Calif.) Rep. Sam Johnson (R-Tex.) Rep. Dennis Hastert (D-Ill.) Rep. Wayne Allard (R-Colo.)	Reduction of Clinton's proposed new taxes on airline and cruise ship passenger fares that were to fund retraining for workers displaced by NAFTA		Ewing suggested cutting food stamps instead to pay for retraining.

217

TABLE 10

(Continued)

Legislator	Project	Cost	Comment
Rep. J. Roy Rowland (D-Ga.)	Administration agreement to negotiate limits on peanut butter imports from Canada.		
Rep. John Spratt (D-S.C.), Rep. W.G. Hefner (D-N.C.), Rep. Nathan Deal (D-Ga.)	Additional funding for U.S. Customs to enforce laws on textile imports	$15 million	Administration pledge to push for five additional years of protection for U.S. textiles textiles at the GATT talks.
Rep. Bill Sarpalius (D-Tex.)	Reversal of Clinton's earlier recommendation to cut helium subsidies	$47 million	
Rep. Norman Mineta (D-Calif.)	Administration promise to protect cut-flower industry		
Rep. Martin Frost (D-Tex.)	Government pledge to protect glass producers		
Rep. Peter Hoekstra (R-Mich.)	Administration promise to protect Michigan asparagus growers		
Rep. Benjamin L. Cardin (D-Md.)	Administration pressure on Canadian government to diminish subsidies for a Quebec chemical plant		
Rep. David Hobson (R-Oh.)	Special protection for flat glass and broomcorn, produced in his district		

Source: Sarah Anderson and Ken Silverstein, *The Nation*, 20 December 1993, 752–753.

The Showdown Vote[414]

The House passed NAFTA 234 to 200 on 17 November 1993, while the Senate approved the pact, 61 to 38, three days later. In the House, three of four GOP members supported the accord (132) compared to four of ten Democrats (102). Groups that backed the legislation included three of four Asian-American members (75 percent), 64 of 91 representatives from states that border Mexico (70.3 percent), and nine of 15 members of the Hispanic Caucus (60 percent). Members who were serving their second through ninth terms favored NAFTA 58.8 percent to 41.2 percent. Of the 172 fast-track advocates still in office, 142 (82.6 percent) supported NAFTA, while 30 (17.4 percent) opposed it. On average, NAFTA supporters were slightly older (52.5 years) than opponents (51.8 years). Geographically, NAFTA garnered support from 140 of the 256 congressmen from coastal states, including Hawaii and Alaska (54.7 percent). Support was disproportionately strong in the Sun Belt, Rocky Mountain, and Pacific regions.

In addition to a majority of Democrats, NAFTA House opponents included 31 of 37 Congressional Black Caucus members (83.8 percent), 27 of 46 female representatives (58.7 percent), 61 of 114 freshmen (53.5 percent),[415] and 33 of 63 men and women serving 10 terms or more (52.4 percent). Unsurprisingly, 70.9 percent of the 134 representatives who had received more than $40,000 per year from labor PACs between 1 January 1983 and 30 June 1993 opposed the accord.[416] Also predictable was the strong opposition to NAFTA in the Northeast, Middle Atlantic, and the Midwest regions. Slightly more than six of every ten (61.9 percent) representatives from states bordering Canada voted against NAFTA.

More GOP senators (34) favored NAFTA than did Democrats (27)—with Dorgan (D-N.D.) not voting. NAFTA attracted the support of six of eight senators from states bordering Mexico (75 percent), four of seven female senators (57 percent), the only African-American (Carol Moseley-Braun from Daley's Illinois), 28 of 46 senators from coastal states (60.9 percent), and a majority of members in each tenure classification from freshmen (51.7 percent) to second-termers (66.7 percent) to those serving four or more terms (60 percent).[417] Pro-NAFTA senators were, on average, younger (56.7 years) than opponents (59.8 years). Like their House counterparts, senators from the Sun Belt and Mountain regions lined up behind NAFTA. In contrast to their House counterparts, however, senators from the Northeast overwhelmingly voted for the accord.

In addition to Democrats, Senate opponents included the two Asian-Americans (themselves Democrats), and a majority of lawmakers from the Middle Atlantic, Midwest, and Pacific regions. Also, 60.9 percent of senators from states bordering Canada voted "nay" on NAFTA.

Of the 51 members who endorsed fast track in May 1991 and were still in the Senate, 42 backed the continental pact (82.4 percent), while nine (17.6 percent) opposed it.

Conclusion

After a protracted, bitter fight, the forces of international engagement emerged victorious. Perhaps the only consolation for the losers was that any signatory to NAFTA could withdraw from the accord after giving six months notice. In theory, therefore, should the Mexicans prove unworthy economic allies, Washington could pull out of the pact. In fact, the NAFTA-impelled acceleration of North American economic integration made future U.S. disengagement from the compact nothing more than a will-o'-the-wisp for foes of the agreement.

Clinton was both the hero and villain of the NAFTA saga. Daley won few if any votes for the pact. Yet, thanks to the Chicagoan's organizational prowess, NAFTA finally loomed large on the presidential radar screen. It grew brighter and clearer despite efforts to diminish the pact's salience by Ms. Clinton's health care team and the consultants. They seemed oblivious to the fact that a congressional victory on the trade agreement would enhance the White House's influence on Capitol Hill and, possibly, pave the way for triumphs on social issues. At the eleventh hour, the president brilliantly spearheaded a campaign to save both the trade venture and the credibility of his administration. If, however, he had known what he wanted and faithfully communicated his intentions with respect to the trilateral agreement early in 1993, NAFTA's foes would neither have managed to frame the terms of the debate nor win so many supporters on Capitol Hill. An early articulation of presidential goals, as recommended by Neustadt, would also have militated against organized labor's concluding that victory was a near certainty. This belief, when shattered, gave rise to the need for herculean fence-mending by the White House to keep a core Democratic constituency enthusiastically in the fold for the 1994 and 1996 national elections.[418]

CHAPTER TEN

NAFTA as a Defining Event

Introduction

It would be naive to suggest that NAFTA's passage rivals the defeat of the Versailles Treaty or adherence to the U.N. Charter in shaping the United States's long-term, overarching definition of its international role. The issues then and now are simply different. Then the fundamental question was posed starkly: return to isolation, or accept a radically new and open-ended role on the world stage. From this perspective, NAFTA was a minor event. With or without the free-trade initiative, Washington would remain enmeshed in world affairs. Regardless of congressional action, presidents would continue to involve themselves in global matters for strategic, institutional, political, and personal reasons. The United States would also remain a party to thousands of commitments abroad through treaties, executive agreements, and memberships in international organizations—engagements that can be liquidated only at unacceptable costs. U.S.-based NGOs, multinational corporations, and private citizens would continue to forge ever more intimate and effective transnational alliances.

Yet, viewed from the perspective of future generations, the adoption of NAFTA is likely to appear as an act every bit as consequential for America's sense of its place in the world as earlier contests over the League and the United Nations. No mere trade agreement, the NAFTA accord proposes to establish a funda-

223

mentally new agenda in this nation's foreign relations; indeed, it has blurred the distinction between "foreign" and "domestic" policy almost beyond meaning. Looming behind the technical arcana, the esoteric compromise formulas, and complex administrative guidelines embedded in the final document's 2,000 pages is a project that impels the integration of the North American continent, beginning with economic systems.

Unlike traditional alliances in which nations trade mutual pledges to make common cause in the event of war, so that each may preserve its own autonomy and national identity, the North American Free Trade Agreement has as its inevitable consequence (if not its stated objective) a revision of traditional definitions of nationhood. In effect, it replaces the traditional bonds of citizen and state in Canada, Mexico, and the United States with a new continental social contract. Without erecting a new Leviathan, the pact expands the boundaries of mutual obligation and redefines economic, social, and even political expectations in all three societies.

At the same time, the NAFTA debate has transformed political awareness in this country about the impact of trade with the world beyond North America. By the 1990s, the world economy had evolved toward a degree of openness—with consequences for everyday life scarcely imagined by the architects of the post-World War II international economic order. Today, the cost of mortgages, the security of industrial jobs, wage rates at local factories, and health and occupational standards are all affected by powerful forces beyond the capacity of any state *alone* to control. Innovative forms of social organization—more than 40 percent of world trade now takes place within the *same* multinational enterprises—new technologies, and a growing awareness of ecological and social linkages across national boundaries have begun to reconfigure the relations of societies. By confirming the role of trade negotiations in restructuring or adjusting to these new facts, the NAFTA agreement broke the mold of international trade discussions and guaranteed that any future negotiations would be viewed and reviewed by an increasing broad array of social actors. It raised new standards of political accountability while leaving uncertain the capacities of governments to direct or channel the market forces unleashed.

APEC and the Uruguay Round

It would be foolhardy to predict what course global market relations will take during the next decade, just as it would have been impossible to predict developments in Europe after the defeat of the Versailles Treaty or the onset of the Cold War after the adoption of the U.N. Charter. In the short run, however, it is clear that the NAFTA vote in the U.S. Congress bristled with political consequences, not the least of which was that the rejection of the accord would have constituted a virtual "no confidence" vote on the new Democratic administration, imperiling its subsequent legislative initiatives. As it turned out, the NAFTA outcome enhanced Clinton's credibility when he met with 14 leaders from Pacific Rim countries two days after the House vote. The occasion was a Seattle gathering of the Asian Pacific Economic Cooperation forum (APEC), an informal grouping that links the United States, Canada, Australia, and New Zealand to 11 Asian nations. Mexico joined APEC at the late 1993 meeting; Chile was the next country to affiliate.

This was the biggest summit of Asian and Pacific officials since 1966, when President Johnson invited regional leaders to Manila to drum up support for the escalating war in Vietnam. Although the balance of trade, not the balance of power, dominated the 1993 agenda, Clinton emphasized the interrelationship of security and economics, which is the trademark of his administration. "Our place in the world will be determined as much by the skills of our workers as by the strength of our weapons," he asserted, "as much by our ability to pull down foreign trade barriers as our ability to breach distant ramparts."[419] In keeping with the guns-and-butter analogy, the *New York Times* suggested that withdrawing trading privileges, such as most-favored-nation status,[420] constituted the nuclear bomb of the 1990s—"a weapon so fearful that no one dares to actually detonate it."[421]

In what one observer called "the biggest rethinking of American policy toward Asia since the days of General Douglas MacArthur,"[422] Clinton sought to lay the foundation for an "Asian-Pacific community." In his view, these nations could work together to combat protectionism, expand trade, and create high-tech jobs. Taking a leaf from the NAFTA debate, he also stressed the political dimensions of community and endeavored to promote human rights and discourage missile proliferation.

Yet the Asian-Pacific nations appeared reluctant to convert the amorphous consultative body into a structured organization, one with free-trade zones, dispute resolution procedures for its members, and uniform investment criteria. In the words of Lee Hong Koo, a former South Korean ambassador and cabinet member, "There is no legacy of communal fellowship in Asia-Pacific. . . . It is much more of a Wild West situation where you have to persuade each country to come along on each issue."[423]

Although he compared the Seattle meeting to early sessions of the North Atlantic Treaty Organization, Secretary Christopher was the first to admit both the absence of a "common enemy" and uncertainty about what "the common economic objective should be."[424] Many countries welcomed the United States as a counterpoise to China and Japan, but they feared that Washington might seek to dominate a more closely knit organization, while attempting to draw its members into security or commercial arrangements that might harm their trading relations elsewhere or among themselves.[425] Officials from China and Indonesia, where political suppression abounds, worried that along with growing commerce the United States would press for improved human rights. For these reasons, Japan's foreign minister, Tsutomo Hata, told reporters that APEC should evolve through "incremental gradualism by consensus."[426]

The White House was encouraged, nonetheless, by the "vision statement"—a largely rhetorical communiqué—issued by the leaders at the close of the meeting. "In this post-Cold-War era, we have an opportunity to build a new economic foundation for the Asia-Pacific that harnesses the energy of our diverse economies, strengthens cooperation and promotes prosperity," the document proclaimed. "Our meeting reflects the emergence of a new voice for the Asia-

Pacific in world affairs."[427]   The leaders also agreed to reduce tariffs on a number of manufactured and agricultural items at the GATT negotiations to spur conclusion of the Uruguay Round.

The Seattle session symbolized the increased economic importance to the United States of the Pacific Rim compared to Western Europe. U.S. exports to APEC members total $128 billion annually, accounting for 5.3 million American jobs, versus $102 billion in sales to Europe and 4.2 million jobs. The addition of Mexico to APEC meant that the three NAFTA members now belonged to an increasingly important organization whose members produce half of the world's output of goods and services.[428]   As in the NAFTA debate, Clinton used the Seattle meeting to alert Americans to the importance of foreign markets for economic growth and the creation of new jobs at home. As the president told workers at the Boeing Corporation on the eve of the conference, "Make no mistake about it, ultimately this meeting is about the jobs and futures and incomes of the American people."[429]

The NAFTA victory, followed by the APEC conference, impelled the conclusion of the Uruguay Round in mid-December 1993—with the official signing accomplished in Marrakech, Morocco, on 15 April 1994. "There is no negotiator in Geneva who isn't breathing a sigh of relief," stated Peter Sutherland, director-general of GATT. Upon hearing of NAFTA's passage, Brazilian representative Luiz Felipe Palmeira Lamreia agreed, saying "NAFTA, this vote against protectionism, has opened the road to ending the Uruguay Round." Added John Schmidt, a U.S. negotiator in Geneva, "It's terrific. . . . This removes a cloud" over GATT.[430]

Other factors contributed to the completion of the sluggish multilateral trade talks that by late 1993 had lasted seven years and attracted 116 countries to the negotiating table. To begin with, France and other European countries looked to expanded exports to uplift their recession-mired economies. In fact, the Organization for Economic Cooperation and Development—a group of 24 leading industrial nations that seeks to expand economic growth, stimulate world trade, and coordinate aid to poorer states—had estimated that a broad deal in Geneva could add $270 billion to the $30 trillion world economy by the year 2002.[431]   Similarly, the United States was anxious for a trade accord to provide momentum to its own uncertain economic recovery. Without NAFTA's approval, however, it is doubtful that the Europeans would have made the concessions necessary to conclude the GATT talks since it established the credibility of the Democratic administration to obtain trade concessions from the legislative branch. "If Clinton can't get a highly favorable three-way deal through Congress," they would have reasoned, "why should we lock horns with powerful domestic interests only to see our agreement eviscerated in Washington?" The fact that the GATT negotiations had ground to a virtual halt during the three weeks before the vote on the continental pact only to resume with momentum after 17 November supports the conclusion that NAFTA's passage was crucial to the success of the Uruguay Round.[432]

The most significant multilateral trade talks ever conducted, the Uruguay Round achieved several important goals. It accomplished a 40 percent cut in industrial tariffs, strengthened protection of intellectual property, and designed new procedures to govern the "dumping" of goods at "unfairly" low prices. In addition, the negotiators phased out 30-year-old textile quotas, brought services under GATT disciplines, and reduced agricultural subsidies, albeit not as much as many farmers outsider Europe had hoped. Also created was a World Trade Organization (WTO), with greater power to resolve trade disputes than the 46-year-old GATT whose decisions could be vetoed by individual members.

The NAFTA triumph enhanced the likelihood that Congress would approve the GATT deal, which too was considered under fast-track authority. The AFL-CIO and environmental organizations voiced opposition to the Uruguay Round accord, as did management and workers in the film and textile industries. And on the new antidumping rules, Gephardt said, "I have worries that the thing won't work right."[433] The majority leader also fretted about how to find the $12 billion in new revenue or spending cuts over five years to compensate for lost tariff income. Still, in the NAFTA struggle Clinton had shown his mettle in moving vital legislation through the legislative obstacle course by forging a bilateral coalition—a lesson that, inexplicably, he had to relearn in August 1994 to obtain passage of a controversial crime bill. Predictably, Bonior opposed the multinational agreement, but Gephardt ultimately endorsed the Geneva agreement, and most key lawmakers followed suit. They did not relish another protracted and divisive fight over a trade bill, especially when the stakes for economic growth were so high. "It'll pass because it'll just be unthinkable if it doesn't," stated Florida's Sam Gibbons, who replaced the indicted Rostenkowski as chairman of the Ways and Means Committee.[434] Besides, the GATT negotiators had postponed action on aircraft subsidies, maritime industries, and telecommunications that might have sparked disputes on Capitol Hill. Most of the controversy surrounding the Uruguay Round focused not on its substance but on ancillary matters that might be included in its implementing legislation—e.g., renewing fast track, granting Caribbean countries equal status with Mexico on apparel imports, and expanding the General System of Preferences under which the United States allows the duty-free importation of non-sensitive items from less-developed countries.

Nevertheless, the proposed WTO did give some lawmakers heartburn. NAFTA champion Newt Gingrich initially sought to alter or defeat the GATT accord because, he complained, it would sacrifice U.S. sovereignty and invest small countries with too much power. "If you look at the mess in Bosnia and the U.N.'s incompetence, this World Trade Organization will have 117 members with one vote each. So, in effect, we could be outvoted by Antigua or by Botswana or by Venezuela," he told interviewers on NBC's "Meet the Press."[435] In response, Jagdish Bhagwati, a Columbia University expert on international commerce, said: "We have so many tools" to apply to small countries to make them see our way on trade. "It's a crazy notion" that the United States would be pushed around.[436] Kantor, who talked to the Republican Whip at length, believed that legislators would approve the GATT agreement—especially because in 1988 Congress had directed USTR negotiators to find a tough way to resolve disputes. Elements of a possible compromise that had emerged by late summer 1994 included periodic review of WTO membership and explicit limitations on negotiating trade agreements that authorize sanctions, such as those found in the NAFTA side deals, for violations of environmental and worker rights laws.

Future Trade Deals

NAFTA's impact on APEC and the Uruguay Round was essentially psychological, but the continental accord did set a practical, new standard for future trade negotiations. NAFTA, as the most modern and inclusive trade deal ever signed by the United States, ensured that issues such as services, government procurement, and dispute resolution for investors would figure prominently on the agenda of prospective bilateral and multilateral talks.

Even more novel was the free-trade agreement's attention to environmental and labor protection. Before NAFTA, it was an article of faith among U.S. trade specialists that environmental questions should be kept separate from trade talks. Carla Hills reluctantly made concessions to environmentalists only to mobilize enough votes to gain fast-track authorization. Among the federal agencies that applauded this action were the Environmental Protection Agency, the Interior Department, the Commerce Department's National Oceanic and Atmospheric Administration, and the State Department's Bureau of Oceans, Environment, and Science. Kantor overcame remaining bureaucratic opposition to insist on an environmental side deal that achieved many of the goals of the National Wildlife Federation, the Natural Resources Defense Council, and other constructive engagers. In return, the moderate environmental organizations lobbied hard in behalf of the North American pact, boosting their stock with USTR and the White House.

The influence of environmentalists emerged too late to have a significant impact on the Uruguay Round. Kantor, for instance, failed to have a Trade and Environmental Working Group embedded in the WTO, which will become effective 1 January 1995, if approved by the signatories. Still, Kantor pledged to do everything possible to make the WTO ecologically sensitive. And the environmentally enlightened Salinas is a candidate to head the new organization. Even though the imposition of NAFTA-related sanctions remains anathema to conservative lawmakers and many big businesses, the environment will receive significant attention in future negotiations, and environmentalists will be part of the bargaining process through advisory bodies and other unambiguous

230

channels specified by the USTR. In addition, the North American accord made it clear that international agreements will not be allowed to compromise U.S. federal and state environmental laws, as long as these statutes have a demonstrable scientific basis.

Future negotiations will also extend to worker rights. As one U.S. Department of Labor official said, "The labor genie is out of the bottle." The next set of trade talks will certainly embrace the minimum wage, child labor, and workplace safety standards that NAFTA introduced. When the AFL-CIO decides to advance rather than obstruct negotiations, pressures will mount in Washington to add gender discrimination, freedom of association, collective bargaining rights, and other sensitive issues to the agenda of future talks. Once environmental and labor issues are on the table, interest groups are certain to urge that the elimination of trade barriers be conditioned on respect for political and human rights. In fact, this thorny question has confronted both the Bush and Clinton administrations as they have weighed continuing most-favored-nation (MFN) treatment for China. Although a politically charged issue in negotiations, noncommercial factors will not necessarily prevail. In late May 1994, for instance, Clinton granted MFN status to the Beijing regime. This action indicated that, as in NAFTA, the greater national interest lay in promoting trade, even as Washington would continue to encourage China to improve its woefully deficient human rights record.

Enterprise for the Americas Initiative[437]

The United States's European and Asian trading partners together account for more than half of its international commerce, and so it was to be expected that NAFTA would influence negotiations with these economically powerful states. Less predictable was the agreement's impact on the Western Hemisphere.

Just as Clinton inherited NAFTA from his predecessor, he also received the Enterprise for the Americas Initiative (EAI). While the groundwork was being laid for the North American pact, Bush wanted to assure other hemispheric nations that despite NAFTA and the end of the Cold War, Washington was intently concerned about their fate. He was especially anxious to communicate this message because in the 1980s most countries of the region rejected military regimes in favor of civilian governments, while many adopted market-oriented reforms of the type advanced by Salinas.

Although pleased by these new economic currents, President Bush still saw a threat emanating from the region. He viewed the Latin America of the 1990s not as an incubator of communism but as the source of illegal aliens, capital flight, and narcotics, sometimes pushed by General Manuel Antonio Noriega and other despots. Yet Washington had no coherent policy toward this area, other than dispatching U.S. troops, pouring in aid, or intervening by proxy with the contras in Nicaragua. Bush came away from a February 1990 drug summit with the chief executives of three Andean nations convinced that the United States had to review its approach to Latin America—a point that he emphasized to several Cabinet members, especially Treasury Secretary Brady. Several months before, Georges A. Fauriol, director of Latin American studies at the Center for Strategic and International Studies in Washington, emphasized the absence of a strategic framework for the region in a widely noted *Foreign Affairs* article that Treasury Department officials believe captured the attention of the National Security Council staff and other presidential advisers. "Attempts to put Latin American affairs on the back burner had by the last quarter of 1989," wrote Fauriol, "stumbled predictably over the renewal of violence in El Salvador, the end of the cease-fire in Nicaragua, the October coup attempt in Panama and subsequent U.S. military operations, a far from complete regional debt agenda and a strong Latin American drug connection."[438] Meanwhile, Luigi Einaudi, U.S. ambassador to the Organization of American States (OAS), invited Carla Hills to address the issue of hemispheric free trade at the centennial meeting of the OAS General Assembly, held in early June in Asunción, Paraguay.

Whether Fauriol's article made an impact at the White House is unclear, but the EAI certainly responded to the analyst's call for "a serious and welcome reassessment of hemispheric policy." As usual, the review began with an interagency task force, created under the auspices of the NSC. Next, Treasury Secretary Brady, chairman of the Economic Policy Committee (EPC), established a Working Group on U.S. Economic Policy toward Latin America. This 15- to 20-member interagency body, headed by David Mulford, under-secretary of the treasury for international affairs, developed the main elements of a new policy toward the region. On 23 May 1990, it recommended to the president a "Partnership of the Americas" initiative that focused on liberalizing trade, promoting private investment, reducing debt, and eliminating barriers to services, goods, and capital. Also proposed was the convening of a summit with a limited number of heads of state. Treasury, USTR, and Commerce insisted that any free-trade agreements with the United States that might emerge under the new policy must be rewards for a Latin American country's having accomplished substantial economic changes, not—as advocated by some State Department officials—a pat on the back for mere promises to reform highly protected, statist economies. With respect to FTAs, the various agencies agreed that (1) none would be signed, except possibly with Mexico, until after termination of the Uruguay Round, although preliminary talks might take place sooner, (2) such agreements would complement liberalization accomplished under the Round and be "GATT consistent," (3) efforts at economic integration should lower, not raise, the external tariff of the nations involved, and (4) the agreements should impose no cost on the U.S. budget.

The presidential speech embracing the new U.S. policy was drafted by Treasury Department officials under Mulford's direction. Roger Porter, a White House domestic and economic policy adviser, contributed to the final version.[439] Although vetted by senior administration officials, the speech was not widely circulated before its delivery. The Export-Import Bank and the Department of Agriculture, for example, had no chance to modify its debt-reduction provisions that affected them. The USTR, which would have to negotiate FTAs, was presented with a virtual fait accompli; the trade agency did get, however, safety-valve language inserted that free-trade agreements would be pursued with "groups of countries" that offered "significant markets" to American exporters. The EPA administrator was not informed of the environmental aspects of the plan until the night before its delivery. After White House speech writers renamed the program the Enterprise for the Americas Initiative (because Partnership for the Americas sounded too much like a Democratic scheme), Bush unveiled the Initiative on 27 June 1990. The programmatic edifice rested on three pillars: investment reform, debt reduction, and trade liberalization.

The chief executive proposed to improve the posture of Latin American nations in the "fierce" competition for investment capital by helping them "clear away the thicket of bureaucratic barriers" that discouraged domestic and foreign entrepreneurs. "In one large Latin city," he noted, "it takes almost 300 days to cut through the red tape to open a small garment shop."[440] Specifically, he endorsed the formation, within the Inter-American Development Bank, of a $300 million fund to improve the investment climate in nations willing to implement reforms congenial to private enterprise. In 1992 the U.S. Congress contributed $100 million to this authority, which will seek annual matching grants from Europe and Japan.

Bush argued that a favorable investment climate was inextricably bound to debt relief in a region that owed more than $420 billion to public and private financial agencies. The Brady Plan, he said, had reduced commercial bank obligations in Mexico, Costa Rica, and Venezuela; still, many countries staggered under the weight of debt held by governments rather than private institutions. He thus proposed "a major new initiative to reduce Latin America's and the Caribbean's official debt to the United States for countries that adopt strong economic and investment reform programs with the support of international institutions."[441] At the centerpiece of this plan lay forgiveness of concessional debt arising from foreign aid or food-for-peace accounts. In addition, Washington was prepared to sell a portion of outstanding commercial loans to facilitate debt-for-equity and debt-for-nature swaps in countries that established such programs. To preserve the "national wonders of the hemisphere," Bush advocated creating environmental trusts, where interest payments on restructured debt owed to the United States would be paid in local currency and set aside to fund environmental projects in the debtor countries.

Finally, the president delineated three steps to promote free trade. To begin with, the United States would pursue deeper tariff cuts in the Uruguay Round on products of particular importance to

Latin American and Caribbean states. In addition, he expressed his eagerness to expand NAFTA into a free-trade zone stretching from Anchorage to Antarctica. Individual nations might affiliate with a hemispheric free-trade pact; regional groupings such as those in Central America, the Caribbean, and the Southern Cone would be encouraged to cut trade barriers among themselves as a step toward collective membership in such a configuration. Even before contemplating participation in a pan-American free-trade pact, countries could negotiate bilateral framework accords with the United States to open markets and develop closer commercial ties. "Framework agreements," said Bush, "will enable us to move forward on a step-by-step basis to eliminate counterproductive barriers to trade and toward our ultimate goal of free trade."[442]

The Initiative was sparse on details and even shorter on resources. Still, Latin Americans applauded the plan; it not only revealed Washington's interest in their economic plight but was mercifully free of the tirades against narcotics and communism that had adorned U.S. rhetoric during the Reagan years. As noted by Peter Hakim of the Inter-American Dialogue, the hemispheric leaders sensed a new era was at hand and acted accordingly:

- In September 1991, Mexico and Chile entered into an FTA, and Mexico, Colombia, and Venezuela set 1995 as the date for creating a free-trade zone among themselves.

- In March 1991, Argentina, Brazil, Paraguay, and Uruguay established the Southern Cone Common Market, known as Mercosur—with a view to establishing a common external tariff and eradicating internal commercial barriers by 1995.

- The five Central American nations reinvigorated their common market, proposed extending it to embrace Panama, and forged closer economic ties to Mexico. Meanwhile, Costa Rica moved ahead to forge an FTA with Mexico.

- In July 1991, the 13 states of the Caribbean Community introduced a single currency and announced plans to remove all barriers to intraregional trade by 1993. In mid-1994, 25 nations established the Association of Caribbean States to pursue mutual interests.

- Although the old Andean Pact was dead, Bolivia, Colombia, Ecuador, Peru, and Venezuela declared their intention to strengthen productive economic ties among themselves and adopt a single external tariff by 1995.[443]

Political crises impeded several of these initiatives. The impeachment of President Fernando Collor de Mello temporarily dampened enthusiasm for liberalizing Brazil's hugely protected economy and stalled Mercosur's progress. Public support for a bold anti-inflation plan proposed by Finance Minister Fernando Henrique Cardoso, himself a strong candidate for Brazil's presidency, combined with Argentina's keen interest in Southern Cone integration gave fresh momentum to Mercosur. Two military coup attempts in Venezuela and the December 1993 election there of Rafael Caldera, a traditional populist, clouded prospects for an Andean Common Market. On the brighter side, most countries have sustained the reform movement to liberalize their economies and preserved civilian regimes. Except in Venezuela and Haiti, armies have remained in their barracks—in part, because they were discredited in the 1970s and 1980s; in part, because they do not want to assume responsibility for the inflation, unemployment, and debt bedeviling many countries; and, in part, because they fear the ire of a post-Cold War Washington that no longer views the region through an anti-Communist prism. Thirty-one hemispheric nations have entered into 16 framework agreements with the United States, and Chile is anxious to join NAFTA as soon as possible. Argentina has also shown interest in affiliating.

The EAI, which caught most officials in Mexico City, Ottawa, and Washington by surprise, faded off the White House's radar screen during Bush's last 18 months in office. To begin with, the venture required tens of millions of dollars at a time when the president was trying to reduce a yawning budget deficit. In addition, Bush's energies were increasingly focused on gaining reelection. The program, moreover, had modest institutional backing. Neither the State Department, USTR, nor the National

Security Council clasped the initiative to their bureaucratic bosoms, and the Treasury Department—which had spawned EAI—has a small international capability. Even worse, no constituency for EAI crystallized on Capitol Hill.

Summit of Western Hemisphere Democracies

The White House is now reconsidering the concept of a bold hemispheric initiative, which undoubtedly will be renamed and reshaped to give it a Clintonian cast. Vice President Gore hinted at what might emerge in a December 1993 speech in Mexico City. In that address, he announced that the United States would host a Western Hemispheric Summit for Democracies in 1994. Some 34 leaders, all except Fidel Castro and Haiti's chief executive, have been invited to the United States. Even though Aspe and Serra Puche playfully suggested to Gore that the conclave be held in Los Angeles to coincide with the World Cup championships in July, the event was scheduled for Miami in December. The Mexicans, though informed of U.S. plans for the meeting, found the consultations to be inadequate. Among other things, they believed Miami to be an infelicitous venue because Cuban-American and Haitian-American demonstrators against the Castro and Cedras regimes, respectively, would increase the salience of democracy at the expense of economic issues that most Latin American states wanted to emphasize. The early December date also presented a problem because Zedillo, sworn in on 1 December, would have been in office only several days and the next Brazilian chief executive, elected in October, would not yet have donned the presidential sash.

The summit offers an opportunity to enlarge the scope of a revised EAI. Tentatively, there are plans to concentrate on three themes:

- "Making Democracy Work: Reinventing Government"—with attention devoted to judicial systems, narcotics, crime, human rights, and responsible public administration (a euphemism for combatting corruption).

- "Making Democracy Endure: Sustainable Development"—with emphasis on education, health, and housing.

- "Making Democracy Prosperous: Hemispheric Economic Integration"—with a focus on the relationship between economic development and political openness.

The summit will afford Washington a prime opportunity to reveal its strategy for promoting democracy, social justice, and regional free trade, although candidates for NAFTA had to be submitted to Congress by mid-1994 when only Chile was named. With respect to broadening integration, one possibility would be the negotiation of bilateral FTAs between the United States and individual (or groups of) Latin American and Caribbean states. Such an approach would speed the bargaining process and give U.S. officials greater control over the contents of accords. An alternative would be "NAFTA-plus"—that is, Latin American and Caribbean basin countries applying singularly or collectively for inclusion in the North American Free Trade Agreement, which would be rechristened to reflect an enlarged membership. Proponents favor this option for promoting uniformity in rules of origin and other trade practices. Canadian and Mexican leaders also like NAFTA-plus because it would make them full partners in future trade pacts and prevent the United States from entering hub-and-spoke arrangements with a dozen or so countries or groups of countries in the area. The NAFTA agreement requires approval by the three signatories, according to their domestic legal procedures, for the adherence of additional members. This language ensures Ottawa and Mexico City a veto over future NAFTA signatories, even though it would be difficult for Mexico to turn thumbs down on a sister Latin American state. Nonetheless, they determine which of the region's countries should enjoy structured access to the world's largest economic configuration. Yet another option would be to admit Chile to NAFTA, but encourage Mexico to negotiate bilateral FTAs with other Latin American states (or groups of states), none of which is now prepared to submit to the disciplines of the trilateral pact. The Mexicans, who have developed a reputation as tough bargainers because of their 14-month-long grueling negotiations with the Americans and Canadians, could—in the words of a senior U.S. official—"do some of the heavy lifting required to liberalize relatively closed economies that eventually might be included in NAFTA." It is also conceivable that for the next decade or so, the Andean states, Mercosur members, and other area groupings will prefer to concentrate on reducing intraregional economic barriers, while strengthening ties with each other, rather than seeking admission to NAFTA.

Health care, welfare reform, and other domestic issues will dominate the Clinton administration's agenda in 1995, and the reelection battle will consume 1996. In view of the prickly negotiations over implementing the Uruguay Round, the White House is unlikely to invest political capital in Western Hemisphere trade issues until the late 1990s. Ultimately, as many countries as possible should adhere to most NAFTA provisions to avoid a farrago of tariff schedules, rules of origin, dispute settlement procedures, environmental rules, etc. Meanwhile, the White House "is likely to focus most of its energies in the near future on engaging individual or groups of Latin American nations in narrow negotiations aimed at such steps as nailing down safeguards for foreign investors or expanding intellectual property protection."[444]

Perestroika and Glasnost

The relationship between economic growth and political democracy, a key item on the agenda of the 1994 Western Hemispheric summit, was a leitmotif of NAFTA—specifically, the belief that trade-impelled perestroika would stimulate glasnost in a political system long characterized by authoritarianism and manipulated elections. Astute, veteran observers of Latin American politics have argued that economic liberalization will expand the limited political openings accomplished in Mexico and other hemispheric nations.[445] First, they suggest, economic progress enlarges the size of the middle class, which in turn serves as a powerful advocate for "political sophistication and democratic choice."[446] Second, experience in making decisions in the economic sphere generates "demands for greater choice in the

239

political marketplace."[447]   Third, multiple free-trade-inspired contacts with democratic trading partners will diminish authoritarianism in Latin America just as Spain and Portugal's participation in the European Community fostered democracy in those once-dictatorial Iberian states.   Fourth, market-focused policies go hand-in-hand with decentralization, which "inevitably diminishes the ability of the state to manipulate economic resources as a tool of political control."[448]   Fifth, economic liberalization tends to weaken the power of undemocratic labor unions that may have enjoyed a privileged, although subordinate, relationship in the traditional political order.   Finally, liberalization diminishes opportunities for under-the-table payoffs, or *mordidas*, as market mechanisms replace the discretion exercised by sticky-fingered bureaucrats on rule enforcement.

Detractors of Mexico's political system claim that economic integration with the United States and Canada will merely tighten the grip of a Tammany Hall-style regime, which, now that NAFTA is a reality, no longer has to practice good behavior to ingratiate itself with the U.S. Congress. They cite the uprising, launched by the Zapatista National Liberation Army (EZLN) in southern Chiapas state, as evidence that Mexico's downtrodden, a disproportionate number of whom are indigenous peoples, suffer political repression and economic neglect as the nation's elite unfurls the red carpet for giant North American corporations.   This point was reinforced by the fact that the rebellion coincided with NAFTA's entry into force on 1 January 1994. The subsequent kidnapping of a prominent businessman and the assassination of PRI presidential candidate Luis Colosio sparked myriad rumors of conspiracy, plotting, and a crackdown contemplated by the outgoing Salinas government.

The Salinas administration responded to the crisis by first deploying the army against the rebels but soon shifted to the political arena. It fired the local supervisor of police and prisons, who had been linked to kidnappings arising from the Chiapan land conflicts that ignited the rebellion. In late January, the government also presented a package of electoral reforms, agreed to by the PRI and seven other political parties. These measures created an independent authority to supervise campaigns and elections, prohibited the use of government funds by any party, and established an office to prosecute alleged "electoral crimes." Also proposed were fair treatment of all parties by the Mexican media, recognizing the role of domestic and foreign observers, imposing spending limits in the August presidential campaign, and slashing the maximum expenditure per candidate from $220 million to $43 million.[449] Opposition parties criticized the PRI for breaking previous pledges to halt political fraud and abuse. "We will have to keep struggling to clean up the system, even with this accord," stated Cecilia Romero, a leader of the center-right National Action party (PAN). "It is a daily struggle of political pressure to break down this monolithic political system." Salinas, to his credit, spurned a scorched-earth policy in Chiapas in favor of negotiations. He realized that the army would have difficulty quelling the rebels in a state partly blanketed by the Lacondona rain forest. In addition, he knew that any action that reinforced stereotypes of his regime as "dictatorial" and "repressive" would play into the hands of advocates of U.S. withdrawal from NAFTA.

Also militating against repression was the fact that the accord has intensified the "continentalization" of political, economic, and social issues. Economic integration will accelerate trilateral contacts between academic, religious, labor, environmental, human rights, and other such groups, many of which participated in the struggle for or against the trade pact.[450] In 1990, for instance, Roman Catholic bishops from the United States, Mexico, and Canada urged debt relief for Mexico and other Third World nations. They also demanded that any free-trade accord contain safeguards against exploiting and displacing workers and farmers unable to protect themselves against more efficient competitors. Two years later, the president of the United Automobile Workers, anxious for Mexican incomes to climb, lambasted the Mexican government's arrest of a labor leader who had organized maquiladora workers in Matamoros. Although egregiously corrupt, the Mexican union chief garnered praise for obtaining for his members the highest wages in the assembly-plant sector.[451]

The advent of the trade pact means that NGOs, trade unions, and other organizations that formerly concentrated on domestic matters will seek increasingly to redress abuses occurring throughout the continent. One avenue of relief will be the NAFTA commissions and their advisory groups. Should these institutions fail to provide solutions, the petitioners, having engaged in coalition-building during the NAFTA struggle, will home in on legislative bodies. Because of the inflexibility of Canada's parliamentary system and PRI's domination of the Mexican Congress, U.S. lawmakers will be asked to play the key role in addressing issues, ranging from immigration and environmental protection to narcotics smuggling and electoral practices, that arise from the Yukon to the Yucatán. To the extent that NAFTA is enlarged, American legislators will be confronted with an ever more ambitious array of questions.

Despite NAFTA's offering the last best hope for achieving sustained growth for Mexico's rapidly increasing population, the pact is by no means the panacea that its most avid supporters claimed during the battle over congressional approval. Arguably, Washington and Ottawa negotiated too favorable a deal for themselves. The result is that Mexico will have to rewrite 21 economic-financial laws even as its business community faces surging competition amid increasing acts of violence and social turbulence. Salinas deserves enormous credit for his unswerving commitment to change. In the idiom of the Reagan years, he "stayed the course." Yet, he was largely coloring by the numbers—that is, he sedulously adhered to an orthodox blueprint for reforming a grotesquely statist, corrupt, and sluggish economy.

No similar prescription exists for the twin challenges that face his successor: implementing widespread, NAFTA-inspired economic and legal reforms while opening up Mexico's authoritarian political system in the face of ever-more aggressive pressure from domestic and foreign interest groups. Large corporations, particularly those that enjoy access to international financing, should prosper apace with liberalization. Their success may swell above 24 the number of Mexican billionaires identified by *Forbes* magazine in 1994. But what will happen to the several million small- and medium-sized firms, long accustomed to protection, that lack affordable credit and technical assistance—and have yet to find a niche in the North American market? Such relatively labor-intensive industries as shoes, furniture, textiles, wearing apparel, and toys have already suffered a record number of bankruptcies. Even more problematic is the fate of the Mexican peasantry. Most *ejido* communal farms, even if reformed or modernized under the 1992 constitutional amendment, will not be able to compete with Cargill, Archers Daniel Midland (ADM), and other world-class grain companies that will gain full entrée to the Mexican market within 15 years. The *campesino* population, most of whom have little or no formal education, will double to 30 or 40 million in a generation.

Conceivably, some 10 million or so peasants could find employment in the light manufacturing sector that neoliberal economists believe will expand when middle-class Mexicans can buy more consumer goods, thanks to paying less for imported food. Yet, market forces alone will not generate employment for millions of rural inhabitants, particularly indigenous peoples who are disproportionately concentrated in Chiapas, Quintano Roo, Oaxaca, Guerrero, Yucatán, and other southern states. A "PROCAMPO" incentives program, introduced in 1993 and expanded in 1994 before the presidential election, encourages several million peasants to produce more efficiently, and complements Solidarity in a piecemeal effort to uplift the country's "have nots." Still, unless the next government launches a concerted effort to build infrastructure and design a comprehensive, rural-focused development strategy that emphasizes irrigation and education, many displaced peasants will pour into already saturated Mexican cities, seek to cross illegally into the United States, or cast their lot with EZLN-style rebel movements.

Mobilizing the resources required to meet Mexico's myriad capital needs is also fraught with political imponderables. Private foreign and domestic firms, for example, would pay dearly to sign risk contracts to explore for, and develop, the nation's vast oil and gas resources. Such ventures, which may take place in the late 1990s, would necessitate amending Article 27 of the Mexican Constitution. Although more palatable after six years of Salinas-directed reforms, attacking any of the "five noes" advanced by Serra Puche during the NAFTA negotiations would inflame the passions of rabid nationalists and test the political acumen of proponents of change.

Conclusion

The enactment of NAFTA has transformed the political environment in which trade negotiations are conducted and reshaped both the means and purposes of U.S. diplomacy. First, it advanced America's goals in international organizations (APEC and GATT) and reinforced the nexus between expanded trade and the nation's vital interests. Clinton played the role of the "President as a Teacher" in lucidly explaining to Congress and the public how American leadership in the world is linked to vigorous participation in the global economy.

Second, passage of the accord demonstrated that in the aftermath of the Cold War, few differences separate moderate Democrats and Republicans in foreign policy. It was even possible for a determined chief executive, despite fierce opposition from powerful leaders and constituencies within his own party, to forge a bipartisan alliance to achieve an objective that was palpably beneficial to most of his countrymen. The obvious self-interest of selling more goods abroad contrasted with the dubious benefits deriving from more spectacular, media-attracting actions such as dispatching Marines to Haiti or bombing Serb positions in Bosnia. Winning the competitiveness battle may form part of a new *Realpolitik*—along with stabilizing a non-Communist Russia, preventing nuclear weapons exports from North Korea, promoting Arab-Israeli conciliation, and balancing power between China and Japan—that advances America's interests more than plunging into international hot spots that are marginal to America's well-being and resistant to its influence.[452]

Third, NAFTA erected a new standard for international trade agreements, which—in the future—will contain provisions for intellectual property protection, environmental safeguards, enforcement of labor standards, and other matters covered by the path-breaking North American pact and its side agreements.

Fourth, the agreement's institutional apparatus furnishes even more opportunities for governmental and private actors to inject themselves into the affairs of the three signatory nations. The most likely target of involvement will be Mexico. Its single-party-dominated government, authoritarian labor regime, and ubiquitous

244

pollution will continue to draw fire from U.S., Canadian, and Mexican reformers. Criticism of Mexico City will mount if President Zedillo, who on 21 August 1994 won the cleanest election in Mexican history, reneges on a pledge to modernize his nation's political system.

Fifth, the North American accord sets the stage for greater economic integration in the hemisphere. Building on Bush's Enterprise for the Americas Initiative, President Clinton may act to eliminate additional barriers to commerce and investment throughout the Americas, giving impetus to sustained growth amid increasing pluralism. Such a program would differ from essentially paternalistic schemes—Roosevelt's Good Neighbor policy, Kennedy's Alliance for Progress, and Reagan's Caribbean Basin Initiative—and provide nations (or groups of nations) with a mechanism to manage their own affairs.

Finally, NAFTA-accelerated reforms in Mexico will furnish opportunities for North American investors and entrepreneurs. These changes could also spark friction—particularly between the United States and Mexico—as more issues and advocacy groups impinge on the bilateral relationship. Unlawful immigration, which is expected to mushroom, will move higher on the bilateral agenda, along with drug-trafficking, environmental matters, and trade disputes. Yet, of even greater concern to Washington will be whether Mexico's next chief executive consolidates economic integration, while promoting a political opening that ensures the stability below the Rio Grande that U.S. policymakers have long taken for granted. Although a defining event for the United States, NAFTA presents Mexico with enormous opportunities; it also illuminates formidable problems whose resolution is of acute interest to politicians and average citizens throughout the continent.

Glossary of Key Terms Related to NAFTA

claw back: To withdraw a concession granted during negotiations.

countervailing duty: Duty imposed by Country A on Country B's exporter if the latter has received a subsidy from its country. If U.S. firms have been materially injured, a duty is usually imposed to offset the subsidy.

dumping: Selling goods in a foreign country at a price below the domestic selling price, after subtracting costs arising from tariffs, transportation, and other factors. Also defined as export sales at a price below the cost of production.

endgame: The final stage of bargaining when, according to conventional wisdom, 90 percent of intractable issues are resolved in 10 percent of the time allocated to the negotiations.

fast-track: An expedited procedure for congressional consideration of a trade bill. Congress must vote within 90 legislative days—no amendments permitted—on a measure considered under fast-track authority.

General Agreement on Tariffs and Trade (GATT): A multilateral tariff-negotiating organization, founded in Geneva in 1948, that seeks to liberalize and expand international trade. Its original membership of 23 nations has mushroomed to approximately 117.

jamboree: A NAFTA negotiating meeting, lasting several days, that brought together the chief negotiators, as well as the 19 working groups, to resolve as many issues as possible.

Most-Favored-Nation Treatment (MFN): One nation's granting to another the lowest tariff applied to goods imported from any other country in the world.

snapback: The right to reimpose a tariff for a limited period in the event of an import surge during the 10 or 15 years when the tariff on the affected product is being phased out.

table a proposal: To offer to reduce a tariff, open a sector to competition, or advance some other initiative during negotiations.

tariffication: The conversion of import permits, quotas, and other nontariff barriers to tariffs, as was done in the case of certain agricultural products in the NAFTA talks.

Uruguay Round: A GATT-sponsored conference, begun in Uruguay in 1986, to negotiate reduced trade barriers in manufactures and agricultural goods and services, as well as the protection of patents, copyrights, and other forms of intellectual property.

World Trade Organization (WTO): A veto-free organization committed to promoting international trade that will succeed the GATT in 1995, if approved by a majority of nations participating in the Uruguay Round.

Schedule of Major Meetings on NAFTA, 1991–92

June 12, 1991	Toronto Ministerial
July 9–10, 1991	Williamsburg Chief Negotiators' Meeting
August 6–7, 1991	Cocoyoc Chief Negotiators' Meeting
August 18–20, 1991	Seattle Ministerial
October 9–10, 1991	Meech Lake Chief Negotiators' Meeting
October 25–28, 1991	Zacatecas Ministerial
January 6–10, 1992	Georgetown Conference
January 16–17, 1992	Watergate Chief Negotiators' Meeting
February 4–5, 1992	Aylmer Chief Negotiators' Meeting
February 9–10, 1992	Chantilly Ministerial
February 17–21, 1992	Dallas Plenary
March 4–5, 1992	USTR I Chief Negotiators' Meeting
March 23–27, 1992	USTR II Chief Negotiators' Meeting
April 6–8, 1992	Montreal Ministerial
April 27–May 1, 1992	Chapultepec Plenary
May 13–15, 1992	Toronto Plenary
June 1–5, 1992	Crystal City Plenary
June 17–19, 1992	USTR III Chief Negotiators' Meeting
June 29–July 3, 1992	USTR IV Chief Negotiators' Meeting
July 7–10, 1992	USTR V Chief Negotiators' Meeting
July 25–26, 1992	Chapultepec Ministerial
July 29–August 1, 1992	Watergate Chief Negotiators' Meeting
August 2–12, 1992	Watergate Ministerial
October 7, 1992	San Antonio Initialing

Notes

Introduction

1. For the Speaker's exact words, I am indebted to the Parliamentarian's Office of the House of Representatives.

2. Quoted in *USA Today*, 18 November 1993, 4-A.

3. Quoted in the *Washington Post*, 18 November 1993, A-10.

4. Quoted in Ibid., A-10.

5. *USA Today*, 18 November 1993, 4-A.

Chapter 1: Defining Events in U.S. Foreign Affairs

6. *Common Sense* (Albany: Charles R. and George Webster, 1792), 26.

7. Quoted in Manfred Jonas, "Isolationism" in Alexander DeConde (ed.), *Encyclopedia of American Foreign Policy*, II (New York: Charles Scribner's Sons, 1978), 498.

8. Henry Steel Commager and Milton Cantor (eds.) *Documents of American History: Volume I to 1895* (Englewood Cliffs, N.J.: Prentice-Hall, 1988), 174.

9. Ibid., 188.

10. U.S. Department of State, *A Short History of the U.S. Department of State, 1781–1981* (Washington, D.C.: U.S. Department of State, 1981), 5.

11. Jonas, "Isolationism," 498.

12. Ibid.

13. Thomas A. Bailey, *A Diplomatic History of the American People* (7th ed.; New York: Appleton-Century Crofts, 1964), 276.

14. Jonas, "Isolationism," 499.

15. John Spanier, *American Foreign Policy Since World War II* (2nd ed.; New York: Praeger, 1965), 7.

16. Quoted in Ibid., 7.

17. The Consular Service expanded much more rapidly—from 236 employees in 1860 to 1,042 in 1890; see, U.S. Department of State, *A Short History of the U.S. Department of State, 1781–1981*, 18.

18. Cecil V. Crabb, Jr., *American Diplomacy and the Pragmatic Tradition* (Baton Rouge: Louisiana State University Press, 1989), 148.

19. *Wall Street Journal*, 28 June 1993, A-1, A-10.

20. Bailey, *A Diplomatic History of the American People*, 617.

21. Quoted in the *Literary Digest*, 29 November 1919, 1.

22. *Congressional Record*, 66 Congress, 1 session, 8768. Letter dated 18 November 1919.

23. Bailey, *A Diplomatic History of the American People*, 621.

24. The *Literary Digest*, 29 November 1919, 1.

25. Quoted in Denna F. Fleming, *The United States and the League of Nations, 1918–1920* (New York: Putnam, 1932), 472.

26. Quoted in the *Literary Digest*, 29 November 1919, 1.

27. William A. Scott and Stephen B. Withey, *The United States and the United Nations: the Public View, 1945–1955* (Westport, Ct.: Greenwood Press, 1958), 15.

28. Bailey, *A Diplomatic History of the American People*, 771; and U.S. Senate, *The Charter of the United Nations*, Hearing before the Senate Committee on Foreign Relations, 79 Cong., 1 sess. (1945), 405.

29. Ruth B. Russell, *A History of the United Nations Charter* (Washington, D.C.: Brookings Institution, 1958), 942.

30. Bailey, *A Diplomatic History of the American People*, 772; in addition to Johnson, four other senators—all supportive of the Charter—were absent. Senators Langer and Shipstead voted against the resolution of ratification. Thus the unofficial tally was 93 to three; see, Russell, *A History of the United Nations Charter*, 942 (footnote 18).

31. Arthur H. Vandenberg, Jr., *The Private Papers of Senator Vandenberg* (Boston: Houghton Mifflin, 1952), 130.

32. *Congressional Record*, 80 Congress, 1 sess., 1981 (12 March 1947).

33. Stephen E. Ambrose, *Rise to Globalism: American Foreign Policy since 1938* (5th rev. ed.; New York: Penguin, 1988), 86.

34. Quoted in Harold F. Gosnell, *Truman's Crises: A Political Biography of Harry S Truman* (London: Greenwood Press, 1980), 386.

35. For the Gallup Poll data, see Bailey, *A Diplomatic History of the American People*, 821 (note 5) and 822 (note 7); for other surveys, consult Scott and Withey, *The United States and the United Nations*, 77 to 86.

36. Diane Shaver Clemens, "Executive Agreements, in Alexander DeConde (ed.), *Encyclopedia of American Foreign Policy*, I (New York: Charles Scribner's Sons, 1978), 349.

37. A. Willis Robertson to Virginius Dabney, 31 July 1953, Dabney Papers, Box 1, University of Virginia Library; cited in Duane A. Tananbaum, "The Bricker Amendment Controversy: Its Origin and Eisenhower's Role," *Diplomatic History*, 9 (Winter 1985): 79.

38. Tananbaum, "The Bricker Amendment Controversy," 75; and Frank E. Holman, *Story of the Bricker Amendment (The First Phase)* (New York: Committee for Constitutional Government, Inc., 1954).

39. Dwight D. Eisenhower, *Mandate for Change* (Garden City, N.Y.: Doubleday and Co., 1963), 281.

40. Alexander DeConde, *A History of American Foreign Policy* (2nd ed; New York: Charles Scribner's Sons, 1971), 778; and Eisenhower, *Mandate for Change*, 284.

41. Holman, *Story of the "Bricker" Amendment (The First Phase)*, 17–19.

42. Quoted in *Facts on File*, 26 February–4 March 1954, 69.

43. Ibid.

44. Ambrose, *Rise to Globalism*, 265.

45. Alfred H. Kelly, "The Constitution and Foreign Policy," in Alexander DeConde (ed.), *Encyclopedia of American Foreign Policy*, I (New York: Charles Scribner's Sons, 1978), 184.

46. Ambrose, *Rise to Globalism*, p. 265.

47. Ibid.

48. While 69 percent of respondents feared that defeat of the anti-Sandinista "contra" forces would be "very" or "fairly" likely to result in communist expansion in Central America, only 31 percent of respondents favored providing U.S. military advisers to the "contras" and only 8 percent supported the deployment of U.S. troops; see George Gallup, Jr., *The Gallup Poll: Public Opinion 1985* (Wilmington Del.: Scholarly Resources Inc., 1986), 71–72.

49. Ambrose, *Rise to Globalism*, 389.

50. *Congressional Quarterly Weekly Report*, 12 January 1991, 70.

51. *Newsweek*, 11 March 1991, 30.

52. Quoted in the *Washington Post*, 30 October 1993, A-1.

Chapter 2: NAFTA: Mexico's New Beginning

53. Professor David Dessler, an esteemed colleague, introduced me to Jagdish Bhagwati's use of ideology, interests, and institutions as tools of analysis in his Ohlin Lectures, published as *Protectionism* (Cambridge, Mass: MIT Press, 1988).

54. David Miller (ed.), *The Blackwell Encyclopaedia of Political Thought* (London: Basil Blackwell Inc., 1987), 235.

55. Norman J. Padelford and George A. Lincoln, *The Dynamics of International Politics* (2nd ed.; New York: Macmillan, 1967), 209.

56. Robert O. Keohane, *International Institutions and State Power* (Boulder, Colo.: Westview, 1989), 3.

57. Thomas E. Skidmore and Peter H. Smith, *Modern Latin America* (3rd ed.; New York: Oxford University Press, 1992), 53.

58. Roger D. Hansen, *The Politics of Mexican Developement* (Baltimore: Johns Hopkins, 1980), 48.

59. Ibid., 49.

60. Michael C. Meyer and William L. Sherman, *The Course of Mexican History* (3rd ed.; New York: Oxford University Press, 1987), 646.

61. *Keesing's Contemporary Archives*, 3–10 February 1968, 22505; G. Pope Atkins, *Latin America in the International Political System* (New York: Free Press, 1977), 366–68.

62. Daniel Levy and Gabriel Székely, *Mexico: Paradoxes of Stability and Change* (Boulder, Colo.: Westview, 1983), 177–79.

63. Luis Rubio F., "The Changing Role of the Private Sector," in Susan Kaufman Purcell (ed.), *Mexico in Transition: Implications for U.S. Policy* (New York: Council on Foreign Relations, 1988), 33.

64. Roberto G. Newell and Luis Rubio F., *Mexico's Dilemma: The Political Origins of Economic Crisis* (Boulder, Colo.: Westview Press, 1984), 110.

65. James N. Goodsell, "Mexico: Why the Students Rioted," *Current History*, Vol. 56, No. 329 (January 1969): 32–33.

66. Newell and Rubio, *Mexico's Dilemma*, 126, 199.

67. Alan Riding, "The Mixed Blessings of Mexico's Oil," *New York Times Magazine*, 11 January 1981, 25.

68. *New York Times*, 22 May 1982, 2.

69. *Excelsior*, 2 September 1982, 1-A.

70. *Latin America Weekly Report*, 19 November 1982, 6.

71. *Washington Post*, 26 September 1982, A-20.

72. *Economist*, 14 June 1986, 74; 21 June 1986, 80.

73. *Economist*, 21 June 1986, 79.

74. Quoted in the *New York Times*, 19 June 1986, D-6.

75. Gamboa controlled de la Madrid's appointment schedule. He readily found time for Silva Herzog's detractors and Salinas's supporters to meet with the president. Supporters of the finance secretary or detractors of the SPP head had more difficulty gaining access.

76. Speech delivered at the Center for Strategic and International Studies, Washington, D.C., 22 September 1992.

77. Carlos Salinas de Gortari, "State of the Nation Address," 1 November 1990, in *Daily Report* (Latin America), 14 November 1990, 12.

78. In 1992, the Finance Secretariat enveloped SPP in order to place responsibility for revenues and expenditures in the same ministry.

79. For this point, I am indebted to John J. Bailey, a Mexican expert and professor of government at Georgetown University.

Chapter 3: NAFTA Faces a Fast-Track Showdown

80. This section has benefited greatly, especially with respect to pithy quotations gathered by the authors, from Alan F. Holmer and Judith H. Bello, "The Fast Track Debate: A Prescription for Pragmatism," *The International Lawyer*, 26, no. 1 (Spring 1992): 183–199.

81. See, *New York Times*, 14 November 1979, A-1, A-24; Wallace C. Koehler, Jr., and Aaron L. Segal, "Prospects for North American Energy Cooperation," *USA Today*, May 1980, 40–43; Herbert E. Meyer, "Why a North American Common Market Won't Work—Yet," *Fortune*, 10 September 1979, 118–124; and George W. Grayson, "The Maple Leaf, the Cactus, and the Eagle: Energy Trilateralism," *Inter-American Economic Affairs* 34 (Spring 1981): 49–75.

82. John Sears quoted in William Orme, *Continental Shift* (Washington, D.C.: *Washington Post*, 1993), 24.

83. *Proceso*, 15 August 1977, and reprinted in Proceso, *Petróleo y soberanía* (Mexico City: Editorial Posada, 1979), 1971.

84. The U.S. Embassy claimed that flights into the storm, which had been authorized by the Mexican government, were made only to record Ignacio's temperature and other vital signs. Without contradicting this explanation, Foreign Minister Jorge Castañeda barred U.S. hurricane-hunters from Mexican airstrips during the summer until a thorough investigation of the matter was completed. See, the *Washington Post*, 7 July 1980, A-1, A-12.

85. *New York Times*, 24 November 1988, 25, 28; Robert A. Pastor, *Integration with Mexico: Options for U.S. Policy* (New York: Twentieth Century Fund, 1993), 20, 114.

86. *Los Angeles Times*, 20 August 1989; less than 25 percent of the respondents thought that Salinas had actually triumphed in the 1988 contest.

87. *Wall Street Journal*, 27 March 1990, A-3; and telephone interview with Julius L. Katz, the chief negotiator for NAFTA, 17 May 1994.

88. For example, CTM Secretary-General Fidel Velázquez, and the body's secretary of education and social communication (now governor of Zacatecas state), Arturo Romo Gutiérrez, contributed pro-NAFTA essays to the *Wall Street Journal* (3 May 1991, A-11) and the *Washington Post* (19 May 1991, D-7), respectively.

89. *Wall Street Journal*, 27 March 1990, A-3.

90. These committees are Ways and Means, Agriculture, Banking, Finance and Urban Affairs, Energy and Commerce, Foreign Affairs, Government Operations, the Judiciary, and Public Works and Transportation.

91. U.S. House of Representatives, *North American Free Trade Agreement Implementation Act*, 103d Congress, 1st sess., Rept. 103–361, Part 1, 15 November 1993, 6.

92. *Washington Post*, 9 September 1990, A-34; and *Maclean's*, 19 November 1990, 17.

93. *Maclean's*, 11 November 1990, 17.

94. *New York Times*, 8 November 1988, A-1, A-7.

95. Roy MacLaren headed the Liberal party's pro-NAFTA contingent, while Lloyd Axworthy led the anti-pact wing.

96. Quoted in *Maclean's*, 16 April 1990, 16.

97. Semiparticipation was never a serious option because of its incompatibility with GATT.

98. Ronald J. Wonnacott, *The Economics of Overlapping Free Trade Areas and the Mexican Challenge*, Canadian-American Committee 60 (Ottawa: C. D. Howe Institute, 1991).

99. Interview with Katz, Washington, D.C., 2 June 1992.

100. Interview with Claude Carrière, counsellor for trade policy, Washington, D.C., 4 January 1994.

101. I. M. Destler, *American Trade Politics: System Under Stress* (Washington, D.C., and New York: Institute for International Economics and the Twentieth Century Fund, 1986), 62–63.

102. Ibid., 64.

103. Holmer and Bello, "The Fast Track Debate," 195.

104. Ibid., 194.

105. Ibid., 193.

106. Cited in Ibid., 192.

107. *El financiero*, 15 May 1991, 12.

108. A U.S. lobbyist, who asked to remain anonymous, reported that Mexican observers in Washington's SECOFI office won the pool on the final vote count in the House and Senate. They underestimated the House majority by only two votes and the Senate tally by just one.

109. *Wall Street Journal*, 11 April 1991, A-14.

110. *Wall Street Journal*, 6 May 1991, C-9.

111. *New York Times*, 19 May 1991, IV, 17.

112. Holmer and Bello, "The Fast Track Debate," 197.

113. I am indebted to Tracy Locklin, a graduate student in public policy at the College of William & Mary, for helping to prepare this statistical analysis.

114. *Congressional Quarterly Weekly Report*, 4 May 1991, 1120.

115. *U.S. News & World Report*, 3 June 1991, 42.

116. *Congressional Quarterly Weekly Report*, 16 March 1991, 661.

117. "Tenure classifications" refer to freshmen, second termers, third termers, and those serving their fourth terms or more. In each of these categories, fast track enjoyed a majority. If, however, the last category is broken down into fourth, fifth, sixth, and seventh termers, we find that a majority of fourth termers backed fast track, the fifth and sixth termers split two-to-two, and the Senate's only seventh termer, Strom Thurmond (R-S.C.) opposed expedited negotiating authority.

118. *Congressional Quarterly Weekly Report*, 25 May 1991, 1359.

119. *Congressional Quarterly Weekly Report*, 18 May 1991, 1257.

120. Ibid.

Chapter 4: The Negotiations

121. *Inside U.S. Trade*. 24 May 1991, 2.

122. Interview with B. Timothy Bennett, vice president, SJS Advanced Strategies, Washington, D.C., 22 July 1993. Although a former USTR official, Mr. Bennett was not the source of the "Type-A" personality quotation.

123. Interview, Washington, D.C., 11 June 1993.

124. Interview with Dr. Von Bertrab, Washington, D.C., 21 June 1993.

125. Quoted in *Maclean's*, 5 October 1987, 22.

126. The number of leads totals 20 because Canada divided Standards between Industrial Standards (External Affairs) and Food Safety (Agriculture).

127. Rubio, *¿Cómo va a afectar a méxico el tratado de libre comercio?* (Mexico City: Fondo de Cultura Económica, 1992), 134–136.

128. Interview with Thomas Gillett, U.S. Department of Commerce official, Washington, D.C., 5 October 1992.

129. Rubio, *¿Cómo va a afectar a méxico el tratado de libre comercio?*, 127–129.

130. Telephone interview with Charles E. "Chip" Roh, Jr., deputy U.S. trade representative, 20 January 1993.

131. Rubio, *¿Cómo va a afectar a méxico el tratado de libre comercio?*, 144–145; interview with Jaime E. Zabludovsky Kuper, Mexico City, 18 March 1994.

132. Ann Hughes, deputy assistant secretary for the Western Hemisphere, U.S. Department of Commerce, and the U.S. lead of the Auto Working Group, objected to the term *jamboree* because the "word connotes fun and these sessions involved nothing but hard work complemented by long hours of waiting." Interview, Washington, D.C., 29 December 1992.

133. *Wall Street Journal*, 13 May 1991, A-11.

134. *Platt's Oilgram News*, 16 March 1992, 5. The other senators were Malcolm Wallop (R-Wy.), J. Bingaman (D-N.M.), Donald Nickles (R-Ok.), David Boren (D-Ok.), Phil Gramm (R-Tex.), and Trent Lott (R-Miss.).

135. Quoted from a letter written to Carla Hills on 24 February 1992, and published in *Inside U.S. Trade*, Special Report, 28 February 1992, S-6.

136. The draft, which contained 1,200 brackets, was summarized in *Proceso*, 16 March 1992, 12–16, and 30 March 1992, 6–10.

137. *Proceso*, 16 March 1992, 12.

138. Ibid., 13.

139. *Proceso*, 30 March 1992, 8.

140. Ibid.

141. Rubio, *¿Cómo va a afectar a méxico el tratado de libre comercio?*, 145–147.

142. Interview with Dunn, assistant secretary for import administration, U.S. Department of Commerce, Washington, D.C., 22 December 1992.

143. Telephone interview, 10 December 1992.

144. Interview with Hughes, Washington, D.C., 29 December 1992.

145. Telephone interview, 19 January 1993.

146. Interview with Jesús Flores Ayala, Mexico City, 18 March 1994.

147. Interview with Zabludovsky, Mexico City, 18 March 1994.

148. Interview with Katz, 2 June 1993, Washington, D.C.

149. The author received this impression from a small-group conversation with Salinas following his presentation of the 1992 State of the Nation address, Mexico City, 1 November 1992.

150. Telephone interview, 19 January 1993.

151. The shirts had to be redone because originally they carried a map of "North America" that showed Mexican territory extending all the way to the Panama Canal.

152. Interview with Barry S. Newman, deputy assistant secretary for international monetary policy, Department of the Treasury, Washington, D.C., 29 July 1993.

153. This section draws heavily on Grayson, *The North American Free Trade Agreement* (New York: Foreign Policy Association, 1993), 43–47.

Chapter 5: NAFTA and the 1992 Presidential Campaign

154. *The Gallup Poll Monthly*, June 1992, 17.

155. *The Gallup Poll Monthly*, May 1992, 10; September 1992, 11; June 1992, 45.

156. *Wall Street Journal*, 2 November 1993, A-17.

157. Orme, *Continental Shift*, 69.

158. *Wall Street Journal*, 2 November 1993, A-17.

159. DLC, *The Road to Realignment: The Democrats and the Perot Voters* (Washington, D.C.: DLC, 1993), i.

160. Jacob Weisberg, "Family Feud," *New Republic*, 20 May 1991, 21.

161. Ibid., 22.

162. *Los Angeles Times*, 6 June 1991, B-7.

163. *Washington Post*, 31 May 1992, A-18.

164. Ibid.

165. Orme, *Continental Shift*, 64.

166. Hobart Rowen, "Perot Talks, Walks Like a Protectionist," *Washington Post*, 21 June 1992, H-5.

167. *New Republic*, 15 June 1992, 22.

168. Orme, *Continental Shift*, 65.

169. *New Republic*, 15 June 1992, 22.

170. Ibid.

171. *Wall Street Journal*, 15 June 1992, A-12.

172. *Wall Street Journal*, 30 July 1992, C-1.

173. Orme, *Continental Shift*, 66.

174. *Wall Street Journal*, 9 July 1992, A-1, A-6.

175. *Washington Post*, 17 July 1992, A-1.

176. *Los Angeles Times*, 17 July 1992, D-1.

177. *Washington Post*/ABC News Poll, reported in the *Washington Post*, 16 July 1992, A-8.

178. "I Just Wanted to Do the Right Thing" (interview with Ross Perot), *Newsweek*, 27 July 1992, 26.

179. Quoted in *Time* magazine, 9 November 1992, 28.

180. Ibid.

181. *Congressional Quarterly Weekly Report*, 4 July 1992, 66.

182. (Boston: Houghton Mifflin, 1992).

183. Orme, *Continental Shift*, 68 and 69.

184. *Wall Street Journal*, 2 November 1993, A-17.

185. *Washington Post*, 19 September 1993, H-4.

186. *Congressional Quarterly Weekly Report*, 12 September 1992, 2699.

187. *Maclean's*, 17 August 1992, 29; and *Congressional Quarterly Weekly Report*, 15 August 1992, 2437.

188. *Business Week*, 21 September 1993, 43.

189. *Congressional Quarterly Weekly Report*, 12 September 1992, 2699.

190. *Business Week*, 21 September 1992, 43.

191. *Congressional Quarterly Weekly Report*, 12 September 1992, 2699.

192. *Washington Post*, 9 September 1992, F-2.

193. *Washington Post*, 19 September 1993, H-4.

194. *Wall Street Journal*, 2 November 1993, A-17.

195. *Wall Street Journal*, 11 November 1993, A-17.

196. Bob Woodward, *The Agenda: Inside the Clinton White House* (New York: Simon & Schuster, 1994), 55.

197. *Washington Post*, 8 October 1992, A-30.

198. *Christian Science Monitor*, 31 January 1992, 6.

199. *The Gallup Poll Monthly*, January 1992, 12.

200. *Los Angeles Times*, 15 December 1991, M-4.

201. *The American Enterprise*, January/February 1992, 92.

202. *Monthly Labor Review*, U.S. Department of Labor, Bureau of Labor Statistics, December 1992, 70.

203. *Congressional Quarterly Weekly Report*, 15 August 1992, 2437.

204. *Maclean's*, 17 August 1992, 29.

205. *National Journal*, 10 October 1992, 2337.

206. *New York Times*, 8 October 1992, A-1, A-30.

207. *Weekly Compilation of Presidential Documents*, Office of the Federal Register, National Archives and Records Administration, 12 October 1992, 1881-1882.

208. Quoted in the *New York Times*, 13 October 1992, A-23.

209. *New York Times*, 5 October 1992, A-16.

210. *Congressional Quarterly Weekly Report*, 12 September 1992, 2699.

211. Ibid.

212. *Weekly Compilation of Presidential Documents*, 12 October 1992, 1881-1882.

213. Ross Perot, *United We Stand: How We Can Take Back Our Country* (New York: Hyperion, 1992), 105-106.

214. Quoted in "Campaign '92: Transcript of the Second Presidential Debate," *Washington Post*, 16 October 1992, A-34.

215. Orme, *Continental Shift*, 71.

216. George Gallup, Jr., *The Gallup Poll: Public Opinion 1992* (Wilmington, Del.: Scholarly Resources Inc., 1993), 5.

217. Network exit polls published in Howard W. Stanley and Richard G. Niemi, *Vital Statistics on American Politics* (4th ed.; Washington, D.C.: Congressional Quarterly Press, 1994), 107.

Chapter 6: The Side Deals

218. "Remarks by Governor Bill Clinton at the Student Center at North Carolina State University, Raleigh, North Carolina," Federal News Service, 4 October 1992, 9.

219. Ibid., 8.

220. Ibid., 11.

221. Ibid., 4.

222. Ibid.

223. Ibid., 5.

224. Quoted in Orme, *Continental Shift*, 69.

225. "Remarks by Governor Bill Clinton," 8–9.

226. Ibid., 10.

227. Ibid., 9–10.

228. The text of this accord appears in President of the United States, *The NAFTA Supplemental Agreements* (Washington, D.C.: Government Printing Office, 1993).

229. Super 301 is modeled after Section 301 of the Trade Act of 1974, which permits the U.S. government to investigate and retaliate against specific foreign trade barriers deemed to be unfair. Super 301, first authorized in 1988 trade legislation, authorizes the U.S. government to identify the foreign countries that impose the most unfair or burdensome overall trade restrictions and to place 100 percent tariffs on their exports unless they satisfy Washington's demands. Obviously, Japan was the target of the "resurrected trade policy sledgehammer." See James Bovard, "A U.S. History of Trade Hypocrisy," *Wall Street Journal*, 8 March 1994, A-16.

230. Principal deputy assistant secretary for oceans, environment, and science.

231. Acting administrator for the Office of International Activities.

232. For a copy of this draft, see *Inside U.S. Trade* (Special Report), 5 March 1993, S-6 through S-9.

233. *Inside U.S. Trade* (Special Report), 9 April 1993, S-6.

234. *Inside U.S. Trade*, 13 August 1993, 18.

235. Interview with Kenneth Thomas, Office of Oceans, the Environment, and Science, the Department of State, 28 December 1993, Washington, D.C.

236. Kantor provided this information at a 29 March 1992 news conference; see, *Inside U.S. Trade*, 2 April 1993, 19.

237. Quoted in *Inside U.S. Trade*, 16 April 1993, 3.

238. Ibid., 3-4.

239. *Inside U.S. Trade*, 28 May 1993, 14.

240. *Inside U.S. Trade*, 21 May 1993, 1.

241. *Inside U.S. Trade* (Special Report), 21 May 1993, S-9.

242. Ibid., S-9 and S-10.

243. Quoted in *Inside U.S. Trade*, 28 May 1993, 1.

244. Quoted in *Inside U.S. Trade*, 28 May 1993, 8. Meanwhile, at a 27 May meeting with National Economic Council Deputy Director Bowman Cutter, seven business associations that belong to U.S. Alliance for NAFTA lodged objections to trade sanctions and an independent secretariat, complaining that the administration failed to consult the business community when preparing its Ottawa draft text; see, *Inside U.S. Trade*, 4 June 1993, 1 and 12.

245. Although at a political impasse, the negotiators had regained the good rapport that dominated the discussions. At one point, Yerxa, whose name was particularly difficult for the Mexicans to pronounce, exclaimed playfully to Herminio Blanco, "If you'll stop calling me 'Jerksa,' I won't refer to you as 'Herman.'"

246. Interview with Thomas, 28 December 1993.

247. Ibid.

248. Interview with Smith, Washington, D.C., 4 January 1994.

249. Quoted in *Inside U.S. Trade*, 18 June 1993, 10.

250. Helms expressed his views in a 17 June letter to Joan E. Spero, undersecretary of state for economic and agricultural affairs; see, *Inside U.S. Trade*, 18 June 1993, 8.

251. Quoted in *Inside U.S. Trade*, 28 May 1993, 11.

252. *Inside U.S. Trade*, 13 August 1993, 18.

253. The text of the side agreements appear in President of the United States, *NAFTA Supplemental Agreements* (Washington, D.C., U.S. Government Printing Office, 1993).

254. *Inside U.S. Trade* (Special Report), 16 August 1993, S-1.

255. Interview with Thomas, 28 December 1993: "Fact Sheet on the U.S./Mexican Agreement on the Border Environment Cooperation Commission (BECC) and the North American Development Bank (NADBank), distributed by the U.S. Department of State, n.d. (mimeo.); and *Inside U.S. Trade* (Special Report), 16 August 1993, S-3.

256. This draft paper appears in *Inside U.S. Trade* (Special Report), 5 March 1993, S-2 through S-4.

257. *Inside U.S. Trade* (Special Report), 5 March 1993, S-1, S-2.

258. Ibid., S-3 and S-4.

259. "Labor Agreement Negotiating Report," a memorandum prepared by the Canadian government and cited in *Inside U.S. Trade*, 2 April 1993, 1 and 19.

260. This body, jointly sponsored by USTR and the Department of Labor, was one of the alphabet soup of advisory groups mandated by Congress for trade negotiations.

261. *Inside U.S. Trade*, 20 August 1993, 6.

Chapter 7: Evolution of Mexican Lobbying in the United States

262. This section benefits from George W. Grayson, "From Cellar to the Lobby," *Hemisfile* 3, No. 4 (July 1992): 4–5.

263. Based on lobbying reports filed under the Foreign Agents Registration Act, U.S. Department of Justice, Washington, D.C.; outlays on trade and countervailing duties are considered "quasi-political."

264. *Proceso*, 24 September 1990, 8.

265. The additional agencies were the Attorney-General, the Office for the Negotiation of the Free Trade Treaty, and the ministries of Fisheries and Finance and Public Credit. Already present were the ministries of Commerce and Industrial Development, Agriculture and Hydraulic Resources, National Defense, Navy, and Tourism, as well as the National Financiera development bank. Data supplied by the Office of Press and Public Affairs, the Mexican Embassy, Washington, D.C., 10 April 1992.

266. Data supplied by the Office of Press and Public Affairs, the Mexican Embassy, 10 April 1992.

267. Interview with Leaman, Washington, D.C., 11 June 1993.

268. Interview with Dr. Herman Von Bertrab, Washington, D.C., 21 June 1993.

269. In 1993 Canela, who specializes in applying statistics to political science, returned to the University of California at Berkeley, which had granted him a leave of absence.

270. For copious information on pro-NAFTA lobbying through 1992, with emphasis on former U.S. government officials, see *The Trading Game: Inside Lobbying for the North American Free Trade Agreement* (Washington, D.C.: the Center for Public Integrity, n.d.).

271. *Washington Post*, 28 September 1993, A-21.

272. Ibid.

273. Jeffrey H. Birnbaum and Alan S. Murray, *Showdown at Gucci Gulch* (New York: Vintage Books, 1987), 17.

274. Ibid.

275. *Washington Post*, 28 September 1993, A-21.

276. Tarullo recused himself from participating in decisions affecting either Mexico or NAFTA.

277. *Washington Post*, 28 September 1993, A-21.

278. Ibid.

279. Jorge Mas Canosa, the head of the Cuban-American National Foundation, quoted in the *Washington Post*, 23 May 1991, A-21.

280. *Washington Post*, 23 May 1991, A-21.

281. Among the Hispanic organizations invited to take part in the program are the National Council of La Raza, the U.S. Hispanic Chamber of Commerce, the Association of Mexican-American Chambers of Commerce in Texas, and the California Hispanic Chamber of Commerce; Press Office of the President of Mexico, *Mexico: On the Record* 1, No. 8 (August/September 1992): 3.

282. The two leaders met in Paris (July 1989), Washington (October 1989 and June 1990), Monterrey (November 1990), San Antonio (February 1991), Houston (April 1991), Camp David, Maryland (December 1991), and San Antonio (October 1992). Salinas also held a meeting with President-elect Clinton in January 1993. Between 1945 and 1988, Mexican presidents met with U.S. chief executives 28 times—with López Portillo (1976–1982) and de la Madrid (1982–1988) holding the most bilateral summits during this period with six apiece.

283. Quoted in *Facts on File*, 18 April 1991, 288.

284. *New York Times*, 30 December 1991, A-4.

285. *Wall Street Journal*, 25 April 1991, A-16.

286. Ibid.

287. Ibid., 20 May 1993, A-18.

288. Ibid.

289. Ibid.; Charles Lewis and Margaret Ebrahim, "Can Mexico and Big Business USA Buy NAFTA?," *The Nation*, 14 June 1993, 826–39.

290. Ross Perot (with Pat Choate), *Save Your Job, Save Our Country: Why NAFTA Must be Stopped—Now!* (New York: Hyperion, 1993), 63.

Chapter 8: Congress: the Last Best Hope for Victory

291. John Rourke, *Congress and the Presidency in U.S. Foreign Policymaking: A Study of Interaction and Influence, 1945–1982* (Boulder, Colo.: Westview, 1993), 171.

292. Ibid., 172.

293. U.S. Department of State, "NAFTA: In the Overriding Interest of the United States," Address of the Honorable Warren Christopher to the Los Angeles World Affairs Council and Town Hall, 2 November 1993, *U.S. State Department Dispatch*, 1.

294. Ibid., 2.

295. Ibid.

296. U.S. Department of State, "Statement of the Honorable Warren Christopher, Secretary of State, before the Senate Foreign Relations Committee," 4 November 1993 (mimeo.), 4.

297. *U.S. News & World Report*, 29 April 1991, 92.

298. *New York Times*, 17 September 1993, A-1 and D-5.

299. Ibid.

300. Ibid., D-5.

301. U.S. Embassy (Mexico), "Mexico: Economic and Financial Report," April 1993, Mexico City, mimeo., 3.

302. Quoted in the *Washington Post*, 1 September 1993, F-3.

303. *Wall Street Journal*, 23 December 1992, A-1.

304. Quoted in *Washington Post* advertising supplement, "Sierra Club to Clinton: Renegotiate NAFTA!," 27 October 1993, A-19.

305. *Washington Post*, 11 November 1993, A-19.

306. *Congressional Quarterly Weekly Report*, 20 November 1993, 3175.

307. *Facts on File*, 9 September 1993, 667. (See Perot's book.)

308. *Facts on File*, 9 September 1993, 667.

309. Quoted in the *Los Angeles Times*, 18 August 1993, B-7.

310. According to studies by Lawrence Mishel and Jared Bernstein conducted for the Economic Policy Institute and published in the *Washington Post*, 28 November 1993, C-4.

311. Challenger, Gray & Christmas compiled this figure, which was published in the *Washington Post*, 6 November 1993, A-10.

312. Thomas B. Edsall, "Age of Irritation," *Washington Post*, 28 November 1993, C-4.

313. Daniel La Botz quoted in the *Wall Street Journal*, 12 February 1991, A-10.

314. Robert E. Baldwin, "The Changing Nature of U.S. Trade Policy since World War II," in Robert E. Baldwin and Anne O. Krueger (eds.), *The Structure and Evolution of Recent U.S. Trade Policy* (Chicago: University of Chicago Press, 1984), 13.

315. Harold W. Stanley and Richard G. Niemi, *Vital Statistics on American Politics* (4th ed.; Washington, D.C.: Congressional Quarterly Inc., 1994), 190.

316. *USA Today*, 18 November 1993, 5A; *Wall Street Journal*, 5 October 1993, B1–B6.

317. Professors Stephen Bronars (University of California at Santa Barbara) and Donald Deere (Texas A&M) cited in the *Wall Street Journal*, 17 April 1990, A1.

318. Calculated from data that appears in U.S. Department of Commerce, *Statistical Abstract of the United States 1993* (Washington D.C.:

Government Printing Office, 1992), 435; and from date provided by the AFL-CIO.

319. Harold W. Stanley and Richard G. Niemi, *Vital Statistics on American Politics* (4th ed.; Washington, D.C.: Congressional Quarterly Inc., 1994), 106 and 108.

320. Telephone interview with Frenzel, 28 July 1994.

321. Perot, more than the AFL-CIO, appears responsible for activating rank-and-file union members.

322. These were the National Audubon Society, the Environmental Defense Fund, the Natural Resources Defense Council, the National Wildlife Fund, the Nature Conservancy, and the World Wildlife Fund; for a description of the event with the vice president, see *Washington Post*, 16 September 1993, D-10 and D-12.

323. Interview, Washington, D.C., 7 December 1992.

324. "American Environmentalism: A Movement Courting Irrelevance," *World Policy Journal*, IX (Winter 1991-92): 74.

325. Interview, Washington, D.C., 7 December 1992.

326. *Washington Post*, 14 December 1992, A-20.

327. Ibid.

328. For a partial list of the RMALC's 80 constituent groups, see *Proceso*, 30 March 1992, 7.

329. U.S. Department of State, "Environmental NGO Developments on the Eve of NAFTA," unclassified cable from the U.S. embassy in Mexico, 15 November 1993, 1-2.

330. Quoted in *El financiero*, 18 January 1991, 25.

331. "Can NAFTA Change Mexico?," *Foreign Affairs* 72 (September/October 1993): 68 (the article is pp. 66-80).

332. In fact, Canada's exports to the United States during CFTA's first three years of operation performed better in sectors—particularly nonresource-based manufacturing—that were liberalized by the accord; see Daniel Schwanen, "Were the Optimists Wrong on Free Trade? A

Canadian Perspective," *Commentary*, C. D. Howe Institute, No. 3 (October 1992).

333. Quoted in the *New York Times*, 25 March 1993, D-4.

334. Ibid.

335. Perot (with Choate), *Save Your Job, Save Our Country: Why NAFTA Must be Stopped—Now!*, i and ii.

336. Ibid., chapters 1 and 2.

337. Ibid., 54.

338. Ibid., 10.

339. Ibid., 14.

340. Ibid., 6.

341. "Correcting the Record," Response of the Office of the U.S. Trade Representative to the Perot/Choate NAFTA book, Washington, D.C., 30 September 1993.

342. Heritage Foundation, "Setting the Record Straight: Evaluating Ross Perot's Allegations Against the NAFTA," Backgrounder No. 959, Washington, D.C., 30 September 1993.

343. *Washington Post*, 6 October 1993, A-6.

344. Quoted in the *Washington Post*, 6 October 1993, A-6.

345. Quoted in the *Wall Street Journal*, 4 October 1993, A-11.

346. *Wall Street Journal*, 2 November 1993, A-24.

347. This figure includes delegates from the U.S. Virgin Islands and Puerto Rico, whose voting privileges are limited; see *Congressional Quarterly*, 2 January 1993, 7.

348. The Center for Responsive Politics reported the PAC figures, which were published in the *Wall Street Journal*, 25 October 1993, A-22; for total outlays, see Stanley and Niemi, *Vital Statistics on American Politics*, 212.

349. The average number of House losses was 26.25; the figure for senators was 4.92. See Stanley and Niemi, *Vital Statistics on American Politics*, 205.

350. *Congressional Quarterly Weekly*, 14 November 1992, 3626.

351. *Washington Post*, 26 October 1993, A-6.

352. The number of House CBC affiliates jumped from 23 to 38, with Senator Carol Moseley-Braun (D-Ill.) representing the 39th member.

353. Forty governors backed NAFTA in a June 1993 survey; see, the Heritage Foundation, *F.Y.I.*, 1 July 1993, 1.

Chapter 9: The Showdown Vote

354. *Presidential Power: The Politics of Leadership* (New York: John Wiley & Sons, 1960), 20.

355. Heritage Foundation, *Mexico Watch*, 39 (July 1993): 1.

356. *Wall Street Journal*, 2 November 1993, A-1.

357. Ibid.

358. Woodward, *The Agenda*, 216.

359. This struggle is a leitmotiv of Woodward's *The Agenda*.

360. Woodward, *The Agenda*, 256.

361. Quoted in Wilbur Edel, *The Reagan Presidency* (New York: Hippocrene Books, 1992), 152.

362. Walter Shapiro, "Whose Hillary is She Anyway?" *Esquire*, August 1993, 84.

363. Gerald Ford's standing was 48 percent (1974) following his pardon of Richard Nixon; see *Facts on File*, 6 May 1993, 326.

364. *Gallup Poll Monthly*, August 1993, 14.

365. Robert Oichter and Ted J. Smith, "Bad News Bears," *Media Critic*, 1 (October 1993), 81-87.

366. Quoted in Sidney Blumenthal, "The Making of a Machine," *New Yorker*, 29 November 1993, 80–81.

367. Quoted in Blumenthal, "The Making of a Machine," 89.

368. *Washington Post*, 15 November 1993, B-8.

369. Frenzel, telephone interview, 28 July 1994.

370. Frenzel, telephone interview, 28 July 1994.

371. Interview with Ambassador Gillespie, Washington, D.C., 7 January 1994.

372. Ibid.

373. James R. Jones, "Letter to Rep. John J. LaFalce," 26 November 1993.

374. Quoted in *Congressional Quarterly Weekly Report*, 18 September 1993, 2501– 2502.

375. Quoted in Heritage Foundation, *Mexico Watch* 41 (September 1993): 1.

376. Quoted in the *New York Times*, 15 September 1993, B-12.

377. Ibid.

378. Quoted in the *Washington Post*, 19 September 1993, H-5.

379. Quoted in Blumenthal, "The Making of a Machine," 92. I sanitized the F-word.

380. *Washington Post*, 15 November 1993, B-1.

381. For example, named to senior White House positions were Joan Baggett (Bricklayers), political director, and Joe Velazquez (AFL-CIO), deputy political director. Appointments in the Department of Labor included: Jack Otero (Transportation Workers), deputy undersecretary for international affairs; Steve Rosenthal (Communications Workers), associate deputy secretary; Joyce Miller (Garment Workers), special assistant to the secretary; Michael Kerr (AFSCME), executive secretary to the secretary; Leslie Loble (Communications Workers), acting assistant secretary for policy; Karen Nussbaum (Service Employees), director, Women's Bureau; Martin Manley (Machinists), assistant secretary, Office of the American

Workplace; and Geri Palast (AFL-CIO), assistant secretary for congressional and intergovernmental affairs.

382. Quoted in the *New York Times*, 11 November 1993, D-9.

383. Quoted in the *New York Times*, 8 November 1993, A-1 and D-9.

384. Ibid., D-9.

385. Ibid.

386. Quoted in the *Washington Post*, 6 November 1993, A-7.

387. NBC/*Wall Street Journal* poll cited in the *Washington Post*, 6 November 1993, A-7.

388. Reported in the *Washington Post*, 31 October 1993, C-2.

389. Even AFL-CIO insiders were irritated by the media attention afforded William H. Bywater, the profane, NAFTA-hating, Clinton-bashing president of the International Union of Electricians. Not only did the 73-year-old, pugilistic union leader present an unflattering image of the labor movement, his union is a minor contributor to movement activities.

390. The debate, which drew an 11.9 rating by the A.C. Nielsen television rating service, attracted the largest audience ever for a regularly scheduled cable TV show; see *Facts on File*, 11 November 1993, 844.

391. Even the vehemently anti-NAFTA Sierra Club estimates that addressing border pollution and constructing necessary infrastructure will cost $20.7 million—a figure much higher than the administration's estimate; see the *Wall Street Journal*, 11 November 1993, A-16.

392. Former Internal Revenue Service Commissioner Sheldon S. Cohen helped Perot obtain a tax break worth at least $15 million from the Ways and Means Committee in 1975. Subsequently, the valuable amendment was killed on the House floor; see the *Wall Street Journal*, 11 November 1993, A-16.

393. For an especially deft analysis of the debate, see Tom Shales' "Perot: Don't Speak When I'm Interrupting!" *Washington Post*, 11 November 1993, C-9.

394. Quoted in Blumenthal, "The Making of a Machine," 92.

395. Quoted in the *Washington Post*, 11 November 1993, A-9.

396. *Facts on File*, 11 November 1993, 844.

397. *Wall Street Journal*, 17 November 1993, A-24.

398. *Washington Post*, 11 November 1993, A-43.

399. Blumenthal, "The Making of a Machine," 92.

400. Quoted in the *Wall Street Journal*, 16 November 1993, A-30.

401. Ibid.

402. *Congressional Quarterly Weekly*, 20 November 1993, 3185.

403. Quoted in the *Wall Street Journal*, 16 November 1993, A-30.

404. Quoted in *Congressional Quarterly Weekly*, 20 November 1993, 3175.

405. Quoted in the *Wall Street Journal*, 16 November 1993, A-30.

406. *Wall Street Journal*, 19 November 1993, A-7.

407. *Congressional Quarterly Weekly*, 20 November 1993, 3175.

408. *New York Times*, 19 November 1993, A-7.

409. Ibid.

410. *Washington Post*, 1 November 1993, A-1.

411. Quoted in the *Wall Street Journal*, 19 November 1993, A-7.

412. Ibid.

413. Quoted in the *New York Times*, 19 November 1993, A-27.

414. I am indebted to Tracy Lochlin, a graduate student in public policy at the College of William and Mary, for analyzing the data presented in this section.

415. The freshmen include 110 members elected in November 1992 and four chosen to fill vacancies in 1993. Forty-five of 66 freshman Democrats (68.2 percent) opposed NAFTA, while only 16 of 48 GOP first-termers (33.3 percent) cast "nay" votes.

416. Raw data on these contributions appeared in the *Washington Post*, 15 November 1993, A-17.

417. A breakdown of the last category finds that seven of ten 4th termers and three of four 5th termers backed NAFTA, while only two of five 6th termers supported the pact. The Senate's only 7th termer (Strom Thurmond) voted "no."

418. Conventional wisdom aside, Clinton captured the White House not because he drew substantial numbers of suburban Republicans, independents, and other middle-class voters; rather, he attracted essentially the same coalition that—in 1968—enabled Hubert Humphrey to claim 43 percent of the ballots cast, the same portion garnered by Clinton in 1992. See, Vic Fingerhut, "The Mythical Clinton Coalition," *Campaigns & Elections* (January 1993), 29-30, 33.

Chapter 10: NAFTA as a Defining Event

419. Quoted in the *New York Times*, 21 November 1993, E-1.

420. This is the practice whereby the United States, for example, imposes on Chinese imports tariffs that are the same as those applied to the products of the country with which we have the lowest duties. The 1989 Tiananmen Square massacre and subsequent human rights abuses have prompted some members of Congress to urge eliminating most-favored-nation treatment for the Beijing government.

421. 21 November 1993, 14.

422. David E. Sanger, "Salesman in Chief," *New York Times*, 11 November 1993, E-1.

423. Ibid.

424. Quoted in the *New York Times*, 19 November 1993, A-6.

425. *New York Times*, 19 November 1993, A-6.

426. Quoted in the *New York Times*, 21 November 1993, 14.

427. Ibid.

428. In addition to Mexico, Papua New Guinea was admitted to APEC, with Chile scheduled for membership in 1994.

429. Quoted in the *New York Times*, 19 November 1993, A-1.

430. These quotations appeared in the *Wall Street Journal*, 11 November 1993, A-7.

431. *Wall Street Journal*, 19 November 1993, A-7.

432. For this point, I am indebted to B. Timothy Bennett, vice president of SJS Advanced Strategies, interview, Washington, D.C., 7 January 1994.

433. Quoted in the *Wall Street Journal*, 15 December 1993, A-6.

434. Ibid.

435. Quoted in the *Washington Post*, 4 May 1994, D-2.

436. Ibid.

437. For the President's announcement of the Initiative, see U.S. Office of the Federal Registrar, National Archives and Records Administration, *Weekly Compilation of Presidential Documents*, "Administration of George Bush 1990," 2 July 1990, 1009–1013.

438. Georges Fauriol, "The Shadow of Latin American Affairs," *Foreign Affairs* 1 (1990): 117.

439. Orme, *Continental Shift*, 160.

440. "Administration of George Bush, 1990," 1011.

441. Ibid., 1012.

442. Ibid., 1011.

443. "President Bush's Southern Strategy: The Enterprise for the Americas Initiative," *Washington Quarterly* 15 (Spring 1992): 100.

444. Bruce Stokes, "Looking South," *National Journal*, 18 December 1993, 2990.

445. For the most developed presentations of this thesis, see Sidney Weintraub and M. Delal Baer, "The Interplay between Economic and Political Opening: The Sequence in Mexico," *Washington Quarterly*, 15

(Spring 1992): 187; and Luis Rubio, "El dilema liberal," *Vuelta*, 191 (October 1992): 70–71.

446. Weintraub and Baer, "The Interplay between Economic and Political Opening," 188.

447. Ibid., 187.

448. Ibid., 188.

449. *Washington Post*, 29 January 1994, A-16.

450. Cathryn L. Thorup has conducted path-breaking research on this subject; see "Redefining Governance in North America: Citizen Diplomacy and Cross-Border Coalition," *Enfoque*, Center for U.S.-Mexican Studies, University of California, San Diego (Spring 1993), 1, 12, and 13.

451. *Journal of Commerce*, 5 February 1992, 1-A and 5-A.

452. Edwin W. Sill, letter-to-the-editor, *Washington Post*, 25 June 1994, A-20.

Bibliography

BOOKS AND MONOGRAPHS

Ambrose, Stephen E. *Rise to Globalism: American Foreign Policy since 1938*. 5th rev. ed. New York: Penguin, 1988.

Atkins, G. Pope. *Latin America in the International Political System*. New York: Free Press, 1977.

Bailey, Thomas A. *A Diplomatic History of the American People*. 7th ed. New York: Appleton-Century Crofts, 1964.

Bhagwati, Jagidsh. *Protectionism.* Cambridge, Mass.: MIT Press, 1988.

Birnbaum, Jeffrey H. and Alan S. Murray. *Showdown at Gucci Gulch*. New York: Vintage Books, 1987.

Commager, Henry Steel and Cantor, Milton, eds. *Documents of American History: Volume I to 1895*. Englewood Cliffs, N.J.: Prentice-Hall, 1988.

Crabb, Cecil V., Jr. *American Diplomacy and the Pragmatic Tradition*. Baton Rouge: Louisiana State University Press, 1989.

DeConde, Alexander. *A History of American Foreign Policy*. 2nd ed. New York: Charles Scribner's Sons, 1971.

Democratic Leadership Council. *The Road to Realignment: The Democrats and the Perot Voters*. Washington, D.C.: DLC, 1993.

Destler, I. M. *American Trade Politics: System Under Stress*. Washington, D.C., and New York: Institute for International Economics and the Twentieth Century Fund, 1986.

281

BIBLIOGRAPHY

Edel, Wilbur. *The Reagan Administration*. New York: Hippocrene Books, 1992.

Eisenhower, Dwight D. *Mandate for Change*. Garden City, N.Y.: Doubleday and Co., 1963.

Fleming, Denna F. *The United States and the League of Nations, 1918–1920*. New York: Putnam, 1932.

Gallup, George Jr. *The Gallup Poll: Public Opinion 1985*. Wilmington, Del.: Scholarly Resources Inc., 1986.

Gore, Albert. *Earth in the Balance: Ecology and the Human Spirit*. Boston: Houghton Mifflin, 1992.

Gosnell, Harold F. *Truman's Crises: A Political Biography of Harry S. Truman*. London: Greenwood Press, 1980.

Grayson, George W. *The North American Free Trade Agreement*. New York: Foreign Policy Association, 1993.

————. *Oil and Mexican Foreign Policy*. Pittsburgh: University of Pittsburgh Press, 1988.

————. *The United States and Mexico: Patterns of Influence*. New York: Praeger, 1984.

Hansen, Roger D. *The Politics of Mexican Development*. Baltimore: Johns Hopkins, 1980.

Holman, Frank E. *Story of the Bricker Amendment (The First Phase)*. New York: Committee for Constitutional Government, Inc., 1954.

Huchim, Eduardo. *TLC: hacia un país distinto*. Mexico City: Editorial Patria, 1992.

Keohane, Robert O. *International Institutions and State Power*. Boulder, Colo.: Westview, 1989.

Levy, Daniel and Gabriel Székely. *Mexico: Paradoxes of Stability and Change*. Boulder, Colo.: Westview, 1983.

282

BIBLIOGRAPHY

Lewis, Sanford. *Rivers in Peril.* Boston: National Toxics Campaign Fund, 1991.

Meyer, Michael C. and William L. Sherman. *The Course of Mexican History.* 3rd ed. New York: Oxford University Press, 1987.

Miller, David, ed. *The Blackwell Encyclopedia of Political Thought.* London: Basil Blackwell Inc., 1987.

Newell, Roberto G. and Luis F. Rubio. *Mexico's Dilemma: The Political Origins of Economic Crisis.* Boulder, Colo.: Westview Press, 1984.

Neustadt, Richard. *Presidential Power: The Politics of Leadership.* New York: John Wiley & Sons, 1960.

Orme, William. *Continental Shift.* Washington, D.C.: Washington Post Co., 1993.

Padelford, Norman J. and George A. Lincoln. *The Dynamics of International Politics.* 2nd ed. New York: Macmillan, 1967.

Paine, Thomas. *Common Sense.* Albany: Charles R. and George Webster, 1792.

Pastor, Robert A. *Integration with Mexico: Options for U.S. Policy.* New York: Twentieth Century Fund, 1993.

Perot, Ross. *United We Stand: How We Can Take Back Our Country.* New York: Hyperion, 1992.

———— (with Pat Choate). *Save Your Job, Save Our Country: Why NAFTA Must Be Stopped—Now!* New York: Hyperion, 1993.

Rourke, John. *Congress and the Presidency in U.S. Foreign Policymaking: A Study of Interaction and Influence, 1945–1982.* Boulder, Colo.: Westview, 1983.

Rubio, Luis, *¿Cómo va afectar a méxico el tratado de libre comercio?* Mexico City: Fondo de Cultura Económica, 1992.

BIBLIOGRAPHY

Russell, Ruth B. *A History of the United Nations Charter*. Washington, D.C.: Brookings Institution, 1958.

Scott, William A. and Stephen B. Withey. *The United States and the United Nations: the Public View, 1945-1955*. Westport, Ct.: Greenwood Press, 1958.

Skidmore, Thomas E. and Peter H. Smith. *Modern Latin America*. 3rd ed. New York: Oxford University Press, 1992.

Spanier, John. *American Foreign Policy Since World War II*. 2nd ed. New York: Praeger, 1965.

Stanley, Howard W. and Richard G. Niemi. *Vital Statistics on American Politics*. 4th ed. Washington, D.C.: Congressional Quarterly Press, 1994.

The Center for Public Integrity. *The Trading Game: Inside Lobbying for the North American Free Trade Agreement*. Washington, D.C.: The Center for Public Integrity, n.d.

Thompson, Kenneth W., ed. *The Presidency, Congress and Political Discourse*. New York: University Press of America, 1987.

Vandenberg, Arthur H., Jr. *The Private Papers of Senator Vandenberg*. Boston: Houghton Mifflin, 1952.

Wonnacott, Ronald J. *The Economics of Overlapping Free Trade Areas and the Mexican Challenge*. Canadian-American Committee 60. Ottawa: C. D. Howe Institute, 1991.

Woodward, Bob. *The Agenda: Inside the Clinton White House*. New York: Simon & Schuster, 1994.

GOVERNMENT DOCUMENTS

Congressional Record. "Letter dated November 18, 1919." 66 Congress, 1 sess.

Congressional Record. 80 Congress, 1 sess., 12 March 1947.

BIBLIOGRAPHY

Congressional Research Service. *North American Free Trade Agreement: Issues for Congress*. Washington, D.C.: Library of Congress, 25 March 1991, updated 12 July 1991.

Federal News Service. "Remarks by Governor Bill Clinton at the Student Center at North Carolina State University, Raleigh, North Carolina." 4 October 1992.

Office of the Press Secretary, the White House. "Integrated Environmental Plan for the Mexico-U.S. Border Area." News release: 25 February 1992.

President of the United States. *NAFTA Supplemental Agreements*. Washington, D.C.: U.S. Government Printing Office, 1993.

Press Office of the President of Mexico. *Mexico: On the Record* 1, no. 8. August/September 1992.

Thomas, Kenneth. "Fact Sheet on the U.S./Mexican Agreement on the Border Environment Cooperation Commission (BECC) and the North American Development Bank (NADBank)." U.S. Department of State, 28 December 1993, n.d. Mimeo.

U.S. Department of Commerce. *Statistical Abstract of the United States 1993*. Washington, D.C.: U.S. Government Printing Office, 1992.

———. *Survey of Current Business*. September 1990.

U.S. Department of Justice. *Foreign Agent Registration Act*. Lobbying reports filed. Washington, D.C.

U.S. Department of Labor. *Monthly Labor Review*. Bureau of Labor Statistics: December 1992.

U.S. Department of State. *A Short History of the U.S. Department of State, 1781–1981*. Washington, D.C.: U.S. Department of State, 1981.

———. "Environmental NGO Developments on the Eve of NAFTA," unclassified cable from the U.S. Embassy in Mexico, 15 November 1993.

————. "NAFTA: In the Overriding Interest of the United States." Address of the Honorable Warren Christopher to the Los Angeles World Affairs Council and Town Hall. United States State Department Dispatch, 2 November 1993.

————. "Statement of the Honorable Warren Christopher, Secretary of State, Before the Senate Foreign Relations Committee." 4 November 1993. Mimeo.

U.S. Embassy (Mexico). "Mexico: Economic and Financial Report." Mexico City, April 1993. Mimeo.

U.S. Congress. House. *North American Free Trade Agreement Implementation Act*. 103d Congress, 1st sess., Report 103–361, Part 1, 15 November 1993.

U.S. Office of the Federal Register, National Archives and Records Administration. *Weekly Compilation of Presidential Documents*. 2 July 1990; and 12 October 1992.

U.S. Congress. Senate. *Charter of the United Nations: Hearing before the Senate Committee on Foreign Relations*. 79 Cong., 1 sess., 1945.

U.S. Trade Representative. *NAFTA Review*. 1. Washington, D.C.: January 1992.

————. "Correcting the Record: Response of the Office of the U.S. Trade Representative to the Perot/Choate NAFTA Book," Washington, D.C., 2 September 1993, mimeo.

ARTICLES AND BOOK CHAPTERS

Anderson, J. W. "Sore Losers." *Washington Post*, 1 October 1993, A-25.

Baldwin, Robert E. "The Changing Nature of U.S. Trade Policy since World War II." in *The Structure and Evolution of Recent U.S. Trade Policy*, edited by Robert E. Baldwin and Anne O. Krueger. Chicago: University of Chicago Press, 1984, 5–31.

BIBLIOGRAPHY

Blumenthal, Sidney. "The Making of a Machine." *New Yorker*, 29 November 1993, 80–93.

Bovard, James. "A U.S. History of Trade Hypocrisy," *Wall Street Journal*, 8 March 1994, A-16.

Castañeda, Jorge G. "Can NAFTA Change Mexico?" *Foreign Affairs*, (September/October 1993): 66–80.

Clemens, Diane Shaver. "Executive Agreements." in *Encyclopedia of American Foreign Policy*, edited by Alexander DeConde, Vol. I, 339–358. New York: Charles Scribner's Sons, 1978.

Cloud, David S. "Bush's 'Action Plan' May be Key to Approval of Fast Track." *Congressional Quarterly Weekly Report*, 4 May 1991, 1120, 1124–1125.

Dowie, Mark. "American Environmentalism: A Movement Courting Irrelevance." *World Policy Journal* IX (Winter 1991–92): 67–92.

Edsall, Thomas B. "Age of Irritation. The New Bitter Politics of Fear." *Washington Post*, 28 November 1993, C-1.

Fauriol, Georges. "The Shadow of Latin American Affairs." *Foreign Affairs* 1 (1990): 116–134.

Fingerhut, Vic. "The Mythical Clinton Coalition." *Campaigns & Elections* (January 1993): 29–30, 33.

Goodsell, James N. "Mexico: Why the Students Rioted." *Current History*, no. 329 (January 1969): 31–35, 53.

Grabendorff, Wolf. "Mexico and the European Community: Toward a New Relationship?" in *Mexico's External Relations in the 1990s*, edited by Riordan Roett. Boulder: Lynne Rienner, 1991.

Grayson, George W. "From Cellar to the Lobby." *Hemisfile* 3 (July 1992): 4–5.

———. "The Maple Leaf, the Cactus, and the Eagle: Energy Trilateralism." *Inter-American Economic Affairs* 34 (Spring 1981): 49–75.

BIBLIOGRAPHY

Hakim, Peter. "President Bush's Southern Strategy: The Enterprise for the Americas Initiative." *Washington Quarterly* 15 (Spring 1992): 93–106.

Holmer, Alan F. and Judith H. Bello, "The Fast Track Debate: A Prescription for Pragmatism." *International Lawyer* 26 (Spring 1992): 183–199.

Jonas, Manfred. "Isolationism." in *Encyclopedia of American Foreign Policy II*, edited by Alexander DeConde. New York: Charles Scribner's Sons, 1978, 496–506.

Kelly, Alfred H., "The Constitution and Foreign Policy." in *Encyclopedia of American Foreign Policy I*, edited by Alexander DeConde, New York: Charles Scribner's Sons, 1978, 177–190.

Koehler, Wallace C. Jr. and Aaron L. Segal, "Prospects for North American Energy Cooperation." *USA Today*, May 1980, 40–43.

Lajous, Roberta. "Mexico's European Policy Agenda: Perspectives on the Past, Proposals for the Future." in *Mexico's External Relations in the 1990s*, edited by Riordan Roett. Boulder: Lynne Rienner, 1991, 81–87.

Lewis, Charles and Margaret Ebrahim. "Can Mexico and Big Business USA Buy NAFTA?" *The Nation*, 14 June 1993, 826–839.

Lichter, Robert and Ted J. Smith. "Bad News Bears." *Media Critic* 1 (October 1993): 81–87.

Meyer, Herbert E. "Why a North American Common Market Won't Work— Yet." *Fortune*, 10 September 1979, 118–124.

Riding, Alan. "The Mixed Blessings of Mexico's Oil." *New York Times Magazine*, 11 January 1981, 22–25, 56, 58 and 59.

Rubio, Luis. "El dilema liberal." *Vuelta*, No. 191 (October 1992): 70–71.

———. "The Changing Role of the Private Sector." in *Mexico in Transition: Implications for U.S. Policy*, edited by Susan Kaufman Purcell. New York: Council on Foreign Relations, 1988, 31–42.

————. "El talón de aquiles de la reforma económica," *Vuelta 200* (July 1993).

Rowen, Hobart. "Perot Talks, Walks like a Protectionist." *Washington Post*, 21 June 1992, H-1.

Salinas de Gortari, Carlos. "State of the Nation Address," 1 November 1990, in *Latin American Daily Report*. 14 November 1990.

Sanger, David E. "Salesman in Chief." *New York Times*, 11 November 1993, E-1.

Schwanen, Daniel. "Were the Optimists Wrong on Free Trade? A Canadian Perspective." *Commentary*, C. D. Howe Institute, 3 (October 1992).

"Setting the Record Straight: Evaluating Ross Perot's Allegations against the NAFTA." *Heritage Foundation Backgrounder, No. 959*, Washington, D.C., 30 September 1993.

Shales, Tom. "Perot: Don't Speak When I'm Interrupting." *Washington Post*, 10 November 1993, C-1.

Shapiro, Walter. "Whose Hillary is She Anyway." *Esquire*, August 1993, 84–87.

"Sierra Club to Clinton: Renegotiate NAFTA!" *Washington Post*, advertising supplement. 27 October 1993, A-19.

Tananbaum, Duane A. "The Bricker Amendment Controversy: Its Origins and Eisenhower's Role." *Diplomatic History* 9 (Winter 1985): 73–93.

Thorup, Cathryn L. "Redefining Governance in North America: Citizen Diplomacy and Cross-Border Coalitions." *Enfoque*, Center for U.S.-Mexican Studies, University of California, San Diego (Spring 1993): 1, 12, and 13.

Wallach, Lori and Tom Hilliard. "The Consumer and Environmental Case Against Fast Track." *Public Citizen's Congress Watch*, May 1991.

BIBLIOGRAPHY

Weintraub, Sidney and M. Delal Baer, "The Interplay between Economic and Political Opening: The Sequence in Mexico." *Washington Quarterly* 15, (Spring 1992): 187–201.

Weisman, Jacob. "Family Feud." *New Republic*, 20 May 1991, 20–23.

Whitehead, Laurence. "Mexico and the 'Hegemony' of the United States: Past, Present, and Future." in *Mexico's External Relations in the 1990s*, edited by Riordan Roett. Boulder: Lynne Rienner, 1991, 243–262.

MAGAZINES AND NEWSPAPERS

American Enterprise. January/February 1992.

Business Week. 21 September 1993.

Christian Science Monitor. 1992–1994.

Congressional Quarterly Weekly Report. 1991–1993.

El financiero (Mexico City). 1991–1994.

Excelsior. 1982–1994.

Facts on File. 1954–1994.

F.Y.I. 1 July 1993.

Gallup Poll Monthly. 1992–1993.

Inside U.S. Trade. 1991–1994.

Journal of Commerce. 1988–1994.

Keesing's Contemporary Archives. 1968–1994.

Latin American Weekly Report. 1982–1994.

Literary Digest. 5 April 1919 and 29 November 1919.

BIBLIOGRAPHY

Los Angeles Times. 1989–1994.

Maclean's. 1990–1994.

Mexico Watch. 1993.

National Journal. 10 October 1992.

New Republic. 15 June 1992.

Newsweek. 11 March 1991.

New York Times. 1979–1994.

Platt's Oilgram News. 16 March 1992.

Proceso. 1977–1994.

Universal. 1988–1994.

USA Today. 18 November 1993.

U.S. News & World Report. 1991–1994.

Wall Street Journal. 1976–1994.

Washington Post. 1980–1994.

UNPUBLISHED WORKS

Aspe Armella, Pedro. Speech delivered at the Center for Strategic and International Studies, Washington, D.C., 22 September 1992.

Jones, James R. Letter to Representative John J. LaFalce, 26 November 1993.

Robertson, A. Willis. Letter to Virginius Dabney, 31 July 1953. Dabney Papers, Box 1, University of Virginia Library; cited in Duane A. Tananbaum, "The Bricker Amendment Controversy: Its Origin and Eisenhower's Role," *Diplomatic History*, 9 (Winter 1985): 79.

BIBLIOGRAPHY

INTERVIEWS BY AUTHOR

Adam, David. Economic Counselor, Canadian Embassy, Mexico City, 13 October 1992.

Audley, John. Staff member, Sierra Club, telephone interview, 9 May 1992.

Barreda, William E. Deputy Assistant Secretary for Trade and Investment, Department of Treasury, Washington, D.C., 12 December 1992.

Bennett, B. Timothy. Vice President, SJS Advanced Strategies, former USTR official, Washington D.C., 6 December 1992; 22 July 1993; and 7 January 1994.

Blanco Mendoza, Herminio. Chief Trade Negotiator, SECOFI, Mexico City, 18 March 1994.

Cardero García, María Elena. Director-General for Bilateral Economic Relations for the American Continent, Secretariat of External Relations, Mexico City, 14 October 1992.

Carrière, Claude. Counsellor for Trade Policy, Canadian Embassy, Washington, D.C., 2 December 1992 and 4 January 1994.

Cleland, Michael. Director General, Energy Policy Branch, Energy Sector, Department of Energy, Mines and Resources, Ottawa, 22 March 1993.

Craft, William. Director, Office of Multilateral Trade Affairs, U.S. Department of State, Washington, D.C., 22 December 1992.

de la Calle, Luis Fernando, Official, SECOFI Office, Washington, D.C., 8 December 1992.

Dunn, Alan M. Assistant Secretary for Import Administration, Department of Commerce, Washington, D.C., 22 December 1992.

Farias de Avila, Maria Emilia. Mexican Consul General in Montreal, Montreal, 21 May 1993.

292

Feigen, Edward M. Organizing Department, AFL-CIO, telephone interview, 25 July 1994.

Flores Ayala, Jesús. Coordinator of Advisers for the Chief Negotiator, the North American Free Trade Agreement, SECOFI, Mexico City, 30 October 1992 and 18 March 1994.

Fisher, Lynn. Staff member, Natural Resources Defense Council, Washington, D.C., telephone interview, 15 January 1993.

Fisher, Robert C. Director, Mexican Affairs, USTR, Washington, D.C., 13 October 1990 and 17 August 1993.

Fraser, Sandra. Legal office, Department of External Affairs, telephone interview, 22 March 1993.

Freiberg, Kenneth P. Deputy General Counsel, USTR, Washington, D.C., 29 June 1993.

Frenzel, Bill. Former congressman, telephone interview, 28 July 1994.

Gillespie, Ambassador Charles "Tony." Jr. U.S. State Department official, Washington, D.C., 7 January 1994.

Gillett, Thomas. U.S. Commerce Department official, Washington, D.C., 5 October 1992.

Hart, Michael. Senior adviser, Department of External Affairs, Ottawa, 22 March 1993.

Houseman, Robert F. Attorney with the Center for International Environmental Law, 7 December 1992.

Hughes, Ann H. Deputy Assistant Secretary for the Western Hemisphere, Department of Commerce, Washington, D.C., 29 December 1992.

Jacobs, Steven. U.S. Department of Commerce official, telephone interview, 10 December 1992.

Katz, Julius L. Deputy United States Trade Representative, 1989 to 1993, Washington, D.C., 2 June 1993; telephone interview, 17 May 1994.

BIBLIOGRAPHY

Kie, Richard. Environmental Protection Agency, Mexico City, 12 July 1994.

Lande, Stephen. President, Manchester Associates, former USTR official, Washington, D.C., telephone interview, 17 January 1993; personal interview, 4 January 1994.

Leaman, Miguel. Minister-Counselor for Commercial Affairs, Mexican Embassy. Washington, D.C., 11 June 1993.

Lonmo, O. Victor. Deputy Co-ordinator, Market Access, Multilateral Trade Negotiations, Department of External Relations, Ottawa, 22 March 1993.

Lowe, John. Director, International Trade and U.S. Relations, Energy Policy Branch, Department of Energy, Mines and Resources, Ottawa, 23 March 1993.

Mackay, Donald. First Secretary, Commercial Affairs, Canadian Embassy, Ottawa, 20 May 1993; Mexico City, 18 December 1993.

Mazur, Sandra. Director of International Trade, Eastman Kodak Corporation, Washington, D.C., 5 January 1994.

Murden, William. Treasury Attaché, U.S. Embassy in Canada, Ottawa, 20 May 1993.

Newman, Barry S. Deputy Assistant Secretary for International Monetary Policy, Department of Treasury, Washington, D.C., 29 July 1993.

Noffle, Francine. Official, Department of Energy, Mines and Natural Resources, Ottawa, 23 March 1993.

Pumphrey, David L. Director, Division of Energy Assessments, Office of International Affairs, U.S. Department of Energy, Washington, D.C., 21 October 1992.

Ramsay, William C., Deputy Assistant Secretary for Energy, Resources and Food Policy, U.S. Department of State, Washington, D.C., 2 October 1992.

BIBLIOGRAPHY

Roh, Charles E. "Chip," Jr. Deputy U.S. Trade Representative, telephone interview, 20 January 1993; personal interview, Washington, D.C., 4 January 1994.

Ryan, Douglas. Official, Office of Mexican Affairs, U.S. Department of State, Washington, D.C., 23 November 1992.

Samuel, Brian. USTR official, Washington, D.C., 7 December 1992.

Santiago, Henry. Division of Energy Assessments, Office of International Affairs, U.S. Department of Energy, Washington, D.C., 9 September 1992.

Smith, Richard J., Deputy Assistant Secretary of State and Special Negotiator, Washington, D.C., 4 January 1994.

Sweeny, Jack. Treasury attaché, U.S. Embassy, Mexico City, 20 December 1993.

Thomas, Kenneth. Office of Oceans, the Environment, and Science, U.S. Department of State, Washington, D.C., 28 December 1993.

Tinsley, Mary. Congressional liaison official, USTR, Washington, D.C., 7 December 1992.

Urteaga-Trani, Raúl. Official, Washington NAFTA Office, SECOFI, telephone interview, 30 December 1993.

Vincent, John. U.S. State Department official, Washington, D.C., 28 December 1993.

Von Bertrab, Herman. Director NAFTA Office, SECOFI, Washington, D.C., 21 June 1993.

Watkins, Richard. Energy attaché, U.S. Embassy, Ottawa, 22 March 1993.

Yancik, Joseph, U.S. Department of Commerce official, Washington, D.C., 23 November 1992.

Zabludovsky Kuper, Jaime E., Deputy Chief Negotiator, SECOFI, Mexico City, 18 March 1994.

BIBLIOGRAPHY

OTHER ITEMS

Sill, Edwin W. Letter-to-the-editor. *Washington Post*, 25 June 1994, A-20.